# "I HEAR AMERICA SINGING"

# "I HEAR AMERICA SINGING"

## FOLK MUSIC AND NATIONAL IDENTITY

RACHEL CLARE DONALDSON

TEMPLE UNIVERSITY PRESS
PHILADELPHIA

TEMPLE UNIVERSITY PRESS
Philadelphia, Pennsylvania 19122
www.temple.edu/tempress

*All reasonable attempts were made to locate the copyright holders for the lyrics published in this book. If you believe you may be one of them, please contact Temple University Press, and the publisher will include appropriate acknowledgment in subsequent editions of the book.*

Library of Congress Cataloging-in-Publication Data

Donaldson, Rachel Clare, author.
  "I hear America singing" : folk music and national identity / Rachel Clare Donaldson.
    pages cm
  Includes bibliographical references and index.
  ISBN 978-1-4399-1078-8 (cloth : alk. paper) — ISBN 978-1-4399-1079-5 (pbk. : alk. paper) — ISBN 978-1-4399-1080-1 (e-book)  1. Folk music—United States—History and criticism.  2. Music—Political aspects—United States—History—20th century.  I. Title.
  ML3550.5.D66 2014
  781.62'13—dc23

                                                                2014010460

♾ The paper used in this publication meets the requirements of the American National Standard for Information Sciences—Permanence of Paper for Printed Library Materials, ANSI Z39.48-1992

Printed in the United States of America

9  8  7  6  5  4  3  2  1

*To my parents,*

*Robert and Carmela Donaldson*

# CONTENTS

# ACKNOWLEDGMENTS

If you read the acknowledgments sections of academic books, you know that numerous people and institutions contribute to the creation of a single monograph; this one is no different. I owe a great debt to many people for their contributions to my research, writing, and sanity while I completed a dissertation and then turned it into a book.

As a graduate student I had the good fortune to work with several people in a variety of disciplines. Robert Bethke lent his expertise in folklore at the very early stages of my research, which helped shape my ideas. William Caferro, Devin Fergus, Yoshikuni Igarashi, Holly McCammon, and, especially during my years as a lecturer, Teresa Goddu were inspiring teachers and mentors. Susan Kuyper provided enormous assistance in applying for research grants and fellowships from the start of my research to the end of my graduate career. For my dissertation, Larry Isaac and David Carlton provided insightful and critical feedback. As my adviser, Gary Gerstle consistently held me to high standards, which significantly aided in the smooth transition from dissertation to book. I am also especially grateful to Kathryn Schwarz for the time and effort she put into helping me revise my proposals and responses to reader reports. Two people who, while serving as models of professional success, were constant sources of encouragement and compassion throughout my graduate career were Sarah Igo and Katherine Crawford. Their support and advice helped me weather the stresses of graduate school and the great beyond.

During my first year of research, I was introduced to Ronald Cohen, and we began a working relationship that continues to this day. Besides being *the* font of knowledge on the folk revival (and thus playing a crucial role as both my research mentor and outside dissertation reader), Ron has become a good friend.

I have had the pleasure of getting to know Ron through lengthy e-mail exchanges, meals out at conferences, and visits with him and his wife, Nancy. I also recently had the pleasure of working with him on a book about the folk revival in the United States and England during the 1950s; I look forward to working with Ron in the future. I am also grateful to those who got me started on this path in the first place, particularly Paul Cimbala, Elaine Crane, and Mark Naison, my mentors at Fordham University.

Many people connected to outside institutions also aided my research. A grant from Western Kentucky University gave me access to the Sarah Gertrude Knott papers, and a Smithsonian predoctoral fellowship enabled me to explore the archives at both the Smithsonian Center for Folklife and Cultural Heritage (CFCH) and the American Folklife Center (AFC) at the Library of Congress. I am thankful to the staff at the CFCH, especially Jeff Place and Pam Rogers, for helping me with their collections, and to Todd Harvey for his help (and humor) at the AFC. Fellowships and grants from Vanderbilt University gave me the time to focus on research and writing and presenting my work at various conferences throughout my graduate career. In terms of transitioning my work into a book, I am grateful for the support of Janet Francendese at Temple University Press and the two readers who took the time to fully engage with my work. Unfortunately, because of the anonymity of the process, I cannot cite them by name, but I am especially thankful to "Reader #1," whose thorough comments greatly aided me in establishing a clear plan of revision. The main title of this book, *"I Hear America Singing,"* which was proposed by the folks at Temple University Press, references the poem by Walt Whitman.

In addition to the support that came from academic circles, my friends and family helped by making the time I spent researching, writing, and revising enjoyable. My friends from graduate school, including Rob Chester, Katherine Fusco, Claire Goldstene, David Gruber, Jamie and Steve Harrison, Jen Holt, Kurt Johnson, David LaFevor, LeeAnn Reynolds, Rick Stone, Nick Villanueva, and Erin Woodruff-Stone, and the beer we imbibed together, created fond memories. I look forward to creating many more. Lee and Elizabeth Jones provided a much-needed connection to the world beyond academe and became my second family. Judy and Wayne Houston welcomed me into their home and family, and they have become a pillar of familial support. I was fortunate enough to stay with Jacqueline Young during my year in Washington, D.C., which made a long time away from home much more enjoyable. Visits with such good friends as Brad Alexander, Martha Clippinger, Lee Crane, Debi Germann, Chris Kondrich, Kate Lasko, and Kim Rudolph always gave me something to look forward to. Many sat through practice presentations ranging from college papers to job talk demonstrations, and I owe them big-time. Throughout my life, my sister, Leah Donaldson, has given me more than she probably realizes. Her sharp wit and non sequitur–filled phone conversations provided a needed distraction from the job hunt and other aspects of academic life. She helped me get through the homesickness of the first year of college, and it was an honor to have her name called out with mine at graduation.

And then, there is Josh Houston. I met Josh during my first year of graduate school, and he soon became my confidant, morale booster, best friend, and favorite drinking buddy. In his wedding vows, he promised always to edit my papers, and he has more than lived up to that pledge. He has read every draft of every chapter and helped me to become a better writer. He has enriched my life more than he knows, and I look forward to many more years with him and the boys, Gus and Charlie.

This book is dedicated to the two people who enabled me to achieve my dream of becoming a historian: my parents. They supported every goal I had—from wanting to become a ShopRite clerk when I was five, to wanting to become a professional trumpet player, to wanting to go to law school, and, finally, to setting my sights on becoming a historian when I was a freshman in college. Their unwavering encouragement throughout my life allowed me to reach each goal I set for myself, and they served as constant models of how to be an effective teacher, critical thinker, and good person along the way.

# INTRODUCTION

In 1965, the musician Pete Seeger published an article in which he explained his interest in folk music. Seeger was sixteen when he first attended the Mountain Dance and Folk Festival in Asheville, North Carolina, in 1935. As the child of two musicians, Seeger was no stranger to different genres of music; yet the festival, he wrote, introduced him to something entirely new. It was then that Seeger fell in love with what would become his musical trademark: the five-string banjo. The banjo, however, was not all that drew Seeger's attention; he became enamored with all facets of the music that he heard that day—the rhythms, melodies, and, most of all, the song lyrics. Seeger explained, "Compared to the trivialities of the most popular songs, the words of these songs had all the meat of human life in them. They sang of heroes, outlaws, murders, fools. . . . Above all, they seemed to be frank, straightforward, honest." Folk songs, Seeger learned, told a great deal about the people who performed them. His subsequent experiences with folk music over the next thirty years led him to conclude that these songs could help Americans "learn about ourselves, and . . . learn about each other." As the music of the people, folk music provided a way to understand "where we came from, the trials and tribulations of those who came before us, and the good times and the bad." Seeger argued that the music also enabled Americans to understand their fellow citizens—the ones with whom they most likely would never interact—by asking, "How many white people have rediscovered their own humanity through the singing of American Negro songs? How many town dwellers have learned a bit about a rougher outdoor life from songs created by men with calloused hands?"[1] In short, folk music introduced Americans of many walks of life to each other, thus rendering the "imagined" national community more tangible.

Seeger published this piece shortly after folk music peaked in popular culture. During the early 1960s, in the years between the end of 1950s rock-and-roll rebellion and before the British Invasion, folk music had become a mainstream musical fad commonly referred to as the folk revival. The actual revival, however, was much more expansive than merely the "boom" of folk music in popular culture. It was, in fact, a movement that began in the early 1930s, which brought public folklorists, cultural preservationists, scholars, musicians, political activists, and musical entrepreneurs together in the effort to protect, preserve, and promote folk music. As with any movement, the revivalists encompassed various, and sometimes conflicting, views and aims. Despite these differences, they shared the core belief that, because it came from the American people and thus depicted American experiences, folk music constituted a critical component of the nation's cultural heritage. The revivalists knew that the music was not dead; what they sought to *revive* was Americans' knowledge and interest in their living, musical heritage—a heritage that revealed the essence of their national identity.

Since the movement's end in the late 1960s, scholars have amassed a considerable body of work addressing various aspects of the folk revival in historical accounts, sociological studies, biographies, and autobiographies. While the quantity of scholarship on the revival is too great to list exhaustively, no study to date fully explores the relationship between the revival and concepts of nationalism; yet influencing the ways in which Americans understood the values, the culture, and the people of their nation was the crux of the movement. Seeger's argument that folk music enabled listeners to "understand" themselves as Americans reveals his belief that there were distinct traits that the American people held in common, traits that united them as a national community.

In many ways, my understanding of the revival and my assessment of its impact on American society borrow from the work of the sociologists Ron Eyerman and Andrew Jamison. Social movements, in their view, are "central moments in the reconstruction of culture," meaning that members of these movements reevaluate societal values and norms, redefining them in the process. These movements also rely on cultural forms to forward political agendas; movement actors often appropriate cultural traditions to define both themselves and their political aims. Although they emphasize political reform, social movements often alter larger social and cultural norms in the process and thus have profound cultural consequences—sometimes beyond what the actors intended—that last even after these movements fade from the national spotlight. By seeking to understand the ways in which social movements alter culture, Eyerman and Jamison also elevate the role of culture within social movements. In doing so, they challenge scholars' tendencies to disconnect culture from politics or dismiss culture altogether in the effort to cast social movements in political terms, relegating culture to the role of a structural "frame" that supports the more properly political activity.[2]

Following Eyerman and Jamison's conceptual framework, I argue that the revivalists used the cultural form of folk music to articulate the values embedded in American identity. Music was the central medium through which the revivalists spread their message, and their work had a significant impact on American society. They not only shaped popular conceptions of folk music, but they also inspired other activists to bring this music into programs of political reform. Social movements, including the Civil Rights Movement, labor activism, and antiwar efforts, incorporated folk music either because the revivalists became directly involved or because the activists drew inspiration from the revivalists' earlier efforts. Even as the revivalists participated in other movements, they remained united in the stewardship of the revival and the effort to advance a pluralist version of democracy as essential to Americanism.

It is no coincidence that the revival emerged during the 1930s, when the magnitude of the Depression threw traditional American values into question. Like many cultural workers of the era, the revivalists sought to solve this collective identity crisis by reminding citizens of the qualities that defined their nation. Scholars, however, have neglected to look at the revival as a part of this effort and to determine how it contributed to national identity constructions during the 1930s and subsequent decades. *"I Hear America Singing"* brings the revivalists into debates about the nation's character by examining the type of Americanism (i.e., nationalism in a specifically American context) that they crafted and publicized through the cultural medium of folk music. Since the revival lasted decades beyond the Depression, studying this movement reveals how constructs of nationalism from the 1930s continued to operate in American society for much of the twentieth century. Moreover, because the revivalists brought folk music into debates about the nation's civic and cultural identity, the revival provides particular insight into American cultural politics during the mid-twentieth century.

Numerous participants drifted in and out of the revival over its forty-year span. Rather than studying the movement from the perspective of rank-and-file folk enthusiasts, as many works in history and sociology have done, *"I Hear America Singing"* focuses on the ways in which leading revivalists interpreted folk music and the programs that they initiated to disseminate this music among a public audience. Although the revival changed over time in response to larger cultural and political shifts, an effort to shape how Americans understood themselves and their nation lay at the revival's core. As with most groups engaged in national identity projects, rhetorical allusions to democracy permeated their programs. Democracy, in their view, had a very specific meaning. In general, the leading members were social and political progressives who believed that cultural diversity and the inclusion of all citizens in the political process was the essence of the kind of democracy that lay at the core of American identity. The revivalists grounded their Americanism in social theories that first appeared in politically progressive circles during the World War I era, drawing on cultural pluralism and cosmopolitanism, which emphasized urban ethnic identities, as well as on regionalism, which highlighted rural identities.

The folk music revival emerged at the nexus of intellectual discourses and social movements that sought to define the nation by cultural traditions from the rural hinterlands *and* the cosmopolitan urban centers. Thus, the American identity that the revivalists generated presented an exceptionally diverse picture of the nation—a picture that they worked to sustain over decades marked by war, political turmoil, and cultural factionalism.

In using the folk music revival to understand projects of national identity conceptualization, my work situates itself within a body of scholarship that investigates the various articulations of American nationalism over the course of the twentieth century. In showing that the revivalists placed civic ideals and cultural pluralism at the core of Americanism, *"I Hear America Singing"* presents the argument that they, along with other political progressives, initiated a version of nationalism that ran contrary to many contemporary views of American identity. In doing so, this book contributes to the conversation that such historians as Rogers Smith and Gary Gerstle have initiated. Smith and Gerstle each contend that the history of American nationalism in the twentieth century has been a continuous contest between two notions of national identity: a democratic, civic nationalism, on the one hand, and a militaristic, racially exclusive nationalism, on the other. The construction of American national identity depended on the interplay between civic nationalism and racial nationalism, two visions that not only defined American values but also determined who counted as an American. The contest between these two concepts of nationalism largely fell along political lines. Smith argues that by the eve of World War I, centrist members of the Progressive era who advocated white supremacy, anti-immigration, and cultural homogeneity opposed leftist progressives who advocated pluralistic, inclusive conceptions of American identity. Smith also claims that leftist progressives were unable to articulate anything distinctive about American national identity because their pluralism led them to believe that no one group could speak for the whole nation.[3] The leftist progressive conception of American nationalism challenges this view because, in the hands of revivalists, it became a mechanism for insisting that regional and ethnic diversity and the democratic values associated with such diversity were precisely what made the United States unique. By collecting, recording, and performing the music of communities ranging from rural towns to urban ethnic enclaves, the revivalists used folk music to illustrate American cultural heterogeneity. The revivalists argued that these communities were united under the umbrella of the nation and, although culturally distinct, embodied essential civic ideals, such as a commitment to democratic political participation. Americans, the revivalists believed, ought to uphold the democratic ideal in the cultural realm as much as the political one—all citizens should be allowed to express cultural differences while maintaining a voice in the political process.

In addition to complicating the scholarship on American nationalism, the folk music revival illustrates how early twentieth-century theories of cultural pluralism laid the groundwork for the emergence of multiculturalism in the

1970s. The revivalists recognized the inherent plurality of American society and worked to ensure that national identity reflected this social reality. By bringing the music of folk communities to a national listening audience, they hoped to achieve that end. Yet they did not just bring the *music* to a mainstream audience; they provided outlets for the musicians of folk communities to present their own traditions directly to the listening public. In this way, the revivalists sought to let the folk speak for themselves. By "giving voice" to these Americans, many of whom were politically and economically marginalized, the folk music revivalists provided a bridge from cultural pluralism to early concepts of multiculturalism, thus revealing that the history of multiculturalism is far longer than it has heretofore been depicted as being.

By showing the connections between cultural pluralism and multiculturalism, I do not imply that they were theoretically one and the same. The contexts from which these theories emerged differed significantly: cultural pluralism was a reaction against the anti-immigrant Americanism of the World War I era, whereas multiculturalism followed on the heels of the racial nationalism and anti-Americanism that characterized the identity politics of the late 1960s. Cultural pluralists sought to secure a place for cultural difference within mainstream American society, but many multiculturalists rejected affiliations with dominant culture and national politics. Furthermore, while both groups encouraged ethnic minorities to sustain their traditions, cultural pluralists emphasized the instrumental value of ethnic traditions—that is, their benefits both for ethnic groups and the nation at large—while multiculturalists emphasized the intrinsic value of ethnic and racial identities, independently of their national consequences. These differences, however, should not obscure the historical connections between these two movements, which hitherto have been largely under-studied.

Currently, there are few studies dedicated to the history of multiculturalism in America. This is not to say, however, that scholars have avoided the subject. Social and educational theorists documented the emergence of multicultural or "multiethnic" education programs from the late 1970s through the 1980s; by the 1990s, historians and sociologists had begun assessing the positive and negative consequences of multicultural theories in American life. In *Postethnic America: Beyond Multiculturalism,* the historian David Hollinger provides the most detailed investigation into the emergence of multiculturalism.[4] Hollinger describes the parallels among multiculturalism and earlier twentieth-century ideas of pluralism. However, his focus is not on explaining *how* early constructs of pluralist Americanism came to influence theories of multiculturalism. The folk music revival provides a way to trace how variations of cultural pluralism continued through the mid-century, changed over time, and helped inform programs of multiculturalism. By conducting a close examination of revival programs from the 1930s to the late 1960s, *"I Hear America Singing"* reveals the complex history of American multiculturalism, a history that extends back to the early decades of the twentieth century. Thus, my explanation of the "long history" of multiculturalism parallels the work of recent historians who have revealed the "long history" of the Civil Rights Movement.

The idea of "giving voice" to racial and ethnic minorities, which became a guiding principle for programs of multiculturalism, permeated the folk music revival and shaped the revivalists' version of Americanism from the beginning of the movement. Embedded in this idea were the moral imperatives to include the traditions of minority communities in the national culture and to ensure that the members of these communities had full access to local and national politics. The latter conviction led many revivalists into left-wing programs that worked to bring politically and economically marginalized Americans into the democratic process. Several scholars have noted the connection between the folk music revival and left-wing politics, especially during the early years of the movement. Others have documented the revivalists' work in programs of the New Left, such as the Civil Rights Movement and the anti–Vietnam War movement. However, no one has followed the revivalists' political activism from the 1930s *through* the rise and fall of the New Left in the 1960s. Many political activists of the Old Left continued to participate in the resurgence of activism that marked the early years of the New Left. While these two generations of leftists differed in many ways, they also shared remarkable similarities, primarily regarding a faith in the promise of American civic ideals as a means to secure social and political justice. Most important, they all worked to reform the political, social, and economic systems to ensure that all Americans would have access to these ideals.

Viewing the Old Left from the perspective of the revivalists, determining what led them to join programs connected to the Communist Party of the United States (CPUSA), reveals that many leftists were genuinely motivated by the ideals that permeated the CPUSA's rhetoric during the second half of the 1930s. This perspective therefore challenges the historical assessment that dismisses members of the Old Left as mere "Stalinists," because it exposes how many left-wing and communist political activists of the 1930s through the 1940s were driven by a faith in the type of democratic pluralism that the CPUSA promoted during the Popular Front era. Recent historical scholarship that examines the left at the grassroots level has revealed that the nature of the Old Left was both more complicated and more rooted in the American context than historians had previously thought. By freeing left-wing revivalists of the Old Left of their Stalinist stigma, a project that Richard Reuss began with his study *American Folk Music and Left-Wing Politics, 1927–1957*,[5] this book sheds light on the full impact that these activists had on political discourse in the United States during the twentieth century. In doing so, I align myself with the perspective that Michael Denning developed in *The Cultural Front: The Laboring of American Culture in the Twentieth Century*. Denning significantly broadens the historical understanding of the left during this period by casting aside traditional investigations of the Old Left via institutional politics that identify a core of card-carrying members surrounded by a periphery of pink-tinged fellow travelers.

Rather, he argues that the Popular Front consisted of myriad leftists who, while working with communists and liberals, generated an independent social movement.[6] Like other Popular Front leftists, the left-wing revivalists had varying degrees of sympathy toward or allegiance to the CPUSA over the course of three decades, but their *social* views did not change. When the CPUSA was a force calling for political reform and social justice, left-wing revivalists sought affiliations with the party; when the party showed its undemocratic colors, they severed ties. By noting the incorporation of folk music in left-wing programs and examining certain figures who were active in revival circles, Denning's work is foundational for my own. *"I Hear America Singing"* furthers the conversation that began with *The Cultural Front* by situating the larger folk revival in relationship to the Popular Front, examining how and why revivalists worked to deploy folk music in political activism during the Popular Front period and afterward.

In situating the revivalists in their political context, I employ the term "progressive," the meaning of which changed over time. The early revivalists of both liberal and left-wing persuasions drew inspiration from left-progressives of the Progressive era—figures who believed in cultural pluralism and shared sympathies with political radicals ranging from socialists to anarcho-syndicalists and communists. By the 1930s, the term "progressive," now removed from the context of the Progressive era, largely became associated with the left, such that the distinction of a "left progressive" fell by the wayside. During this period, I apply the term "progressive" when referring to left-leaning and communist revivalists who believed in the pluralist, politically inclusive, and internationalist Americanism that characterized the Popular Front. The progressive label still applied to those revivalists who sustained this Americanism through the Cold War and into the early 1960s. Although the early members of the New Left tended to eschew labels, their understanding of American ideals had remarkable similarities to aspects of Popular Front Americanism; thus, they generated a new variant in the history of American progressivism. However, the term "progressive" would no longer apply to the young leftists of the late 1960s that rejected the belief that American ideals could provide a path toward social justice. While the events of the late 1960s threw the left into turmoil, I explain how the effects proved especially devastating to concepts of progressive Americanism.

The revivalists were able to bring folk music into programs of political, social, and cultural activism because they believed that folk music was a grassroots tradition that expressed the concerns, interests, values, and experiences of the American populace. As such, this music was an intrinsically democratic art form, because the songs belonged to an ongoing oral tradition in which people across generations adapted them to suit their present interests and circumstances; folk songs had no official version. Based on this view, many revivalists defined folk music by the simple maxim: "Folk music is what the people sing."[7] Yet simmering below this seemingly simple statement was a cauldron of contentious issues that academic and public folklorists, amateur song collectors, musical enthusiasts and entrepreneurs, educators, and musicians debated throughout the late nineteenth century and twentieth century. The obvious question this definition raises is: who are "the people"? By arrogating to themselves the power to determine who qualified as legitimate folk, early revivalists began a process of determining which traditions belonged in the canon of folk music, a process that grew increasingly complex as the movement developed.

The evolution of the revivalists' understanding of folk music operated dialectically: when existing conceptualizations of folk music encountered new political and cultural trends, novel definitions emerged. As the sociologist Thomas Rochon explains, "culture" consists of a temporally situated and evolving "stock of ideas that define a set of commonsense beliefs about what is right, what is natural, what works." As such, the revivalists' varying definitions of folk music reflected the shifting cultural conditions in which each generation of revivalists operated. Rochon further explains that social movements articulate a particular "discourse," which is the "linguistic expression of a system of thought" that includes "a shared set of concepts, vocabulary, terms of reference, evaluations, associations, polarities, and standards of argument connected to some coherent perspective on the world."[8] The folk revival's primary discourse centered on music, and the revivalists each had their own reasons for appreciating folk music. To some, like Seeger, the music was more "honest"—the opposite of the oft-cited "June-moon-croon" rhyme scheme of Tin Pan Alley pop songs. To later revivalists, beginning with the generation that came of age during the 1950s, the music was a far cry from the teenage rock-and-roll and adult pop standards that infused their suburban surroundings. For these revivalists, folk music became a "vehicle to carry an ideological message," according to the sociologist William G. Roy, a message that entailed their rejection of popular, mass culture.[9] Some revivalists focused on the music of rural, native-born citizens, especially in underdeveloped regions in the Southeast; others emphasized the music that immigrant groups carried with them and sustained in urban ethnic enclaves. Some believed that folk music could be composed only in culturally and socially isolated communities, whereas others included music from almost any group. Even Seeger recognized that definitions of folk music varied over time and chose to refrain from delving into the debate by acknowledging that "definitions change." My approach is similar to Seeger's. Rather than establishing my own definition of folk music or engaging in questions of musical authenticity, I address the various definitions without claiming that some were more legitimate than others. The importance for this project lies not in establishing a concrete definition of folk music but, rather, in understanding *why* the revivalists defined folk music in particular ways and how those definitions related to the social, political, and cultural contexts from which they emerged.

## *Tuning Up*

The beginning of the folk music revival dates back to the 1930s, when the initial revivalists began to infuse folk music into mainstream culture, with the dual purpose of reforming both the cultural landscape and popular concepts of Americanism. Although their understanding of folk music and its place in the pantheon of American cultural heritage was largely shaped by the context of the Depression, many revivalists rooted their ideas in the work of folklorists, scholars, and musical enthusiasts stretching back to the late nineteenth century. To understand the folk music revival and its place in twentieth-century America, therefore, we need to begin before the beginning.

Although the British collector Cecil Sharp was not the first to study folk music on American soil, folklorists largely credit him as one of the earliest scholars to identify Anglo folk music traditions in the United States. Sharp believed that British ballads dating back to the Elizabethan era survived in the hollows of the southern Appalachian Mountains. Like the novelists, collectors, and reformers who also turned their attention to the southern mountaineers, Sharp believed that the mountain communities' geographical isolation protected them from the corruptions of mass culture. His interest in the Anglo ballads, coupled with the fear that this cultural isolation would not last long, precipitated his song-collecting recording expeditions around the southern highlands. Seeking only Anglo ballads, Sharp was drawn to the mountain communities as places that time forgot, where Anglo-Saxon settlers preserved an unadulterated British ballad tradition. This view, of course, did not take into account that many of these communities were situated near large towns or middle-class tourist destinations. In his quest to find a connection to the British past, Sharp also conveniently ignored the mountain communities' racial and ethnic diversity.[10] Even as he amassed his collection by listening to local musicians, Sharp included only song lyrics and refrained from documenting the music of the songs. His ballad collections, such as *English Folk Songs of the Southern Appalachians,* which he jointly published with Olive Dame Campbell in 1917, focused exclusively on the song texts rather than the accompanying tunes. Despite these shortcomings, Sharp's methods of collecting songs inspired other song collectors, amateur and professional. Indeed, the image of a white mountaineer singing an Anglo ballad became the ideal of authentic folk music in America for many enthusiasts, especially in the South.

While ballad collectors championed the music of white mountain communities as the epitome of folk music in America, others worked to broaden the definition of the genre. Scholarly folklorists connected to the American Folklore Society (AFS), a professional organization that began in the late nineteenth century, operated concurrently with the Anglo ballad collectors but turned their attention to other ethnic groups, such as American Indians. Much like the Anglo ballad collectors, these folklorists rushed to record their music, crafts, and other cultural artifacts before these traditions disappeared, as the folklorists presumed they would. The anthropological folklorists followed in the footsteps of Franz Boas, who helped establish the AFS in 1888. On the basis of his studies of American Indians in the Pacific Northwest, his scholarship on black folklore, and his experiences living in the multiethnic metropolis of New York

City, Boas rejected the racialized evolutionary theories that dominated anthro-pological thought and developed the theory of cultural relativism. Evolutionary theories held that cultures evolved over time and that folkways served as build-ing blocks in that process; cultures that continued to practice folk traditions (i.e., those of the Nordic and Western regions of Europe) remained in a primi-tive stage of development and had not advanced to the level of modern societies. Boas's work challenged this view by stipulating that all cultures maintained validity and that anthropologists should appreciate the plurality of cultures on an equal plane rather than arrange them in a hierarchical order. By recognizing the cultural significance of non-Western groups, Boas and other folklore an-thropologists succeeded in opening up the field of folklore to include non-West-ern people.[11]

Working alongside other folklorists in the AFS, Boas sought to make the study of folklore a social science worthy of scholarly pursuit. Despite these ef-forts, the society often lacked funds and public respectability. To counter these deficiencies, AFS leaders encouraged members to organize local chapters in the hopes of garnering more grassroots support. Not surprisingly, these chapters largely catered to the local members' needs instead of following the national organization's guidelines. For example, the members of local chapters in recent-ly settled states were interested in using folk culture more to establish their local identities than to preserve indigenous cultures.[12] Often they used their chapters to stage musical performances such as festivals, concerts, and fiddle conventions that showcased the musical traditions that settlers had brought with them and adapted or new songs that spoke to and of local conditions. In so doing, these regional AFS chapters opened the canon of folk music to include new traditions that people generated based on their experiences migrating to and settling down in frontier regions. This understanding of folk music effectively challenged the ballad collectors' Anglo focus and the anthropologists' emphasis on American Indian cultures—both of which grounded folk traditions in historical epochs and removed them from contemporary, mainstream culture.

While the AFS remained a largely academic organization on the national level, local chapters did succeed in attracting amateur enthusiasts. Mediating between the two groups were the new public folklorists who joined the ranks of academic folklorists in studying, collecting, and defining folk music during the first two decades of the twentieth century while remaining connected to a pop-ular audience. The public folklorists moved beyond the ballad collectors by seeking traditions generated on native soil rather than transplanted by Anglo settlers—shifting the focus from folk music *in* America to *American* folk music. They worked both to generate wider interest in folk music and to use this music to understand the people who continued these musical traditions. Soon, many of these folklorists began arguing that folk music did not just provide insight into small communities throughout the country, but, when taken as a whole, also provided a way to understand the American people as a national body. One of the earliest members of this new cohort was the song collector John Lomax.

In 1947, Lomax opened the memoir of his song-collecting adventures with a sweeping assessment of his personal motivations: "All my life I have been interested in the songs of the people—the intimate poetic and musical expression of unlettered people, from which group I am directly sprung." By defining the American folk as the "unlettered" of society, Lomax implied that they were unaffected by such modernizing forces as public education and commercial culture. While this definition follows in the same vein as his scholarly predecessors, Lomax set himself apart from figures like Sharp and Boas by declaring that he himself was from that ilk, describing his family as hailing from "the upper crust of 'po' white trash," a hard claim to make considering his Ivy League education.[13] One badge that Lomax could use to separate himself from his academic predecessors was that he was a southerner, born and raised. He was born in Mississippi in 1867, and his family moved to Texas while he was a child. He turned his love for the music of his adopted state, particularly the songs of cowboys, into a scholarly pursuit when he began a master's degree at Harvard University in 1907.

Lomax's first major work was *Cowboy Songs* (1911).[14] Although the collection consisted entirely of the songs of men working in a single occupation, it marked a turning point in the study of American folk music. In *Cowboy Songs*, Lomax parted from the Sharp precedent by providing musical notations and anecdotes to illustrate the songs' subject matter of life on the range, which situated them in a specifically American cultural and geographical context. In another important respect, however, he continued in the Sharp legacy: he asserted that truly authentic folk music existed only in communities isolated from mainstream society. Cowboys, to Lomax, fit this criterion. Driving cattle herds up and down the rural western states, cowboys were transitory figures disconnected from dominant society, living in their own communities and creating songs that spoke directly to their circumstances. Lomax regarded cowboys as not only isolated but also embodying a close-to-nature primitivism, which stemmed from the context of their work. As the historian Daniel Walkowitz explains, this "folk-as-antimodern" view regards the folk as untainted by mass culture and closer to nature. One problem with this view is that it fails to account for the "folk's" cultural dynamism, instead interpreting their traditions as frozen in time and disregarding how members of different communities borrowed from one another in crafting their own traditions.[15] Indeed, cowboys did not exist solely on the open plains; rather, they frequented towns and cities whenever they could. Yet Lomax's myopic view of the cowboys' circumstances was not necessarily intended merely to ascribe an authentic primitivism to them. It was also intended to portray them as products of uniquely national conditions; their authenticity lay in their situatedness in a distinctly American way of life. While the overwhelming majority of their countrymen did not share the cowboys' experiences, Lomax categorized their music as American because, in his view, they created it in response to uniquely American climatic, geographical, and labor conditions.

Besides cowboy music, the other distinctly American folk music in Lomax's estimation came from black communities in the rural South. A popular interest in black folk music had percolated in American society since the mid-nineteenth century. One of the earliest collections of black music was a series of spirituals that missionaries to the Sea Islands off the coast of Georgia and South Carolina published after the Civil War. Lomax had developed an interest in black folk songs as early as 1904, although he set it aside to concentrate on *Cowboy Songs*.[16] After publishing *Cowboy Songs*, Lomax returned to black folk music, asserting that it was the "most natural and distinctive" of all American music. He often lamented scholars' tendency to ignore black folk music, which, without scholarly attention, was in danger of being lost—corrupted by romantic whites who often adulterated the material in their local color literature, or ignored by educated blacks who, Lomax believed, often shunned the music of their ancestors and that of rural black communities. Lomax's interest in black folk music sharply contrasted with that of most folk song enthusiasts of the era, who were interested in only white traditions. It is even more remarkable that in the early years of the twentieth century, Lomax treated black music as part of the national musical heritage rather than solely that of an allegedly inferior subculture.

In spite of his populist approach and his interest in protecting black folk music traditions, Lomax did not transcend the racism of his time and place. In his writings, Lomax went beyond merely romanticizing southern black music to exoticizing it as the product of a strange, primitive people. He often reinforced racial stereotypes by describing African Americans as "childlike" or resorting to physical descriptions that he rarely applied to the white singers he encountered.[17] In his memoir, Lomax even mentioned with perplexity that northern audiences sometimes viewed his presentation of black folk songs with hostility, finding in it racist elements that Lomax either overlooked or dismissed. His ambiguity on race is displayed throughout *Adventures of a Ballad Hunter*. While he peppered his autobiography with racial stereotypes, he also demonstrated a profound respect for black folk traditions, as he revealed in one passage: "All my life I have laughed with my negro friends—never at them. In particular, I do resent 'takeoffs' of Negro religious ceremonies and spiritual singing such as I have often heard in northern cities."[18] Although he ultimately retained a strong social conservatism that often translated into overt racism, Lomax did view southern black culture as a legitimate form of folk culture. Furthermore, he argued that black secular musical traditions made significant contributions to the development of an American folk music canon and that recordings of black folk music should be preserved and maintained in the Library of Congress, to which he bequeathed all of his recordings.

Lomax was not alone in his effort to broaden the definition of American folk music to include the traditions of other native-born Americans, particularly African Americans, during the early decades of the twentieth century. In 1909, the sociologist Howard Washington Odum completed a doctoral dissertation at Clark University in Mississippi based on African American secular and religious folk songs that he had collected. Odum first attempted to delineate the psychological and social aspects of black music in his article "Folk-Song and Folk-Poetry: As Found in the Secular Songs of the Southern Negroes" (1911). While Lomax focused on collecting and preserving black traditions for posterity, Odum used them to understand a marginalized racial group. According to the historian Lynn Moss Sanders, Odum believed that folk songs provided insight into African American culture and society because they revealed what blacks "are" instead of "what [they] *appear to be*."[19] Like Lomax, Odum recognized that as a white scholar he knew little about African Americans and turned to their musical traditions as a way to cross social and cultural divides. Odum was a sociologist, and his work in African American folk music, much of which was done in collaboration with his student and eventual colleague Guy B. Johnson, interpreted folk music through a sociological lens. Odum and Johnson's study, *Negro Workaday Songs* (1926), achieved acclaim because it both contained original scholarship on black secular music and provided an analysis of how the songs functioned in society. Through this work, Odum came to believe that black folk music should be preserved and studied not only for its own sake but also because it could be employed in the effort to improve American race relations.[20]

Despite their often erroneous adherence to the "folk-as-primitive" view, Lomax and Odum, by opening up the canon of American folk music to distinctly national groups such as southwestern cowboys and former slaves and their descendants, broadened the understanding of folk music to include songs generated on American soil that related to American conditions. Lomax hoped that his collection of cowboy songs would encourage others to take up the task and collect other variations of national folk music, including "Negro folk songs" and lumberjack, mountaineer, and sea songs.[21] Odum took a more academic path and used folk music to understand American social conditions.

While insisting that American folk music was an indigenous creation, both men restricted their song collecting to specific communities of native-born Americans who were (allegedly) isolated from mass culture. Other folklorists of this era, however, encouraged the collection and preservation of both native and naturalized Americans. As early as 1914, for example, the folklorist Phillips Barry called for members of the AFS to collect the songs "of our fellow-citizens whose power of English is an acquired trait," in addition to collecting from native-born and American Indian groups. Barry listed German, French, Spanish, Gaelic, and Yiddish as "folk" languages, and the "new settlers of our crowded cities," including other white and non-white ethnic groups, such as Italians, Greeks, Slavs, Armenians, Magyars, and Syrians, as some of the neglected folk groups.[22] Few folklorists of the World War I era cared about the folklore of the foreign masses that filled the country's urban and industrial centers. Barry was thus an anomaly in early twentieth-century folklore circles, but his views were very much in line with a new group of public intellectuals who looked to protect and preserve immigrant cultures, both for the sake of the ethnic communities and for the nation as a whole.

## Theoretical Influences

Horace Kallen, a philosopher and co-founder of the New School for Social Research in New York City, was one of many social theorists who grappled with issues of cultural diversity during the era of mass immigration and migration of the early twentieth century. Kallen opposed programs that forced ethnic minorities to assimilate into dominant culture and advocated what came to be known as the theory of cultural pluralism. Kallen proposed that the United Stated adopt a "federation" approach similar to Switzerland's, in which all ethnic groups could participate on equal footing in political and economic life. Citizens would be united through the official language of English and would have access to dominant political and economic institutions. At the same time, however, they would be permitted to engage in their own cultural practices. Kallen scorned the popular melting-pot theory as a policy of forced homogeneity that stripped away citizens' ethnic heritage. The consequences of this could be devastating, for ethnic identities, according to Kallen, were the roots of individual identities; one could change almost every aspect of one's personal identity, but no one could alter his or her ethnicity. All Americans were hyphenated, even Anglo-Americans, and the time had come for the country to recognize that the national ideals of "individual freedom and liberty" included the right to cultural difference. Kallen's federation idea presented one of the earliest unity-within-diversity views of American society: it characterized the United States as a multicultural society that should protect the rights, both cultural and political, of the various ethnic groups living within its borders.[23]

Many urban progressives shared Kallen's views, particularly activists in the settlement house movement. As part of their effort to assist immigrants living in urban ethnic enclaves, settlement houses often offered classes in ethnic literature, art, and music. The houses even opened their doors to ethnic societies to stage community events that would bring immigrants of different backgrounds together. Jane Addams, a leader of the settlement movement, believed that aspects of the folk traditions of new immigrants from southern and eastern Europe needed to be preserved. Settlement workers collaborated with others interested particularly in folk dance to stage pageants that included the traditions of ethnic groups living in the area in the hope that the incorporation of these practices into mainstream culture could enrich American life and help the immigrants assimilate into their new environment.[24] Through these pageants, the settlement house workers aimed to aid in the immigrants' Americanization process while also enabling them to retain aspects of their cultural heritage. Several folklorists and folk enthusiasts operated in the same vein as the settlement house workers. Some members of regional chapters of the AFS even advocated a culturally pluralist position years before Kallen debuted his theory. As early as the 1890s, for example, the Philadelphia branch emphasized the diverse character of the city by instructing its members to collect the traditions of various groups residing there, including "Anglo-American," "Africo-American," and "Local Foreign" (Italian, German, Chinese, and "Gypsy" communities). The organization's guidebook instructed members to collect the living traditions in these communities that provided the groups with their distinctive identities—identities that also shaped the city's overall cultural character.[25]

Shortly after Kallen began challenging efforts to eradicate ethnic identity, Randolph Bourne, a leftist progressive, debuted his own proposal for how America should deal with its diverse populace. Bourne's views were foundationally similar to Kallen's, although his ultimate vision of American identity diverged from Kallen's federation. In the essay "Transnational America," Bourne claims that assimilation programs not only were detrimental to immigrants but also undermined their own intended goal of cultural homogenization. By forcing naturalized citizens to renounce all ethnic ties, 100 percent Americanizers had actually caused immigrants to cling steadfastly to their Old World identities. As did Kallen, Bourne supported cultural diversity, but whereas Kallen argued that ethnic identities were primarily important to the people of different ethnic groups, Bourne argued that these identities were important for individual citizens and for the nation as a whole.

Claiming that Anglo conservatism had been the nation's "chief obstacle to social advance," Bourne maintained that America needed the flow of new immigrants "to save us from our own stagnation." The end result would be a cosmopolitan nation that incorporated the best aspects of different global cultures. Bourne's vision of the ultimate American identity was "a transnationality, a weaving back and forth, with other lands, of many threads of all sizes and colors," predicated on a constant interchange with ethnic cultures present in the United States.[26] By arguing thus, Bourne moved beyond the limits of cultural pluralism by ignoring group boundaries and promoting voluntary over involuntary affiliations, meaning that individuals could adopt from a variety of cultural sources, in addition to relying on the traditions of one's ethnic heritage, in constructing a personal identity. In Bourne's system, individuals could indeed change their identities regardless of their lineage. This idea strongly resonated with folk revivalists who later argued that all ethnic, regional, and racial folk music traditions found throughout the nation contributed to an overarching national identity; thus, all citizens, not just those who emerged directly from these groups, could borrow from and partake in these American traditions.

The progressive intellectuals and folklorists generated a vision of Americanism grounded in cultural diversity. Yet there were points of division among the approaches. Kallen and Bourne focused largely on urban groups of naturalized citizens, whereas folklorists such as Lomax and Odum emphasized rural communities of native-born citizens in their work. To overcome the division between rural and urban cultures, a movement that attempted to bring them together within an overarching American national identity emerged in the

1920s. The regionalist movement, as it became known, connected writers, artists, folklorists, sociologists, urban planners, and scholars who eschewed mass
culture in favor of folk cultures. While the movement appreciated both urban
and rural cultures, many regionalists specifically looked to rural groups in their
effort to locate a distinctly national culture. However, rather than simply advocating rural culture in toto, the regionalists, as their name implies, acknowledged the cultural differences of American regions and tried to determine how
the traditions of the Northeast, Southeast, Southwest, Midwest, and West could
be woven into a single national fabric. Because they viewed regions as constitu-
ent parts of the national whole, the regionalists held a culturally pluralist view
of American identity that promoted "heterogeneity over homogeneity" and that
provided a means for contesting the homogenizing effects of mass culture by
bringing local folkways into mainstream culture. As the regionalist folklorist
Benjamin Botkin noted, regionalism emerged as "an effect of the cultural diversity and change due to the geographical distribution and historical diffusion of
culture."[27] The regionalists' task was to ensure that American identity reflected
the diverse nature of its citizenry.

Regionalists ardently believed that American culture needed to be rooted in
the nation's primary folk communities: rural communities, Indian tribes, immigrant folk groups, and African Americans in the South.[28] Near the end of the
decade, Botkin described the movement as "developing a new feeling for local-
ity—not the idle small-town spirit of curiosity, gossip, and boosting but the
genuine need of taking root, of finding solidarity and unity in identifying one-
self with the community, a need growing out of a world unrest and conflict
during and since the War."[29] Botkin concluded with a reference to World War I
because the social transformations wrought by the wartime domestic policies
profoundly affected the early regionalists. The increased xenophobia, heightened vigilance, and open suppression of cultural and political dissent that characterized these years worried regionalists, many of whom were politically
progressive. The labeling of political dissenters or ethnic Americans as "un-
American" continued with the anti-pluralist 100 percent Americanizers during
the postwar years. The regionalists strongly advocated cultural heterogeneity
and abhorred programs that limited diversity, such as the Quota Act of 1924,
which severely curtailed the number of immigrants from southern and eastern
Europe and eliminated new immigrants from East Asian and South Asian nations altogether, and groups that stifled political and social dissent, such as the
American Legion and the Ku Klux Klan. Regionalists worked to counteract this
restrictive, xenophobic nationalism through their literary and artistic works
and public programs. According to the editor of the *Saturday Review of Literature,* regionalism, "already booming underway in this country," was ushering in
a new concept of nationalism that directly challenged the reactionary nationalism that allegedly patriotic groups such as the Klan espoused. Calling for "a
dynamic and realistic defining of the concept of Americanism to take it out of
any possible shallow connotation of reaction or conservative implication," the

*Review*'s editor firmly situated regionalism in a socially progressive vein. Lest there was any doubt as to his social views, he continued: "Classifying people and policies as 'American' or 'un-American' is a poor substitute for reality in a day when the nation needs to go on as a nation, set in the American scene."[30] As with cultural pluralists, regionalists recognized the importance of group identities embedded in local cultures throughout the nation. They sought to preserve the customs and traditions that these communities had generated and sustained over the course of American development while ensuring that citizens in all groups had access to the political process. Ultimately, they advocated a unity-within-diversity interpretation of American identity that included native-born and ethnic citizens in the national composite.

Although the regionalist movement consisted of members from all areas of the humanities and social sciences, literary figures interested in folklore were particularly prevalent. Legends, tall tales, jokes, and other aspects of storytelling appeared in regionalist novels, plays, and story collections. Several regionalists also turned their attention specifically to folk music. Perhaps the most notable figure in this area was Carl Sandburg. A writer and poet, Sandburg often roamed the country, a practice he developed as a young man looking for work. Over the course of his travels, Sandburg collected songs from friends, colleagues, and other people he met on lecture tours, publishing them in a large volume entitled *American Songbag* (1927).[31] Sandburg's primary objective in releasing his collection was to get Americans singing—and singing these particular songs; hence, his inclusion of piano arrangements to accompany the song lyrics. Sandburg often sang these songs himself, generally breaking out into one or more before he ended a public lecture. He arranged his collection thematically, dividing the songs under such headings as "Lumberjack," "Sea Chanties," "Mountain," "Cowboy," and other established categories of folk music. However, he also extended the definitional boundaries by including sections such as "Hobo Songs" and "Prison and Jail Songs" five years before John Lomax began collecting songs from prisoners in southern penitentiaries. He even included a section on urban songs called "Big Brutal City." In so doing, Sandburg ignored the stipulation among academic folklorists that folk songs arose only in isolated communities and that those communities were predominantly rural.

By including urban material in his definition of folk songs, Sandburg followed Barry's inclusion of city dwellers in his definition of folk communities. Sandburg also included in his collection songs from known musicians, breaking from another folk music convention that folk songs were a community affair and not the creations of individuals. He attributed an overwhelming majority of his songs to individual authors, many of whom had composed the songs recently and related them to relatively current events. In these respects, Sandburg represented a trend that the historian Karl Miller argues developed in the 1920s: that of folklorists including commercial music in their collections of American folk music. This can be attributed to two trends: the fact that the view that rural folks were still creating folk songs, a view that both Lomax and Odum advocated, had gained popularity in folklore circles and the rise of commercial race and hillbilly recordings, which consisted of relatively unknown regional musicians performing material not composed by professional songwriters. The latter trend led some to investigate how commercial music entered regional folk communities, which in turn led them to reevaluate the stipulation that folk groups—especially those in the rural South—were isolated from mass culture.[32] Sandburg combined these trends by asserting that folk songs were both "as ancient as the medieval European ballads brought to the Appalachian Mountains" and "as modern as skyscrapers, the Volstead Act and the latest oil-well-gusher," and that all of them contributed in some way to the making of an identifiable national identity.[33]

The melodies and verses presented in *American Songbag* were from "diverse regions, from varied human characters and communities . . . sung differently in different places," as Sandburg wrote in the introduction to the collection; they were all "ditties brought together from all regions of America. . . . It is an all-American affair, marshaling the genius of thousands of original singing Americans."[34] One of the defining features of America for Sandburg was diversity itself. He did not merely state that this collection was indicative of the pluralist nature of American society; he demonstrated this in the songs he included: Mexican songs such as "La Cucaracha," cowboy ballads such as "Streets of Laredo," mountain fiddle tunes such as "Turkey in the Straw," southern blues such as "Levee Moan," and songs from the Caribbean such as "John B. Sails." Sandburg's recognition of pluralism as a critical feature of American identity would continue among every succeeding generation of folk revivalists.

As with the folk music collectors like John Lomax, social scientists like Howard Odum, and public folklorists like Benjamin Botkin, Sandburg believed that folk music provided particular insight into different groups of Americans and that deciphering what musical variations revealed about these communities would provide a deeper understanding of American society as a whole. His diverse collection of "American" folk songs also reflected the theories of cultural pluralism and cosmopolitanism because it incorporated ethnic songs from communities of recent immigrants. Sandburg, however, went beyond celebrating cultural diversity and became an advocate for the people whose music he collected. For him, folk music was a way to champion economically, socially, and politically marginalized citizens. Through this music, Americans expressed their disillusionment with their circumstances and their hope for a better life. The fact that he included songs from labor strikes and other protests indicates that Sandburg also believed that folk music could be used as a tool in people's struggles. This interest largely stemmed from the radical political views that he developed at an early age. Indeed, Sandburg's belief that the music of the people could be used to help aid movements for social justice became a guiding principle for the initial folk music revivalists, and for the generations that followed.

In his collections of folk songs, Sandburg added a class dynamic to popular understandings of American folk music. This was the final element of the foundation on which the early folk music revivalists constructed their own view of Americanism. Sandburg's working-class Americans joined with the ethnically, racially, and regionally diverse citizens that other scholars, public intellectuals, and folklorists celebrated in their definitions of the American folk, definitions that the folk revivalists used in constructing their understanding of American folk music and an overarching American identity.

## *The Medley*

In conducting an intellectual history of the folk revival, *"I Hear America Singing"* follows the movement chronologically. Chapter 1, "Hearing the People," explains how and why the revival began during the era of the Great Depression by exploring the reciprocal relationships that the revivalists had with cultural and political leaders/workers. This investigation into how the revivalists contributed to the shaping of dominant cultural norms during the World War II era continues in Chapter 2, "The People's War." The political culture of the wartime years, much like that of the New Deal era, was conducive to the revivalists' music and their larger message, and they ensured that folk music became a vehicle for pro-democracy and pro-diversity propaganda. Many of the leading members of the revival were leftists—either communists or fellow travelers. The history of the Old Left of the Popular Front generation is therefore crucial to the story of the folk music revival; thus, Chapter 3, "Illusion and Disillusionment," examines leftist revivalists during their political heyday, between the Popular Front and the beginning of the Cold War. Chapter 4, "Keeping the Torch Lit," follows the revivalists into the Cold War era and explores how they struggled to survive the anticommunist crusades of the McCarthy period. This chapter also addresses the new, postwar generation of revivalists and determines how they reacted to the cultural and social contexts of the 1950s. In doing so, it adds to the developing historiography that challenges the view that American culture and society was ruled by consensus politics and cultural conformity during the 1950s. Specifically, the revival projects reveal that many Americans continued to believe in the promise of progressive Americanism and voiced their outrage at the disjuncture between democratic rhetoric and constitutional rights, on the one hand, and the political reality of anticommunism, on the other. Through specific musical programs, members of the revival expressed their cultural and political dissent and reaffirmed their faith in cultural and political democracy, all of which served as a precursor to the rise of New Left activism.

Chapter 5, "The Boom," charts the major turning point in the movement—the advent of the folk music fad—tracing the explosion of popular interest in folk music during the early 1960s and the implications this had on the core revival. While teenyboppers fueled the folk music craze in pop culture, a new generation of political activists incorporated folk music in efforts of social and political reform, as had the Popular Front generation. During the 1940s, leftist revivalists viewed folk music as a valuable cultural tool for struggles for eco-

nomic reform, civil rights, and peace; in the 1960s, leftist revivalists of the baby
boom generation brought folk music into the contemporary variations of these
same struggles. Therefore, examining how and why political actors of both generations used folk music in their programs helps to draw the connections between these two eras of heightened leftist activity. /in Mass Media

As with many fads, the folk boom did not last long. During its height, the
revivalists responded to the popularity of folk music in different ways, which
made it difficult to regroup after the boom subsided. Many had established trajectories that separated them from the main movement and had little interest in
returning to the revival. Similarly, young political activists of the early New Left
divided into smaller, special interest groups rather than remaining as a large-
scale political movement. Chapter 6, "A Bust and a Beginning," charts the almost simultaneous disintegration of the folk music revival and of the early New
Left. Yet as the political and revival movements collapsed, a new movement
designed to generate a culturally and civically democratic American identity
was on the rise: multiculturalism. The second half of the chapter explores how
the revivalists set the stage for this cultural turn by examining the emergence of
multiculturalism and connecting this development to similar programs that the
revivalists created during the late 1960s and into the 1970s.

Post Mod.

Each chapter explores a stage in the evolution of the folk music revival over
the course of the mid-twentieth century. As a cultural movement that lasted for
decades, the revival went through phases: sometimes the revivalists were in the
cultural spotlight, while at other times they played on a small side stage below
the cultural and political radar. Yet despite the varying degrees of the revival's
cultural and political significance, each phase gave new shape and form to the
revival as a whole. Therefore, *"I Hear America Singing"* does not privilege any
particular period of the revival or group of revivalists. In addition to explaining
the revival's rise and fall as a movement and its relationship to American culture and society, the book provides an account of how and why the revivalists
sustained their culturally pluralist and politically democratic Americanism
over this tumultuous period in American history. The rhetoric and tactics that
the revivalists used changed in response to larger political and cultural shifts,
but the message remained the same. Although the revival has long since ended,
both the ideas of democratic Americanism and the music of the movement continue to be vital parts of the American cultural identity—past and present.

# 1

## HEARING THE PEOPLE

When the 1930s began, the community of folk music enthusiasts that had started to form during the previous decade had little holding it together other than shared musical appreciation. As the decade progressed, however, these individuals came together to form a network, united by their efforts to use folk music to influence how Americans conceptualized their nation. The timing for this kind of program was apt, for the country was in the midst of an identity crisis as citizens struggled to adapt to the chain of disasters that accompanied the onset of the Depression. Distressing levels of unemployment and underemployment challenged the old adage that America was the land of opportunity where hard work was the key to success. Amid the emotional turmoil that the Depression engendered, intellectuals began to examine the underlying values and traits that formed the national character. Many aimed to redefine the American identity, often by seeking to unearth cultural traditions that could aid Americans in their struggle to stay afloat, both economically and psychologically.[1] In the effort to do just that, the public folklorists, musicians, and musical entrepreneurs of the revival combined ideas embedded in cultural pluralism, cosmopolitanism, and regionalism to generate an interpretation of nationalism predicated on cultural and political democracy. In addition to borrowing from social theories, these budding revivalists also incorporated the politics of the era in the version of Americanism that they crafted during this period. Combining racial, ethnic, and religious pluralism with the celebration of the economically marginalized common within left-wing and liberal circles, the revivalists solidified their pluralist view of democracy, a view that they forged through folk music.

The revivalists were in good company. The general malaise that settled over the country after 1929 prompted many intellectual, cultural, social, and political leaders to turn to "the people" to locate the traits of the nation's identity. In the 1930s, artists and intellectuals who had fled the provinces in the previous decade returned home and attempted to reconnect with American society. One way they aimed to do so was by incorporating images of the quotidian in their work. Throughout the decade, scholars conducted oral histories, painters depicted scenes of everyday life, writers dabbled in realist literature, and photographers became preoccupied with capturing images of average and downtrodden Americans. During the Depression years, many artists and intellectuals defined the people as Carl Sandburg did: displaced farmers, southern sharecroppers, unemployed industrial workers, migrants, hoboes, and other groups of the economically dispossessed. As the understanding of the people fell along economic lines, other identities based on race, gender, or ethnicity tended to fall by the wayside in popular discourse.[2]

Leading liberal intellectuals, government officials, and labor leaders may have lost interest in cultural identities, but they remained fascinated with the cultural traditions practiced within various communities. Cultural and civil leaders encouraged the collection and cataloguing of these traditions in the midst of the economic crisis in an effort to understand the American cultural heritage. To achieve this goal, many of these figures used what they found to identify a "usable past"—traditions that had sustained the American people throughout the nation's history and that they believed Americans could now employ to aid them through the present crisis. While the effort to locate a usable past originated in the 1920s, the Depression turned it into a widespread mission.[3]

In an era dominated by the iconography of the people, public folklorists found a receptive audience for folk music. Some scholars have argued that the populist sentiments that pervaded New Deal rhetoric and policies focused on the white rural ideal.[4] Yet although liberal politicians, conservative folk preservationists, and even some leftist folk enthusiasts tended to focus on rural communities of native-born citizens—regarding these people as either the last racially pure Anglo-Saxon Americans or as exemplars of a native radical tradition—their conceptions of the folk were not the only ones that circulated during this period. Most Depression-era revivalists recognized the ethnic, racial, and geographic diversity of America, a view that borrowed heavily from the theories of regionalism that became predominant during the 1930s. Regionalists were primarily interested in locating a national heritage that contained traditions to which Americans could turn to reestablish a collective identity during an era of social, cultural, and economic transformation. The search for an American identity manifested itself in the regionalists' collections of folk culture and their studies of the relationships between folk groups and the regions in which they lived. Regionalism during the 1930s emphasized an idea of "place," both in the literal sense as a geographically defined location and in a figurative sense as characterized by the people who lived there—in their patterns of daily life, the history of their shared traditions, and the ways in which they viewed themselves as belonging to a community that was simultaneously part of the nation and still culturally distinct.[5]

While they shared a belief that national identity should be predicated on cultural heterogeneity, regionalists varied in their views of what the movement entailed and in their political outlook.[6] During the early years of the movement, most regionalists believed that cultural products were born out of particular social, cultural, and geographical conditions, and they focused exclusively on the cultural differences among regional communities, often ignoring issues of social stratification and economic disparity. As the Depression progressed, however, many regionalists began to adopt more progressive, or even radical, political and social views as they became active in public programs. As a result, these regionalists turned their attention to groups that they had overlooked during the prior decade—economically marginalized members of rural communities, as well as urban and labor groups.[7] On the one hand, many of these regionalists were politically aligned with New Deal liberalism. On the other hand, the more politically progressive regionalists' racially, geographically, and economically inclusive definition of regional groups more closely mirrored the views of the American left of the 1930s. Several nascent folk revivalists participated in the latter wing of the movement and carried the ideas of left-wing regionalism into their own interpretations of both American folk music and the overarching American identity.

By combining cultural pluralism and regionalism, the revivalists defined the American people as an array of different groups. This led some revivalists to join in left-wing causes, which suited their interpretation of Americanism. Others remained committed to New Deal liberalism, and their work during the Depression era challenges the assessment that liberal concepts of the people focused solely on economic groups over cultural ones. Although not all revivalists shared the same political views—some remained in the political center—they all ultimately believed that the American national identity rested on a foundation of cultural diversity. Yet this diversity did not divide citizens along cultural fault lines because a collective faith in democratic civic ideals united Americans as a national body politic. Indeed, this view became dominant in mainstream politics during the Depression and the World War II era. Two key revivalists, Benjamin Botkin and Alan Lomax, summarized this view by explaining that the rise of interest in folk music during the 1930s resulted from the "deep need for art, literature and music that reflected U.S. democratic and equalitarian political ideals."[8] By the end of the decade, the revivalists had crafted a notion of nationalism that brought the appreciation of cultural diversity found in cultural pluralism and cosmopolitanism together with an interest in securing political and economic rights for all citizens, rights that the revivalists believed formed the basis of American political democracy.

The folk revivalists found the political and cultural atmosphere of the New Deal conducive to both their understanding of Americanism and their efforts to spread this view through folk music. A fan of folk music, Franklin Roosevelt hosted concerts at the White House and often patronized local festivals when he visited Warm Springs, Georgia. The Roosevelt administration also supported efforts to collect, preserve, and present folk music to the public, and several of the early revivalists found homes in government agencies and New Deal cultural programs. As many revivalists became enmeshed in the New Deal milieu, some of the leading figures also drew inspiration from the Popular Front. Members of Popular Front programs often worked on behalf of disadvantaged Americans—many of whom came from the folk groups that the revivalists championed. The leftist politics of the 1930s offered some revivalists a political outlet that enabled them to move beyond merely advocating the people's music to acting as advocates for the people by engaging in new programs of political and social activism. The revivalists' version of Americanism was thus motivated by a strong social impulse that combined liberalism's emphasis on equal opportunity, freedom of expression, and political progress with left-wing demands for economic and social justice.[9] Their version of nationalism therefore emphasized pluralism and demanded the inclusion of all citizens regardless of cultural, racial, or economic differences. For the young revivalists, the essence of the democratic national heritage—cultural and ideological—could be found within different types of folk songs, and they began a movement with the intention of introducing (and sometimes reintroducing) Americans to their national music.

## The Rise of Folk Festivals

The rise of interest in folk music during this era was most notable in the proliferation of musical performance, specifically in festival form. Some folk festivals, especially those in urban areas, maintained the spirit of cultural pluralism that had begun in the previous decade. In 1932, organizers in St. Paul, Minnesota, attempted to inaugurate an annual event that featured more than eighteen nationalities. According to the program book for the 1934 "International Folk Festival" in St. Paul, "All nationalities, races, religions, ages and occupations are represented. Men, women, and children of various degrees of education, of every economic and social level, the privileged and the unemployed, descendants of early settlers, [and] the latest arrivals are friends in a common enterprise." Mutual understanding and an acceptance of cultural diversity were essential to the national image that these festivals promoted.[10] Occasionally, the urban festivals were lengthy events, as was the case in Hartford, where a year-long festival in 1935–1936 commemorated the three hundredth anniversary of the founding of Connecticut in 1635. In orchestrating the event, festival planners studied census records to determine which ethnic and racial groups lived in the city. Representatives from each group participated in organizing the events, and the different groups performed several times throughout the year. Event planning was left entirely to the participating groups. The festival debuted on August 31, 1935, with a German presentation. Norwegian, Danish,

Chinese, African American, Ukrainian, French Canadian, Armenian, Swedish, Irish, Italian, Hungarian, Russian, and Portuguese groups sponsored programs the rest of the year. Like other festivals of the era, this one focused on enabling different ethnic groups to present their traditions. James H. Dillon, one of the main organizers of the festival, noted its success by observing that the audience for each event was always diverse and never limited to members of the groups that were presenting.[11]

Not all festivals shared the pluralist approach of the organizers of the Hartford and other urban folk festivals. Some festivals, particularly those in the South, promoted the view that the *real* folk of America were rural mountaineers of Anglo-Saxon descent. In 1928, Bascom Lamar Lunsford, a musician and lawyer, designed a folk music program as the entertainment portion of the annual Rhododendron Festival in Asheville, North Carolina. By 1930, the success of Lunsford's program had led him to establish it as a separate event named the Mountain Dance and Folk Festival. The same year, Jean Bell Thomas debuted her American Folk Song Festival in Ashland, Kentucky. Both festivals included only self-taught musicians who presented music and dances allegedly handed down through the generations. Lunsford and Thomas focused exclusively on white Appalachian mountain culture, ignoring music influenced by other racial and ethnic groups or by mass culture. Another popular festival of the era was the White Top Festival that Annabel Morris Buchanan organized in southwestern Virginia with the help of the composer John Powell. The White Top Festival, according to the organizers, presented only the "finest" examples of American folk music to preserve, in Buchanan's words, "the best native music, balladry, dances, traditions, and other arts and customs that belong to our [white] race. . . . The White Top activities, if they are to endure, must be wrought slowly, carefully, measure by measure, for a race." White Top was for "the folk," and, as she proclaimed, "We are the folk."[12] Despite its racial exclusivity and myopic definition of the "folk," White Top was a popular event; it even attracted Eleanor Roosevelt as a visitor.

In the midst of southern regional festivals such as White Top and the Mountain Dance and Folk Festival, a new festival emerged under the direction of Sarah Gertrude Knott. Born in 1895 and raised in southwestern Kentucky, Knott grew up among people who maintained similar social and cultural mores as Buchanan and Lunsford. Despite these similar circumstances, Knott took her program in a very different direction from that of the other regional festivals. With a penchant for theater, Knott became active in the Carolina Playmakers during the 1920s, a student playwriting and acting troupe at the University of North Carolina, Chapel Hill, under the direction of Frederick Koch. In 1929, Knott left Chapel Hill for St. Louis, where she became the executive director of the city's Dramatic League. During the early years of the Depression, Knott sought to bring theater to the people and even received some funding from the Federal Emergency Relief Administration for her programs. One of the league's most successful events was "The Theater of Nations," a performance that featured new immigrants presenting plays and stories in their own languages. Eventually, this expanded into a citywide event called a "Festival of Nations." This festival sparked Knott's interest in developing a national event that would display a variety of American regional folk traditions. In 1933, Knott brought together several prominent businessmen from St. Louis to finance the operation, the playwright Paul Green to serve as the festival's president, and the former showman M. J. Pickering to act as the business manager for the first National Folk Festival (NFF) production.[13]

Although Buchanan, Lunsford, and Thomas all became affiliated with the National Folk Festival, Knott's views on what constituted American folk traditions differed remarkably from those of her predecessors. Rather that focus exclusively on Anglo-Saxon music and dance, the NFF featured an array of regional traditions performed by a variety of cultural groups. Perhaps this deviation from the norm stemmed from the fact that Knott had never attended a southern festival prior to designing her own, and she drew much of her inspiration from the regional dramatists who began staging theatrical productions based on rural and agrarian folk culture during the 1920s. Koch was part of this camp, and he often incorporated southern, rural African American folklore collected by his colleague Howard Odum into his plays about North Carolina. This interest in local folklore and his affiliation with the University of North Carolina, Chapel Hill, led Koch, along with many other local dramatists, into the burgeoning regionalist movement. Koch shared a high opinion of regionalism, stating in 1925 that "the only way we can be truly national is to be loyally local."[14] Knott's association with folk dramatists like Koch had a profound effect on her, and their regionalism greatly influenced how she staged the NFF during its formative years.[15] Other members of the loosely connected regionalist movement also had an impact on Knott's festival planning. Knott, who was not an academic, often sought out scholars for advice on festival planning. One of her earliest advisers was Arthur Campa, a folklorist who specialized in the Southwest. Other regionalist writers, such as Constance Rourke and Zora Neale Hurston, were involved in the festival from the beginning, and Botkin, a leading regionalist, became a prominent member of the National Folk Festival Association (NFFA).

When reflecting on the origins of the NFF, Knott believed that it benefited from starting at the right time. In many respects, the festival reflected the forms of cultural pluralism that characterized New Deal liberalism, particularly the cultural gifts programs, which had gained ascendance during the interwar period. After the passage of the quota acts that stymied the flow of immigration in the mid-1920s, hard-line Americanization programs fell out of favor as attitudes toward ethnic groups began to gradually soften. Led by founding member Rachel Davis DuBois, cultural gifts proponents rejected the forced assimilation of the melting-pot metaphor and instead promoted a unity-within-diversity view of American society reminiscent of Horace Kallen's cultural pluralism, in which the cultural distinctiveness of ethnic groups would be protected. DuBois and her cohort helped move discussions of racial and religious bigotry from the pages of intellectual magazines and scholarly journals into the public realm and worked to secure widespread acceptance of ethnic groups in mainstream society by celebrating their cultural contributions to American life. This approach would not only teach citizens to appreciate the inherent plurality of American culture but also help to assimilate those immigrant groups who were already here. Ultimately, cultural gifts leaders hoped that their programs would teach Americans to appreciate cultural diversity at home and around the world.[16]

While Knott's views on American identity were in line with DuBois's unity-within-diversity view, she did not share Dubois's desire to galvanize support for an international peace movement among American citizens.[17] Instead, Knott designed her program as a presentation of the traditions that shaped the creation of a distinctly American cultural heritage, a design that she believed further enhanced the popularity of the festival. According to Knott, a "spirit of nationalism" marked American culture during the 1930s—a Zeitgeist that included a strong interest in American folk traditions.[18] Indeed, the festival's organization and execution clearly reflect a nationalist vision, but one that was rooted in conceptions of American regionalism as it developed during the Depression decade. Because regionalists focused on the communities that gave regions their cultural characteristics, they often identified regions by the different ethnic groups that resided within them. Regionalists who focused on folk culture (folk regionalists) particularly tended to concentrate on ethnic and racial groups (e.g., Pennsylvania Germans, southern African Americans, southwestern Hispanics, and mountain whites) and sought to create an American national identity that incorporated both the ethnic cultures of immigrant communities and the native-born traditions that developed in the rural provinces.[19]

The inaugural festival in 1934 established the precedent of identifying the participants by their home regions in addition to their race or ethnicity. The program commenced with Kiowa Indians from Oklahoma and moved on to French folk songs and songs from Vermont, and closed with southern African American spirituals. The second day featured shape-note singers presented by George Pullen Jackson, a Spanish folk play, and more American Indian songs and concluded with Spanish folk songs. The third day began with a group of sailors from Snug Harbor on Staten Island singing sea chanteys. Cowboy music and ballads opened the fourth day's program, and the final performance of the festival featured a "Negro Chorus of Three Hundred Voices," which combined different choruses from St. Louis. Knott later explained that she gave the American Indians, the "first Americans," the honor of opening the festival because the program was arranged historically, beginning with the oldest traditions and ending with the most recent. She further justified her decision to begin with non-Anglo traditions by explaining that American Indians had already established a strong folk tradition on American soil that predated the arrival of Europeans.[20]

Much like the cultural gifts proponents, the festival treated each tradition as a separate and distinct entity frozen in time. While Knott emphasized a chronological approach, she did not treat these traditions as a progression wherein older forms influenced recent folk traditions; the music and dance that the festival featured did not indicate any cultural intermingling or change over time. Similarly, cultural gifts initiatives romanticized ethnic traditions as quaint relics partly because new immigrants were not present to challenge the representations of Old World culture. Furthermore, cultural gifts proponents viewed cultural heterogeneity through the lens of American values; thus, they promoted only those traits that were compatible dominant national ideals.[21] These criticisms also apply to the early National Folk Festivals. The festival focused exclusively on ethnic traditions by early immigrant groups rather than on ethnic groups that had recently arrived in the United States, because Knott emphasized those groups that were either the most assimilated or the most closely tied to the nation's past.

While the failure to recognize the contributions that recent immigrant groups made to the development of the American national heritage hampered Knott's pluralist outlook, she would refine her position over the next few years. Despite its general lack of ethnic diversity, Knott consistently advocated for racial inclusion in the festival's planning and performances. When Zora Neale Hurston did not assist in the second festival, held in Chattanooga the following year, Knott enlisted the help of African American civic, educational, and religious groups to recommend black performers. The resulting presentations, while celebrating African American traditions, often veered from accepted definitions of what constituted folk music and dance. The festival featured the highly professional Fisk Jubilee Singers and a large-scale choral performance, in addition to students from the Bonny Oaks School singing spirituals and a YWCA group's presentation of "Negro games." Besides highlighting black spirituals, this festival also included a sampling of work songs by a group from the Booker T. Washington Civilian Conservation Corps camp in Oglethorpe, Georgia. That same year, Thomas E. Jones, the president of Fisk University in Nashville, joined the NFFA's executive committee. The politically progressive side of the festival was shown by the performance of Paul Green's play *Fixin's*, presented by a group of students from Black Mountain College in eastern North Carolina.[22]

Knott faced one of the more significant challenges to her racial inclusivity when the third National Folk Festival took place in Dallas in 1936, timed to coincide with the Texas centennial. A primary problem was that the city's strict policy of segregation made it difficult to stage an interracial show. Although Knott did concede to Jim Crow policies by staging racially separate preliminary programs and showcasing African American traditions in the "Hall of Negro Life" (funded by the federal government rather than the centennial committee), she did not alter the overall design of the program to appease the festival's hosts. Despite the centennial planning committee's efforts to prevent African Americans from participating in their celebration, Knott insisted on the inclusion of black performances in her festival and continued working with African American groups to find strong performers. Furthermore, the program book indicates that the nightly concerts on the main stage continued as planned, with black and white groups performing on the same stage.[23]

Although Knott omitted many groups that others in the Depression era celebrated for their contribution to the national cultural identity, the design of the annual festivals indicates that she largely embraced the culturally pluralist populism of the New Deal era. She particularly desired both to bring art to the people and to include the people in artistic creation. Believing that citizens from politically and economically marginalized folk groups played a role in shaping American culture, Knott concluded that their cultures should be a part of the nation's identity. One way to ensure this democratization of American culture and identity was to incorporate folk traditions into mainstream culture and society. Writing on the eve of the Dallas festival, Knott argued, "Before we ever have a genuine culture in America or a truly creative nation, the interest in creative endeavor must not only touch the lives of the people of higher educational and artistic levels, but it must be so democratic that it will include people of every class."[24] She therefore designed the NFF to bring people from across the nation (and from across racial and socioeconomic divides) together in an atmosphere of appreciation and exchange. Rather than mere entertainment, Knott emphasized that the music and dance performed at the festival was the essence of American heritage and that, by highlighting these performances, the festival "keeps alive the fine traditional customs associated with the founding of the nation."[25]

The following year marked a broadening of Knott's cultural pluralism as the festival moved to Chicago. The first group of recent immigrants to perform on the festival stage was a troupe of Lithuanian dancers led by Vyts Beliajus, a Lithuanian immigrant who was a key member of the International Folk Dance movement in Chicago and who became an active member of the NFFA.[26] Before the opening of the Chicago festival, Knott used an interview on WCFL, the Chicago Federation of Labor radio station, to explain the purpose of the NFF. Echoing a belief that served as a justification for some New Deal cultural programs such as the Federal Writers' Project's American Guide Series, Knott pointed out that Americans had been so busy building up the nation that they never took the time to appreciate the cultural riches scattered throughout the country. When Americans had money to travel, they usually chose to go abroad rather than to explore the varied regions of their own land, the very places that gave America its "warmth and color" as well as its "beauty." Through the festival, Knott endeavored to make the public aware of their country's folk music traditions, which would lead to the development of a "national consciousness" of the American cultural heritage. She also explained that the NFF illustrated the culturally diverse nature of the American people. Yet rather than including all groups in America, she continued to emphasize that the NFF highlighted only those groups that had "integrated more into the American cultural life," which indicated that, even as it slowly broadened, Knott's pluralism still had its limits.[27]

Even though the NFF began during a period of popular interest in folk culture, it struggled to stay afloat. The first two programs lost money, but Knott persisted, moving around the country and working to reflect the regional identities of the places in which the festival operated. When she took the NFF to Chattanooga, she included performers from the Eastern Band of Cherokee; when she hosted it from Texas, the program featured more Hispanic groups. True to her regionalist influences, Knott designed each festival to educate audiences about both their local and their national cultural heritage and, through that, the evolution of the American national identity. According to Benjamin Botkin, two main ideas gave shape to the version of Americanism that Knott presented to festival audiences: the sociological view that stressed the importance of diversity in an effort to counteract the forced assimilation programs of the early twentieth century, and the idea that both folk music itself and the study of folk music encouraged common people to actively participate in American society.[28] These two traits were manifested in the NFF's presentation of a diverse array of regional, ethnic, and racial groups and Knott's desire to incorporate these traditions into the dominant national culture.

Many of Knott's limitations and omissions were common to her place and time. Like the programs that emerged from the cultural gifts movements, the festival disregarded the dynamic nature of culture and instead treated traditions as fixed and unchanging. It also failed to account for the socioeconomic differences and disparities within the groups that presented on-stage or in the United States as a whole; even as it celebrated black folk culture, any recognition of racial inequality was largely absent.[29] Despite these shortcomings, the festival was remarkable in that it did not concentrate solely on celebrating white ethnics, as did many cultural gifts programs; nor did it focus entirely on white rural traditions, as did the southern festivals. Rather, Knott emphasized that racial and ethnic minorities such as American Indians, Latinos, and African Americans all made important contributions to the American cultural heritage, and by the beginning of the next decade, the number of groups that the festival commended for their contributions to American life had grown significantly.

## The New Deal Revivalists

The New Deal significantly influenced not only the politics of the 1930s but the culture of the decade, as well. The Roosevelt administration fostered that culture by establishing Federal One, a section of the Works Progress Administration (WPA) that encouraged the arts and employed American artists, writers, musicians, and actors in such initiatives as the Index of Design, the Federal Writers' Project, the Federal Music Project, and the Federal Theater Project. The New Dealers' populism led them to promote art that was relevant to the people, and public folklore suited this objective well. Botkin described the folklore and folk music research projects of the WPA and other government agencies as efforts that demonstrated "the relation between art and life, between work and culture." Many public folklorists sought to weave traditional songs and tales into the fabric of mainstream culture. Botkin defined the mission of New Deal public folklore as "the public support of art and art for the public, in research not for research's sake but for use and enjoyment by the many." The Federal One programs that incorporated folk culture, therefore, aimed "to assimilate folklore to the local and national life by understanding . . . the relation between the lore and the life out of which it springs." This effort, according to Botkin, was the "greatest educational as well as social experiment of our times."[30]

Botkin had a long history in the field of public folklore by the time he joined the Writer's Project. In 1901, he was a born into a Jewish family in Boston to parents who were recent immigrants. After teaching English at the University of Oklahoma and at settlement houses in New York City, Botkin continued his education in folklore and English under Louise Pound at the University of Nebraska. Relocating to Washington in 1937 under a Julius Rosenwald fellowship to research southern folk and regional literature at the Library of Congress, Botkin remained in the area and became a co-founder and chairman of the Joint Committee on Folk Arts of the WPA, served as the Library of Congress's Fellow in Folklore in 1941, and became the head of the Archive of American Folk Song (AAFS) in 1942. Throughout his career, Botkin was both a scholar and an unabashed popularizer of folk culture; he assembled popular folklore anthologies, served on the board of the National Folk Festival Association, and wrote about popular folk music activities for the *New York State Folklore Quarterly* and other journals. Botkin saw his work as advancing something greater than just the scholarship of American folklore, and he often raised the ire of academically inclined folklorists who disapproved of his disinclination to follow academic standards of analyzing folk music.[31] To Botkin, folklore and folk music played important roles in the communities that maintained certain traditions, and studying these traditions would shed light on the cultural life of the nation as a whole. He wrote, "The material collected will have important bearings on the study of American culture in both its historical and functional aspects, including minority groups (ethnic, geographical, and occupational), immigration and internal migration, local history, regional backgrounds and movements, linguistic and dialect phenomena." The folklorists' task, therefore, was to understand the relationship between folk groups and national society, and Botkin believed it was necessary both to study "folklore as a living culture" and to comprehend "its meaning and function not only in its immediate setting but in progressive and democratic society as a whole."[32] In Botkin's estimation, incorporating folk traditions into the larger national context would connect Americans to their cultural heritage while bringing the nation closer to achieving the political ideal of a democratic society.

By the 1930s, regionalism had come into its own as a movement, and regionalist theories often guided Botkin's work in the WPA. Indeed, many regionalists worked closely with revivalists in the cultural projects of Federal One, which highlighted local artistic expression in literature, theater, and art. These regionalists justified their efforts by arguing that folk culture provided the precise kind of usable past that cultural workers sought during a time of social instability because it consisted of traditions that had sustained generations of Americans through hard times. Seeking to determine how folk traditions could survive in modern America, many regionalists concluded that folk cultural practices were not merely antiquated cultural expressions but, rather, served a purpose for those who practiced them. Among these New Deal regionalists were the early folk music revivalists, who included Botkin, the public folklorist Alan Lomax, and the musicologist Charles Seeger. The figures in this "Washington establishment" used their positions in programs such as the Federal Writers' Project, the AAFS, the Radio Research Project at the Library of Congress, and the Resettlement Administration both to preserve and to popularize folk music and to spread their pluralist Americanism.

In addition to following the tenets of regionalism and theories of cultural pluralism, these folklorists also relied on the anthropological theory of functionalism to buttress their claims regarding the utility of folk music. Developed by the British anthropologists Bronislaw Malinowski and A. R. Radcliffe-Brown, functionalism held that all cultural practices existed because they served important purposes in the communities that maintained them. The theory effectually put an end to nineteenth-century ideas of cultural evolution, which held that cultures advanced over time and folk cultures were archaic vestiges from a bygone era.[33] This theory was particularly important to Depression-era folk regionalists because it justified their belief that folk traditions provided insight into contemporary society as well as historical conditions and events. Among the many public folklorists who relied on regionalism and functionalism as guides for their projects relating to American folk culture, specifically music, was Alan Lomax, the son of John Lomax. Alan Lomax believed that, because folk music served a function in folk communities, it granted insight into how regional communities operated, and he put this theory into practice through song-collecting expeditions.

In many ways, Alan Lomax followed a trajectory similar to that of his father. He was born in Texas in 1915 and educated for a time at Choate, the elite New England boarding school; thus, his identity was shaped by both northern and southern influences. Like his father, Alan Lomax began his college education at the University of Texas, transferred for one year to Harvard, then returned to the University of Texas and graduated in 1936. Throughout the 1930s, Lomax collected songs across the United States, as well as in the Caribbean, with the help of other folklorists, including Mary Elizabeth Barnicle and Zora Neale Hurston. By the end of the decade, he had become a premier figure in public folklore and a leading member of the burgeoning revival. Lomax became the "Assistant in Charge" of the AAFS in 1937, when his father was serving as the Honorary Consultant to the archive. Established in 1928, the AAFS was originally intended as a repository for "all the poems and melodies that have sprung from our soil or have been transplanted here, and have been handed down, often with manifold changes, from generation to generation as a precious possession of our folk."[34] Yet rather than treating the archive as a mere musical library, the Lomaxes turned it into a facility that would both preserve folk music and make it available to a public audience.[35] Through their work in the archive, the Lomaxes used folk music to shape American culture and, subsequently, American identity.

Unlike his father's, Alan Lomax's views regarding the significance of folk music were shaped by current trends in anthropology. During his first solo fieldwork trip in Haiti in 1936–1937, he consulted with Melville Herskovits, a prominent anthropologist, student of Franz Boas, and pioneer on the field of African diaspora studies. Through his studies and personal associations, Lomax followed in the vein of Boasian anthropology, which strongly influenced his views on both folk culture and race. Anthropologists in the Boasian tradition worked to combat racial prejudice by teaching Americans that racial diversity reflected *cultural* differences, based on learned behavior, rather than fixed, inherited traits. Lomax incorporated these ideas into his proposals for research funding, justifying his work in terms of its social science and national significance. In 1941, he began an intensive investigation of musical practices within black communities in the Mississippi Delta region, working in collaboration with several professors at Fisk. When requesting support from the AAFS for the project, Lomax explained:

> The agreed upon study was to explore objectively and exhaustively the musical habits of a single Negro community in the Delta, to find out and describe the function of music in the community, to ascertain the history of music in the community, and to document adequately the cultural and social backgrounds for music in the community. It was felt that this type of study, carried on in a number of types of southern communities would . . . describe music in the community objectively, giving all criteria for taste and the relationship of music to the dynamics of social change.[36]

Like Boasian anthropologists and sociologists in the Odum tradition, Lomax explained that a grassroots study of African American music would grant insight into social conditions and help in the wider understanding of how cultures change over time, a diachronic view that was largely absent in cultural gifts programs.

As regional folk music provided insight into specific communities, it also revealed larger historical processes, according to Lomax. Even before his trip to the Delta, he characterized his song-collecting efforts as important investigations into distinctly American sociological conditions. When he sought funding from the AAFS to conduct fieldwork around the Great Lakes during the late

1930s, Lomax explained that the region was likely a repository for lumberjack songs. He then proclaimed that by focusing on this region, the archive would be able to "explore the musical potentialities of the many foreign language groups of the area (Swedish, Norwegian, Finnish, Gaelic, French-Canadian, etc.) and to observe what have been the results of the mixing of these cultures with the Anglo-American matrix."[37] For Lomax and other folk regionalists of the New Deal era, racial and ethnic pluralism gave the nation its character, and it was incumbent on scholars and public officials to preserve these cultural traditions.

Lomax and Botkin recognized the importance of imparting their views of regionalism and pluralism to a public audience through folk music. One of the most successful means of reaching this public was through the medium of performance, as they wrote in a joint passage on folklore in the *Encyclopedia Britannica*: "Folk, folklorists, and the growing folklore audience met at folk festivals. . . . As cultural expression, it enabled regional and ethnic groups to preserve their own identity and to understand one another better."[38] In effect, they argued that the popularization of folk culture during the 1930s would actually put the appreciation of cultural diversity found in theories of cultural pluralism and cosmopolitanism into practice.

Lomax clearly recognized the important role that folk festivals played in illustrating and promoting American cultural diversity, because he attempted to stage one to suit that very purpose. In 1939, organizers of the World's Fair in New York City sought to incorporate folk traditions into the fair's programs. Envisioning a large-scale folk festival with an international flair to honor the occasion of "bringing the world's nations together" during a troubled time, the organizers commissioned Olin Downes, music critic for the *New York Times*, to plan music and dance activities. Downes strongly encouraged public folklorists such as those in the Folk Festival Council of New York City to be a part of the planning process. Alan Lomax, among others, enthusiastically answered the call to duty.[39] In a letter he wrote to Downes, Lomax described his program, entitled "Yankee Doodle Comes to Town":

> Central Idea: New York City, during her first hundred and fifty years, from 1639 to 1789 exemplifies the growth and the struggle for independence of the whole nation. . . . Nationalities: New York City has always been a cosmopolitan town and it will be amusing to portray the arrival of the first Chinaman, the first Negro, and the first Jew. Music: For musical material we will utilize Dutch and English folksongs, and shanteys, pirate songs, the popular airs of the revolutionary period, and Indian music.[40]

Lomax's pluralist vision reached beyond New York City to the rest of the country. He proposed to Downes that the folk music exhibit should offer four main pavilions: one a "Negro honky-tonk" and second a "mountain square dance hall," and two more drawn from such "almost endless" possibilities as the New Orleans

French Quarter, a Pennsylvania Dutch tavern, a "Haitian house with voodoo dances," a western saloon, "a down-Easter fish house," a "Mexican patio," an "Acadian Fais-do-do hall," a Hawaiian house, and a "Negro church social."[41] Unlike Knott, who structured her festival as an event in which the audience observed the artists on a stage (a structure common among many folk festivals of the era), Lomax sought to generate an atmosphere of active engagement. The purpose of the pavilions was to educate through participation: rather than passively watching folk traditions, audience members were to interact with the tradition-bearers. Lomax believed that, by learning different techniques of dancing, singing, and cooking, audience members would come to understand and appreciate these traditions and learn to respect the people who practiced them.[42]

Revivalists like Botkin and Lomax had developed their pluralist Americanism before they began working in government agencies such as the WPA and the AAFS. Being connected to these institutions, however, enabled them to reach a larger audience (not to mention that it provided them with a steady paycheck). The fact that progressive revivalists found employment through the federal government also reveals the extent to which the New Deal was receptive to the type of Americanism that the revivalists promoted. Ethnic pluralism was a central component of New Deal cultural nationalism. For example, in the fall of 1935, President Roosevelt provided funds to the Office of Education for radio broadcasts that would commemorate American social and cultural diversity; the series *Americans All . . . Immigrants All* (1938–1939), the largest cultural gifts initiative, exemplified this effort. Programs like this were symptomatic of the government's rejection of nativism during the New Deal years and of a widespread effort to celebrate the contributions that ethnic minorities made in shaping American life.

On the one hand, New Deal officials could symbolically embrace ethnic Americans because by the 1930s concerns over ethnic divisions or cultural strife had declined after the National Origins Act slowed the flow of immigration to barely a trickle. On the other hand, racist and anti-immigrant attitudes persisted in American society. Some of these attitudes were exacerbated by the rise of fascism abroad. The United States had its own share of pro-fascist groups, particularly the German American Bund and the Silver Legion of America (Silver Shirts), that attached themselves to Nazi Germany. However, anti-immigrant attitudes were not restricted to fringe groups on the radical right. Even the American Federation of Labor and the U.S. Chamber of Commerce continued to spew nativist rhetoric. The economic depression and fears that recent immigrants took jobs away from native-born citizens generated fertile ground for nativist attitudes to take root, and public opinion polls conducted over the decade revealed staunch opposition to suggestions of relaxing the quotas established in the prior decade. The persistence of nativism and xenophobia even after the curtailing of new immigration indicates that ethnic prejudice continued to be a common feature of the people's decade.[43]

Public officials, along with cultural and social workers, tried to counteract this nativist undercurrent by promoting a version of Americanism that celebrated racial, ethnic, and religious pluralism as the essence of the national identity throughout the Depression decade. By the late 1930s, they had initiated social and educational programs that rejected ideas of racial inferiority and white supremacy and defined the American national community as united by shared civic ideals. Their arguments against racial prejudice were buoyed by the work of anthropologists such as Boas, who wrote radio shows that disseminated this message through dialogues and skits and designed an exhibit in the Hall of Science and Education for the 1939 World's Fair that presented anthropological refutations of pseudoscientific arguments for white racial superiority.[44] The fact that scholars, cultural workers, and government officials, including the president, advocated such an Americanism during an era of increasing racial and ethnic tensions at home and abroad made these efforts all the more noteworthy. Overall, the government's rhetorical acceptance of cultural pluralism helped to spark a still different kind of nationalism during this period. Because the Depression affected almost all Americans, many who attempted to define an American national identity emphasized shared conditions rather than shared racial traits.[45] For them, the varied examples of the American *experience* became the defining feature of the nation's identity—an idea that many folk music revivalists had been articulating since the early 1930s.

By the end of the decade, when debates raged over the meaning of American identity and who qualified as an American, the revivalists were using folk music to push a democratic, pluralist Americanism. They argued that folk songs illustrated a shared national heritage because they came directly from the American people; these songs illustrated the national democratic ideal because all performers of folk songs participated in adapting the music and lyrics to suit their tastes and needs. The revivalists' message and their music therefore fit well with the pluralist, democratic populism of the Roosevelt administration. Yet the New Dealers were not the only ones who espoused this view, and soon more political figures, particularly on the left, adopted a similar interpretation of national identity and used folk music to illustrate their version of Americanism.

## Regionalism, Pluralism, and Race

As a folk song collector who took his children on song-collecting trips, John Lomax clearly influenced his son Alan's career choice. Yet, the Lomaxes' shared interest in, and ideas regarding, folk music did not translate into similar social and political views, particularly those regarding race. John Lomax viewed southern black communities, especially those in the Mississippi Delta, as primitive and isolated, and therefore untainted by mass culture. Penitentiaries contained an even greater repository of folk songs, in John Lomax's view, because prisoners were completely removed from mainstream society and mass culture. During his extensive song-collecting trip in 1933, John focused on recording songs in large prisons such as Angola in Louisiana, and at prison farms such as Sugar Land in Texas and Parchman in Mississippi, and several smaller ones in between. He mostly collected field hollers and other work songs—setting up his recording machine sometimes in the field and at other times indoors, where guards brought prisoners in to sing (sometimes by force). When later reminiscing about the trip, Lomax wrote, "I felt carried across to Africa, and I felt as if I were listening to the tom-toms of savage blacks . . . and I realized that Alan and I were now enjoying a unique experience and a people we really knew very little about."[46] Lomax's views on rural black traditions illustrated the folk-as-antimodern view that many song collectors in the southern mountains espoused. While most of these collectors simply ignored black traditions, Lomax sought them out, thus lending a racial dimension to this view.

As his first time in the field, this trip thrust Alan Lomax into the world of folk song collecting, which would become his life's work. However, unlike John Lomax, Alan Lomax became involved with progressive politics during his stint at Harvard and continued to shift leftward, particularly in his views regarding racial equality, while working with progressive and left-wing folklorists such as Botkin and Charles Seeger during his time in Washington. Throughout the 1930s and 1940s, he stressed the importance of black musical traditions for shaping larger folk music styles. Alan Lomax interpreted black traditions as a hybridization of multiple musical strains, African and European, that merged on U.S. soil and reflected distinctly American conditions. To him, this process of cultural melding was the essence of the American heritage. Because of these factors, Alan Lomax believed that black folk music was the epitome of American music.[47] He even used black folk music to illustrate an American cultural tradition that was pluralist and inclusive and that transcended racial and ethnic prejudices by referring to the song "John Henry" in an article for the *New York Times Magazine*: "'A MAN ain't nothin' but a man!' In this sense America has reached out and welcomed the folklore of all the minority groups, racial and national. Jim Crow prejudice has been inoperative in folklore."[48] While this view was certainly more wishful thinking than reality, it does reveal how Lomax tried to use folk music to realize the egalitarian potential inherent in the American democratic ideal.

One of the most notable aspects of the Washington establishment folklorists was their success in securing widespread acceptance of African American folk music as *American* music. In 1938, Alan Lomax "rediscovered" and recorded the early jazz impresario Jelly Roll Morton, and several folklorists participated in a massive project in conjunction with the Historical Records Survey to record oral histories of former slaves. Some folklorists went even further than Lomax, viewing black folk music as an intrinsic component of the American musical matrix and seeking to eliminate racial distinctions in music. For example, in the music manual for the New Deal Resettlement Administration, Charles Seeger wrote, "The African strain, probably the largest and most powerful of the racial minorities, is thought by many to constitute a separate category." This, however, was a false distinction, for, as Seeger argued, African American "folk music has been so modified as to have become part and parcel of the American traditional idiom."[49] If white music did not have a racial label affixed to it, then neither should black music.

Born in 1886, Charles Seeger was a senior member of the New Deal revivalists, and one of the most politically radical. Seeger began his career in music after graduating from Harvard and accepting a position teaching music at the University of California, Berkeley. His move from classical music to folk music resulted from his affiliation with political radicals—particularly, the Industrial Workers of the World (IWW). Early in Seeger's career, an economics professor at Berkeley informed him that he did not know America, that he did not live in America, and he took Seeger to see the living and working conditions that migrant farmers endured. It was this experience that turned him into a socialist and an advocate of the music of the people he encountered—folk music.[50] After being dismissed from Berkeley for opposing America's entry into World War I, Seeger accepted a position at Juilliard and then the New School in New York City. In 1935, he moved into the New Deal and became the "technical advisor to the head of the Special Skills division" of the Resettlement Administration. The job entailed aiding rural people displaced by ecological and economic hardship by establishing music programs in the resettled communities. He was charged with promoting the preservation of the community residents' cultural traditions, in addition to tending to their needs.[51] Unlike many folk regionalists, Seeger was very selective in his definition of folk music, believing that it was rural by nature, and he aimed to teach urban people to appreciate the folk music of the American provinces. Seeger eloquently summarized the connection between America's rural folk music and national identity in a memorandum he wrote to Nikolai Sokoloff, the director of the WPA's Federal Music Project. The programs of folk music were designed, according to Seeger, "to present a living rural art to urban sections with the idea not only of gaining more respect for it, but even of inculcating a basic conception that there is such a thing as American folk music." As with many revivalists, Seeger believed that "present in [folk] music is a more truly American cultural reality than any other musical idiom."[52] For all those looking to "find" America, they could locate it in folk music.

Seeger, Lomax, and Botkin each looked to marginalized groups in their effort to collect American folk music. Geographically isolated, politically disfranchised, economically disadvantaged, or oppressed ethnic and racial groups were the people of America. Although this view appears to be in keeping with the populism of the New Deal, it took on a radical dimension that was associated with the Communist Party. During the 1930s, the CPUSA became the most prominent—or, at least, the loudest—advocate of marginalized Americans. The relative political fluidity of the era enabled revivalists to share social views with leftists while remaining involved in New Deal programs.

## The Left Side of the Revival

The conditions of poverty, economic migration, unemployment, and labor strife that came to define the Depression years were nothing new to many sectors of the population. It was the depth of economic suffering that made these problems visible on a national scale. Because these conditions occurred in a capitalist economy, alternative systems such as socialism became particularly attractive as a viable solution to the crisis.[53] As artists and intellectuals sought to reconnect to the American people and make their work socially relevant, many turned to the left, particularly to the Communist Party. In his memoir of the 1930s, Malcolm Cowley explained that communism appealed to many people because they viewed it as a movement that arose from the ashes of capitalism and united intellectuals with the working class in a common pursuit of justice. Throughout the 1930s, writers, artists, musicians, actors, and intellectuals joined in various working-class causes—from the mining strikes in Harlan County, Kentucky, to labor rallies in New York City. Many believed that communism offered the possibility of both economic and social regeneration because, while every capitalist country suffered the effects of the global Depression, the communist Soviet Union appeared to be thriving industrially. Artists and intellectuals like Cowley believed that by joining with the left, they could transform a nation that exalted rugged individualism into a unified national community.[54]

Although the CPUSA was tied to the Soviet Union on organizational and ideological levels—the organizer A. B. Magil noted that many communists "felt that the Soviet Union had all the answers"—something more inspired CPUSA members than just the beacon in the East.[55] During the late 1920s, CPUSA leaders started establishing mass organizations to mediate between the party and the public. The Unemployed Councils, the League of Struggle for Negro Rights, and the United Farmers League were just a few of the organizations that developed between 1929 and 1934. These organizations were not necessarily party organs, but party members largely served as the leaders.[56] As shown by their very names, these groups addressed problems endemic to the United States. Their existence, however, was not enough to garner public attention; it took the crisis of the Depression to expose social and economic disparities on a mass scale, which opened the door for communists to present their programs as solutions. Bess Lomax Hawes, Alan's sister and a fellow revivalist, directly attributed her political awakening to the leftist writers, journalists, and other social commentators who documented "the amount of social injustice that was going on in this country . . . [s]tories of lynching in the South, stories of the National Guard being called in against unarmed working people who were organizing in factories and in the mines."[57] Communists made these conditions headline news while advocating on behalf of oppressed citizens, which rendered the party especially attractive to Americans who believed in social and economic justice.

By the mid-1930s, left-wing sympathizers and liberals had a relatively easy time reconciling with communists because of a shift in party policies. American communists began recognizing in the late 1920s that the revolution was unlikely to come to the United States anytime soon. This doubt became moot during the mid-1930s, however, because the revolutionary emphasis that previously marked the CPUSA subsided as fascism spread across Europe. Now, rather than initiate a global revolution against capitalism, party leaders directed communists to work with others to fight the fascist menace. Emerging in 1934, the Popular Front united communists and other social progressive forces in a mutual effort to defeat fascism. On an institutional level, the front encouraged communists in different nations to turn to their national cultures and connect with their societies rather than operate as isolated revolutionary forces. This policy change suited American circumstances well, especially since the prospects of an anticapitalist revolution were bleak. Many social and political activists responded positively to the CPUSA once Earl Browder, the leader, adopted the Popular Front platform. Revolutionary sentiment declined among communists and their sympathizers because even though many of these recruits wanted a socialist economy, they were more concerned with fighting against fascism abroad and for social and political reform at home.[58]

While the Popular Front was tied to communism, Michael Denning argues, historians need to look beyond party politics to adequately understand this period of leftist activity. Rather than viewing it through the lens of institutional communism, Denning regards the Popular Front as an "insurgent social movement" wrought by the Congress of Industrial Organizations (CIO) organizing drives, international antifascist efforts, and left-leaning New Dealers. Led by communists and other social activists, the Popular Front was a "radical historical bloc uniting industrial unionists, communists, independent socialists, community activists, and émigré anti-fascists around laborist social democracy, anti-fascism, and anti-lynching." Taking up the oft-cited mantle of "the people," Popular Front activists worked to generate alliances across racial and ethnic lines that balanced dominant Anglo-American culture, African American culture, and ethnic working-class culture.[59] Whether they were native-born or immigrant activists, the members of the Popular Front often drew from what they perceived as indigenously American radical traditions, which they enhanced and augmented with their own cultural products.

The years from 1935 to 1939 are generally understood as the heyday of the Popular Front. As Browder directed efforts at the macro level, younger communists, many of whom came to the party through the unemployed and student movements during the early 1930s, led the efforts to fight labor oppression, lynching, and fascist threats on the local level. Engaging in these struggles not only prompted communists to work with liberals but also enabled progressive social reformers to join forces with communists. In 1938, the CPUSA referred to its program as a "Democratic" front that united all groups opposed to fascism, including workers, farmers, and middle-class liberals.[60] One way leftist activists attempted to reach out to all citizens—urban and rural—was by generating initiatives that specifically addressed American conditions, among which, in Denning's words, was "proletarian regionalism." Among the members of this cohort, Denning cites Howard Odum, the painter Thomas Hart Benton, and other regionalists who were never card-carrying CPUSA members.[61]

Although Denning gives a nod to rural regionalists as members of the left-wing coalition of the 1930s, he focuses largely on urban culture in his study of the cultural and artistic products that members of the Popular Front generated. This emphasis is reasonable because, as some members of the front later recalled, it was difficult to get a party that was strongest in urban areas to connect to the countryside. The composer Norman Cazden articulated the difficulties of this reorientation: "Earl Browder at the time called for a turn toward rediscovering the American roots because he felt [the] left-wing movement, which was very largely centered in New York City was also very largely centered among recent immigrants rather than grassroots America."[62] Left-leaning revivalists, however, had just the solution for targeting people on the local level while also moving into the cultural mainstream: folk music.

Even before communists adopted the broad platform of the Popular Front, they recognized the importance of addressing the people through art. In 1928, when communists were in the midst of their revolutionary Third Period, the party adopted an art-is-a-weapon ideology that became especially popular among American communists. Members of the CPUSA soon began searching for a proletarian art that would be effective in reaching the people, and it was through this search that communists first became acquainted with folk music. Since folk music came from the people, it was most likely infused with class-consciousness—or so many communists believed. American communists continued to look for ways to use art as a tool in their programs as the Third Period segued into the Popular Front era. Following Soviet directives, many activists adopted the artistic theory of socialist realism, which held that artistic products should be socially useful and grounded in real events. To qualify as "socially useful," artistic products had to educate and uplift the masses, and artists could do that only if they communicated in ways that common people understood. Anything too abstract, esoteric, or incomprehensible was therefore to be rejected.[63]

Folk music suited those seeking to make their work socially useful insofar as it was a simple and direct cultural form that was easily malleable. In 1934, shortly before the official beginning of the Popular Front, the communist writer Mike Gold declared in the *Daily Worker,* the party's newspaper, that through folk music, communists could both connect to the people and use the medium to achieve their goals: "Our movement must learn to SING. With song the marching workers find new courage. A song is really a slogan that has been emotionalized and put into a form where it catches the imagination of great masses of people, and sets them on fire." Even though Gold was not a revivalist, he proceeded to praise singers who had become icons in the movement, such as

Ella May Wiggins, a ballad composer who was active in the textile strike in Gastonia, North Carolina, during the late 1920s; Aunt Molly Jackson, who composed songs in response to the mining strikes in Harlan County, Kentucky; and Joe Hill, a legendary songwriter and organizer for the IWW before World War I, for using folk music to rally workers to organize.[64]

To facilitate the use of music for left-wing causes, musically oriented activists formed the Composers' Collective in February 1932. Charles Seeger, one of the founders of the collective, later explained that the group developed from the same sense of immediacy that spurred most leftist activities of the era. "We felt urgency in those days . . . the economic system, the social system is going to hell over here. Music might be able to do something about it," he said. "Let's see if we can try. We must try. The musician who doesn't feel he must try is . . . no good."[65] Members of the collective composed and performed revolutionary songs and established guidelines for others who were interested in writing songs for political action.[66]

A problem for the collective, however, was that the music in which the composers were interested was avant-garde and almost entirely disconnected from what the majority of Americans enjoyed. Some, like Gold, recognized this disjuncture, opining in the *Daily Worker,* "What song do the masses of America now sing? They sing 'Old Black Joe' and the semi-jazz things concocted by Tin Pan Alley. In the South they sing the old ballads. This is the reality; and to leap from that into Schoenberg seems to me a desertion of the masses."[67] Charles Seeger also came to realize that the American people needed to be reached through their own music. As Seeger recalled, "The whole Socialist and Communist parties were city-oriented, slum-oriented and addressed to and springing from minorities of the population that didn't know America. . . . [T]he Communist Party, as I look back, didn't know the United States. They didn't know the country." Seeger believed that, by ignoring the needs and interests of rural Americans, party leaders and members of the collective failed to account for a large sector of economically struggling Americans. Since the collective was not going to the folk, Seeger tried to solve the problem by bringing the folk to the collective. In 1933, he arranged for Aunt Molly Jackson to sing for the group, a get-together that did not turn out well. Members disliked her musicianship and dismissed her songs as antiquated and irrelevant to present concerns.[68]

Although leftists could not get on board with rural white folk music, they did appreciate black folk traditions. The CPUSA had been one of the strongest advocates for black civil rights dating back to 1920s. The communist "Negro question" policy stemmed from the party's interest in marginalized "national minorities." In the United States, African Americans were the largest and most oppressed minority group. The nation's racist legal and social practices illustrated the double standards of the American "democratic" system. In 1928, the party answered the Negro question by resolving that African Americans were "an oppressed 'nation within a nation'" who had the right to "self-determination." Therefore, for the revolution to be successful in America, communists had to get blacks on board. To increase these chances, the party organized rural sharecroppers, worked in southern cities, fought for the Scottsboro Nine, campaigned to defend Ethiopia from Italian imperialism, organized the National Negro Congress to register blacks into CIO unions, and launched a massive educational campaign to purge any instances of "white chauvinism" from within the party itself throughout the 1930s.[69]

Some activists particularly sought to enhance the struggle for civil rights through black folk music. Lawrence Gellert, an organizer in the South, was perhaps the most famous contributor to this initiative. Gellert became one of the first song collectors to recognize that southern black secular music contained bitter protests against oppressive conditions. Other collectors such as John Lomax and Howard Odum believed that black music could grant sociological insight into the southern black community, but they often turned deaf ears to messages of overt protest in the music. Gellert, by contrast, focused on these messages. Even though he dedicated much of his time to collecting black folk music, Gellert did not claim to be a folklorist. Rather, he believed that black folk songs could be used as a weapon in the struggle for political rights and compiled work songs, chain-gang songs, field hollers, and blues songs to help in the fight. Blues music was particularly important in Gellert's view because the lyrics often expressed rage against racial oppression and economic exploitation. The communist press largely agreed and lauded Gellert's efforts.[70] Even when the CPUSA abandoned the push for revolution during the Popular Front years, it still strongly advocated racial justice and continued to use folk music to aid that effort throughout the succeeding decade. By bringing folk music into efforts for political reform, Gellert was one of the earliest members of a political wing of the revival that developed during the following decade.

With the turn to the Popular Front, the Composers' Collective and many activists in the CPUSA changed their tune and soon embraced both black and white folk music in their effort to recruit more activists. Many leftists viewed folk music as a particularly viable tool because it was so adaptable. Traditional songs could be reformulated to inspire real and potential comrades, and music was even more accessible than theater or dance because it was easier to perform and allowed for audience participation. The communists' approach of using folk music as a weapon often reflected the regional cultures and local circumstances where the party organized. The major regional difference lay between northern, urban, middle-class leftists who used folk music to articulate their hatred of the capitalist system and fight for reform on a national and international scale, and the southern, working-class activists whose radicalism stemmed from personal experiences and who used music to change regional conditions for rural poor whites and blacks. Although regional groups equally despised the class system and warned about the "excesses of capitalism," they arrived at their conclusions from very different experiences.[71]

Long before northern left-wing composers realized that reaching out to the American public through atonal music was not a sound decision, southern radicals recognized that the best way to connect to the people was through their own traditions and group experiences. One regional organization that operated on this principle was Commonwealth College in Arkansas. Originally founded by Debsian socialists in the early 1920s, Commonwealth was a labor school designed to educate working people. In 1931, Lucien Koch, a communist sympathizer, became the director of the college. Shortly thereafter, the last of the socialists left, which allowed Koch to align the school with communist causes. Following his self-proclaimed motto that "Commonwealth is not an institution, it is a movement," Koch instructed students to conduct "fieldwork" that included joining strikes, creating radical groups, and serving as union organizers.[72] After Koch left during the mid-1930s, Claude Williams, a radical Presbyterian minister from Arkansas, took over and continued in the radical vein that Koch established. Williams had been active in efforts to bring unions to the South—he was one of the original members of the Southern Tenant Farmers' Union—and he recognized the need to approach the people through their own cultural forms to achieve any success. Since Williams worked in the Bible Belt, he often approached the people through religion—changing the words of popular biblical stories and well-known hymns to suit contemporary circumstances.

All told, Commonwealth was largely a failure: the labor movement that the "Commoners" hoped to spark in the region never came to fruition, and the school was shut down in 1940 due to its affiliations with the CPUSA. However, the school was successful at transforming the lives of its members—students and teachers.[73] Lee Hays, an Arkansas native who began directing labor drama at Commonwealth in 1938, combined his love of southern folk music with a zeal for social and political activism. While Hays had developed an interest in socialist politics at an early age, the Depression heightened his political awareness, as it did for many activists. Left-wing artists introduced him to the extent of inequality in American life: "I became aware of the plight of the Dust Bowl refugees and the coal miners first through the work of the great American photographers who went out and photographed the face of America during the 30s, when for the first time America got a good look at itself."[74] Other activists such as Claude Williams directly affected Hays's political views and activist tactics. Williams taught Hays the art of changing words to traditional songs and introduced him to such union classics as "We Shall Not Be Moved," "Roll the Union On," and "Union Train" as well as traditional regional songs that Hays brought with him when he relocated to New York City in 1940.[75]

Hays was not the only one who traveled this path. Another member of the southern radical scene who experienced a political awakening through Commonwealth College was Agnes Cunningham. Known as "Sis," Cunningham grew up in Oklahoma and became politically active during the 1930s when she participated in Southern Tenant Farmers' Union activities and helped local organizing drives in Oklahoma to get WPA jobs for more people. With her background in music and music education (she had previously worked as a music teacher), Cunningham joined the Red Dust Players, a group of actors in Oklahoma who traveled off the state's beaten paths to perform plays on contemporary conditions during the mid-1930s. The Red Dust Players presented scenarios that the rural farmers would understand, such as bank companies trying to foreclose farms (presented as a love story, with the "land" portrayed as a damsel in distress, the "mortgage" as the evil villain trying to steal her away, and, finally, the "union" as the hero who saves her and the day). The group performed at schools, in the open air, and on farmers' porches in towns, the names of which even the traveling Federal Theater Project troops forgot.[76]

In his exploration of the culture of the Popular Front, Denning recognizes that southern labor schools like Commonwealth were important for disseminating left-wing ideals in that region.[77] While this may have been the case, Commonwealth was rather isolated from southern society; therefore the impact that it had on southern radicalism is difficult to adequately assess. The political significance of Commonwealth, rather, lay in the organizing tactics and tools that members learned during their time at the college. Through their association with southern radicals such as Williams, Cunningham and Hays learned the importance of reaching people through their own musical, social, and religious traditions. They carried both this organizing tactic and the folk songs from their region with them when they relocated to New York City and joined the left-wing culture of that metropolis.

Another musician who brought regional music from the South and Midwest to New York City was Woody Guthrie. Although he hailed from a family that shuttled between poverty and middle-class status, Guthrie came to symbolize the itinerant, down-and-out everyman of the Depression era to many left-wing activists and revivalists. During the 1930s, Guthrie traveled extensively across the South and West, often leaving his young family for large stretches of time, while observing the effects of the Depression. Guthrie is especially known for his songs about the midwestern exodus to California during the Dust Bowl. To many folk music enthusiasts, especially in the later years of the revival, his look and sound epitomized the American rural folk.

Guthrie's folk style was not so effortless as it outwardly appeared; rather, it was a deliberately politicized portrayal of the American folk. The crisis of the Depression and Guthrie's interactions with suffering Americans had pushed him to the left. Through his narrative talking-blues style, Guthrie's songs became social commentaries that called attention to issues of poverty, labor strife, and civil rights.[78] Indeed, Guthrie became active in communist circles because he saw leftist activists as the only ones who truly fought for the downtrodden and marginalized populations in the United States. At the same time, he recognized that affiliations with the left had negative consequences: "If your work gets labeled as communist or even as radically leaning in the general direction of bolshevism, then, of course, you are black balled, black listed, chalked up as a revolutionary bomb thrower, and you invite the whole weight of the capitalist machine to be thrown against you."[79] Disregarding the difficulties that his political stances and affiliations posed, Guthrie consistently used folk music as a call to fight for people's rights.

During the 1930s and 1940s, Guthrie released albums with songs about various leftist causes with the help of Moses Asch. They included an album that Asch commissioned Guthrie to write about the trial of Nicola Sacco and Bartolomeo Vanzetti, a leftist cause *célèbre*, in 1945, and *Struggle: Documentary #1*. The *Struggle* album originally consisted of six songs, including "Pretty Boy Floyd," a Robin Hood portrayal of the infamous outlaw; "Buffalo Skinners," about mistreated workers in the nineteenth century; "Ludlow Massacre," about the killing of union members and their families during the Colorado Coal Strike of 1914; and "1913 Massacre," about the deaths of seventy-three members of mining families who were on strike in Calumet, Michigan, when someone falsely yelled "fire" during a union Christmas gathering. Guthrie wanted *Struggle* to be one of a series of albums depicting working people's struggles and spreading the word about injustice.[80] The album summarized Guthrie's views about his own music and the purpose of folk music in general, which he described in a letter to Asch: "Every folk song that I know tells how to fix something in this world to make it better, tells what is wrong with it, and what we've got to do to fix it better. If the song does not do this, then it is no more of a folk song than I am a movie scout."[81]

One of the people primarily responsible for opening leftist circles to the songs that Guthrie and others were singing was Alan Lomax. A key form of Popular Front civic culture was the advocacy of civil liberties; activists used the rhetoric of civil liberties specifically to fight against labor oppression and racial injustice.[82] The Popular Front's emphasis on the democratic ideal as a means to secure social and economic justice opened the door for leftist sympathizers like Lomax to promote folk music as the ultimate example of both a democratic and proletarian tradition. Lomax's belief that American folk music was both radical and natively American rendered it the music *of* the American people. As such, it was part of the national democratic heritage with which Lomax identified as both a citizen and a radical.[83]

While Lomax embodied the ethos of the Popular Front, he remained employed by the New Deal establishment, working first for the AAFS, and then the Office of War Information (OWI) during World War II. Because the rhetoric of democracy pervaded New Deal programs and wartime propaganda campaigns, Lomax had an easy time moving between leftist and liberal circles during the late 1930s and early 1940s. Lomax emerged on the political stage in 1948 when he became active in Henry Wallace's Progressive Party presidential campaign. Prior to this, while he supported labor and civil rights, his kept his political views somewhat quiet, while others of his revival cohort, including his sister,

Bess Lomax, loudly proclaimed their political views and affiliations through music—with Lomax helping from the sidelines.

Musical revivalists such as Guthrie, Cunningham, Hays, Charles Seeger, and even Alan Lomax encouraged activists to use folk music in efforts to generate political and social reform. Their efforts were mostly successful with political activists who already had a proclivity for southern-style folk music or who became active in the revival, rather than for leftists as a whole. Many communist organizers could not get on board with rural folk music, the kind that these musicians learned from Aunt Molly Jackson and other singers, preferring formal music or the more familiar tunes of Tin Pan Alley. As some revivalists continued to focus primarily on rural traditions, others solved this disjuncture by composing music that, while still maintaining the *spirit* of rural folk music, addressed the more urban-oriented activists' tastes.

Earl Robinson, a classically trained musician, was one of the key left-wing revivalists who bridged the world of rural folk music and mainstream pop music. Robinson was a member of the Composer's Collective in the early 1930s, alongside Charles Seeger and composers such as Aaron Copland. Working in collaboration with the lyricist John Latouche, Robinson composed the epic musical tribute to the common American "Ballad for Americans" for *Sing for Your Supper,* a Federal Theater Project play. In 1939, a year after "Ballad" debuted, Paul Robeson, the famed concert singer and communist, performed the piece on CBS Radio. Robeson's performance received rave reviews and launched the piece into the American musical mainstream.

"Ballad for Americans" traces the popular history of the United States through iconic moments—the Revolution, the Civil War, the Industrial Revolution, and the Great Depression—from the perspective of the "everybody who is nobody," the "nobody who's everybody," and the "'etceteras' and the 'and so forths' who do the work."[84] In addition to celebrating the working class, Robinson and Latouche define Americans as a multitude of ethnicities and religions, thus couching their Americanism in cultural, ethic, and socioeconomic pluralism. It illustrated the left-wing version of Americanism that was steeped in "an anti-racist ethnic pluralism imagining the United States as a 'nation of nations.'"[85] It also reflected the Popular Front's emphasis on racial equality through the line, "A man in white skin can never be free while his black brother is in slavery." Although this line refers to the institution of chattel slavery, its implications during an era in which left-wing sympathizers advocated for civil rights are quite clear. Besides promoting equal rights, "Ballad for Americans" also embodied Denning's concept of "proletarian regionalism" because it referenced different regions across the United States, deliberately bringing them together into the national whole. Robinson's radical regionalism came across even stronger in another cantata, "Lonesome Train," that he co-wrote with Millard Lampell in 1942. "Lonesome Train" depicts a train trip that carried Abraham Lincoln's casket through several states. In addition to depicting the geographical diversity that regionalists emphasized, "Lonesome Train" takes a populist approach by listing "Lincoln's people" as "A Brooklyn blacksmith, a Pittsburgh preacher / A small-town tailor, a back-woods teacher," among others. Robinson and Lampell maintained their radical edge by using language that, as Robert Cantwell notes, was reminiscent of the Communist Manifesto: "While there are whips and chains and men to use them, there will be no peace!"[86] Like "Ballad for Americans," "Lonesome Train" gained widespread popularity in the immediate aftermath of Roosevelt's death in 1945.

Robinson and the other revivalists of this era solidified the relationship between folk music and left-wing causes by the early 1940s—a relationship that would last for the duration of the revival. While southern musicians such as Guthrie, Hays, and Cunningham bridged the gap between regional variations of activist culture—bringing southern music into northern causes—Robinson and Seeger helped lead activists who favored popular music to appreciate folk music, as well. Robinson also helped alter popular perceptions of folk music, achieving recognition that the category of folk music included both music that came *from* the people and topical music written *for* the people that became popular in left-wing circles. They popularized the idea that folk music was an important tool in the struggles for political, social, and economic change and they continued this effort in the postwar years via a collection of left-wing musicians called People's Songs. Indeed, various activists from the post–World War II era up through the 1960s turned to the type of folk music the New Deal and Popular Front revivalists popularized to promote political and social reform.

## Conclusion

The folk music revival emerged during the 1930s as public folklorists, musical entrepreneurs, musicians, and folk music enthusiasts began to coalesce as a definable community. Situated in the cultural milieu and political atmosphere of the Depression, these figures belonged to a coterie of social and cultural workers who sought to devise ways to help Americans survive the economic and psychological devastation of the Depression and to reform the nation in the process. Believing that folk music was an intrinsic part of both contemporary life and the nation's cultural past, the early revivalists argued that folk music traditions were part of the "usable past" that Depression-era cultural leaders sought to find. The revivalists viewed folk music as a major—if not *the* major—facet of national culture because it came from American communities. It spoke to the experiences and concerns of all types of Americans.

By adopting aspects of regionalism, cultural pluralism, and cosmopolitanism, and by using experiences to define the nation and its people, early revivalists established that naturalized Americans were as much a part of the nation's "folk" as native-born citizens and that black Americans were as intrinsic to the national body as white ones. In so doing, they rejected the belief that other identities (e.g., racial, ethnic, and religious) barred citizens from participating fully in the national community. Now people who took part in westward expansion, fought in national wars, labored in regional occupations, and even emigrated from other countries to begin new lives in the United States were *Americans* because they experienced uniquely national events and contributed to the country's development. Furthermore, folk music illustrated the nation's democratic character because, as songs passed down from one generation to another, all singers had a hand in adapting them to suit their own tastes and needs. The revivalists brought their interpretations of the music to the larger public, not only to encourage the rest of the country to appreciate, protect, and revive these musical traditions, but also to accept their version of American identity that was grounded in democracy—a civic ideal that, in their view, was rooted in an acceptance and appreciation of cultural and social difference. Initially these ideas were vague, but the revivalists refined them over the course of the decade and soon established an understanding of folk music and American identity that guided the movement through the next three decades.

In a populist era, when images of, and references to, the people abounded, the revivalists turned their attention to the singers of folk songs as much as the music itself and presented socially and economically disadvantaged citizens—native and immigrant—as their examples of the American people. The musicians of the revival also worked to incorporate the struggles of the American people into their music, in much the same way that many writers of the era did in their literature. Like the photographers and writers of Depression-era America, the revivalists were cultural brokers—middlepersons who operated between folk culture and the mainstream public. While they tried to adhere to standards of authenticity, they tailored the music they presented to accommodate the type of Americanism that they believed it represented, weeding out those elements, such as racist commentaries, that they deemed unsuitable. Whether they were New Deal liberals or Popular Front leftists, the revivalists were deeply concerned with larger social and political issues. Folk music was not just a cultural form that needed to be preserved for posterity; it was a means for teaching Americans to appreciate their democratic heritage and thus to put that idea into practice. Over time, the revivalists would hone their programs and their message to address more specific programs of activism, but it was during the Depression era that they forged connections among folk music, nationalism, and domestic reform—connections that would characterize the revival for its duration.

While they all participated in forming the folk music revival, the revivalists of the 1930s did not all approach folk music in the same way. Traditionalists such as Sarah Gertrude Knott and John Lomax viewed folk music as cultural traditions from a bygone era. Functionalist folklorists such as Benjamin Botkin and Alan Lomax recognized that, although rooted in the past, folk music remained culturally relevant for the communities that maintained the traditions. Left-wing revivalists, such as Charles Seeger and Lawrence Gellert, interpreted

folk music as a grassroots cultural form that came from the people or was written for the people, such that it could be used in people's struggles for social and
political rights. Despite the revivalists' various political views and different
opinions regarding the nature of folk music, they shared an understanding of
Americanism that grounded the nation's identity in cultural pluralism and political democracy. By the end of the decade, these folklorists, musicians, and
collectors had turned a general interest in American folk music into a social
movement. The folk music revival had officially begun.

# 2

## THE PEOPLE'S WAR

The New Deal and Popular Front eras began to wane even before the 1930s came to a close. Mounting conservative opposition slashed funding for the Work Projects Administration (WPA) arts projects in 1938, and the Popular Front's grand coalition of antifascists ended with the Molotov-Ribbentrop Pact of 1939, leaving many communist and left-wing cultural workers in political limbo. Reaching the American public became particularly challenging for these cultural workers as the larger political and cultural movements of which they were part began to collapse around them. The end of the movements that grew out of the Depression era did not, however, stymie the revivalists, who learned to adjust their message and adapt their work to suit circumstances that developed from a new crisis: World War II. Most significant for the revival, the war united revivalists of varying political and social views in the mutual effort to use folk music to strengthen Americans' faith in democracy and rally the nation in the fight against fascism.

Like many Americans, leftist revivalists initially opposed America's entry into another international war, but the end of the Nazi-Soviet pact in 1941 and the bombing of Pearl Harbor a few months later caused even many skeptics to rally behind the war effort. Public opinion remained divided over the war, however, prompting the government to initiate a concerted propaganda effort to rally citizens to the cause. The revivalists who had survived the political shifts of the late 1930s tailored their programs to suit the new political and cultural climate. Still envisioning the nation as a cultural and political democracy, the revivalists were able to employ the new wartime rhetoric, permeated as it was with the language of democratic ideals, cultural pluralism, and tolerance, to further validate their beliefs and programs. Although some of the venues changed, the message that the revivalists promoted, and the music that they used to spread that message, remained the same. In their effort to garner a public audience, revivalists increasingly employed media such as radio and recording technology. Although folk music enthusiasts and educators had used recording technology since the early years of the twentieth century, their efforts during the war years mirrored a governmental emphasis on using mass media, especially radio, to spread patriotic and morale-boosting messages to the American listening public.[1] Revivalists in the Office of War Information (OWI) and the Archive of American Folk Song (AAFS) designed folk music radio programs for audiences of adults and children to suit this very purpose. By adapting to the political and cultural shifts, the revivalists managed to sustain the movement through the wartime years, when they found a receptive audience, and even into the postwar years, despite mounting political opposition.

In 1939, as war spread across Europe, the philosopher John Dewey called for Americans to turn to their democratic heritage as a source of strength against the threat of European totalitarianism. In his study *Freedom and Culture*, Dewey championed democracy because it was a system in which all could participate; the pragmatic participation inherent in democracy gave the system its egalitarian quality. Dewey noted that all aspects of a democratic society served to secure and enhance its egalitarian character. Unfortunately, Dewey argued, many political and social figures, "even those who call themselves good democrats," ignored the importance of cultural products for enhancing democracy, and he hoped that they would change their minds in light of how fascist countries had begun to operate. "Works of art," according to Dewey, "once brought into existence are the most compelling of the means of communication by which emotions are stirred and opinions are formed." Under fascism, art and recreation outlets "have all been brought under regulation as part of the propaganda agencies by which a dictatorship is kept in power without being regarded by the masses as oppressive." Dewey recognized that these cultural sources were politically important because they played to citizens' "emotions and imagination," which he considered "potent in shaping public sentiment and opinion." One cultural form that Dewey recognized as particularly salient for influencing public opinion was music. "Long before the present crisis came into being," Dewey noted, "there was a saying that if one could control the songs of a nation, one need not care who made its laws."[2] Many revivalists shared this belief, maintaining that music could secure American citizens' faith in democracy as much as it had rallied German citizens to embrace fascism. On the eve of America's entry into World War II, they began mobilizing to bring folk music into wartime propaganda.

Near the close of the 1930s, the celebration of the downtrodden, which was the cornerstone of both New Deal populism and Popular Front Americanism, had gained widespread acceptance. These citizens' ability to endure hardship made them the symbol of that nation's strength in the face of adversity and the vigor of the American spirit.[3] The populist spirit of the New Deal era that located a usable past in the traditions of diverse Americans now became a way to unify a nation on the brink of war. Instead of the forced conformity of 100 percent Americanization of the World War I era, government officials, cultural and social leaders, and propagandists tried to rally the nation under a banner of diversity. Because of this broader shift toward an inclusive nationalism, cultural differences now were not only accepted but also *celebrated* as defining American nationality. Propagandists pushed the notion that, although Americans practiced different traditions, they all came together in a democratic society, united by the civic ideals stated in the Declaration of Independence and codified in the U.S. Constitution. The OWI propaganda cast the war in terms of an ideological battle between tolerance and democracy on one side and intolerance and totalitarianism on the other. Therefore, many programs advocated a unity-within-diversity view of the American people and encouraged ethnic and racial tolerance to both ease heightened racial tensions and create a national unity necessary for the war effort. The historian Zoe Burkholder argues that these initiatives, however, consistently tried to encourage cultural inclusivity while upholding white middle-class values.[4] Although the revivalists engaged in wartime propaganda may have outwardly appeared in line with this balancing act, many, particularly those who sustained a faith in Popular Front Americanism, subtly challenged the call for middle-class conformity, particularly by calling attention to the values they attributed to racial and ethnic groups and those that they found embedded in working-class culture.

During the war years, many revivalists began arguing that folk music could help Americans survive the new crisis, much as it had helped them through the Depression years. Echoing the wartime populism and celebration of American civic ideals, revivalists claimed that folk songs were inherently democratic because they were songs that the people created, and anyone who played these songs over the years could (and often did) amend them in response to his or her own experiences. Thus, this music could be infused into mainstream culture to help the American people sustain their commitment to their democratic national heritage. The revivalists originally promoted this argument during the Depression, but they easily adapted it to rally Americans to support a war that was cast in ideological terms. According to the wartime rhetoric, the Allied Powers were engaged in a battle against the totalitarian "Axis of Evil," a battle in which the very survival of democracy was at stake.

This scenario precipitated what the historian Philip Gleason labels the "democratic revival," a moment in which democracy became the catchall signifier of American identity. During the war, liberal cultural, social, and political leaders crafted an ideology of democracy that became the essence of American nationalism. Even during war, they sustained their understanding of democracy as rooted in ideas of equal opportunity and individual rights. Gleason argues that the democratic ideal provided normative guidelines for American society as a whole; "democracy" became synonymous with "America." Even though Americans did not live up to their democratic creed, as evidenced by an entrenched racial discrimination and adherence to maintaining the barriers of segregation, they theoretically embraced its principles of political equality. After war broke out in Europe and Americans were confronted with the horrors of Nazism, many liberals as well as religious and civic groups resumed efforts to combat prejudice, promote diversity, and thus make American democracy more inclusive of marginalized groups. More than simply generating an appreciation of American diversity, the war sparked an ideological renaissance centering on the values to which Americans committed themselves. This "ideological revival" promoted a resurgence of assimilationist tendencies, but along civic rather than ethnic/racial lines. Now, cultural leaders pushed an "ideological consensus" that promoted the civic ideals of political democracy, social tolerance, and an appreciation of cultural diversity as quintessentially American characteristics.[5]

What Gleason omits from his account of the democratic revival, however, is that this surge of interest in a pluralist vision of democracy was really an extension of ideas of Americanism that liberals and political progressives had developed during the Depression era. The major factor that enabled public leaders to segue from New Deal democratic populism to pro-diversity propaganda after the United States entered World War II was the political character of the enemy. Propagandists in the OWI reinforced the notion that totalitarian regimes rooted their conceptions of nationalism in racial characteristics, which led to oppressive policies of forced homogeneity. They then contrasted these policies with the "American way," which idealized Americans' ability to work together regardless of racial and ethnic differences. This type of civic ideal consensus celebrated cultural and ethnic diversity in the United States as a quality that distinguished American-style democracy from totalitarian fascism. Yet pursuit of a racially/ethnically inclusive notion of national identity also resulted from the fear that entrenched cultural differences would eventually lead to violent factionalism—a Balkanization of America. To thwart this, pluralists argued that the nation must gather its diverse citizenry under a common umbrella of civic consensus.[6] As long as all U.S. citizens believed in the same "universally" American ideals of democracy and liberty, they could practice any cultural traditions they wanted and still be accepted as good citizens. Although this view may have created space for ethnic and racial diversity, it simultaneously created conditions that would isolate those who challenged this civic consensus view of American identity—a problem that would become glaring by the end of the decade.

## *Making America Safe for Democracy*

On the eve of America's entry into the war, many academics, public intellectuals, civic leaders, and cultural workers joined the effort to inculcate this celebration of diversity in public life. Regionalists in particular shifted their rhetoric from advocating social policy reforms to arguing that regionalism could help unite diverse citizens—and thus save American democracy. As early as 1938,

Howard Odum proclaimed, "The theme of American regionalism is . . . that of a great American nation, the land and the people, in whose continuity and unity of development, through a fine equilibrium of geographic, cultural, and historical factors, must be found not only the testing grounds of American democracy but, according to many observers, the hope of western civilization."[7] By adopting a regionalist approach that emphasized conveying messages via cultural media specific to local populations, regionalists argued that the government could both reach more people and spread messages more effectively. Folk revivalists shared this opinion, and some used the regionalists' logic to justify their own programs.

In 1942, Alan Lomax appealed to this regional emphasis on the local and the lingering New Deal populism to explain the importance of his wartime activities. "Since this is a people's war," he said, "it is essential that, so far as possible, information about the war should be distributed equally to all groups of people." The "people" with whom he was concerned consisted of "a large body of the American public that is not sufficiently literate or sufficiently accustomed to reading to be reached through the press." A large percentage of these people also did not have access to national organizations or media; "lumped together," they constituted "the underprivileged, the undereducated, the isolated and certain racial and national minorities, [which] make up what the social scientist, when he is thinking in cultural terms, calls the 'folk.'" Lomax argued that American folk groups had their own forms of cultural expression that they conveyed through folk music, tales, stories, religious services, and speech patterns, all of which were "orally transmitted and from being chewed over thoroughly by the group comes to express the group, stylistically as well as ideologically." Therefore, communication officials must channel information through these forms of cultural expression "in order that folk groups may be reached with war information and with the ideals and principles of their people's war."[8]

Educating Americans about the war according to this regionalist emphasis on local traditions had larger social implications, as well. In 1943, shortly after he joined the OWI, Lomax wrote to William Lewis recounting how they had discussed certain regional concerns, such as the nature of racial tension in the rural South. Lomax knew southern racism well and recognized how detrimental it could be for the war effort. "We spoke of the urgent necessity of reaching rural Negroes and whites with the facts about the war," he wrote, "not only in order to keep them informed, but also in an attempt to undercut the race issue by raising the more important issues of the war. We agreed that getting to these groups at their own level, in their language and through their own media—local radio programs, rural churches, etc.—was the best way to go about the job." In the letter, Lomax complained that members of the OWI did not believe that it was their job to reach "those Americans who are isolated by race or nationality or geography or language or lack of education or poverty." Lomax, however, believed that "in order to win this war and make a decent peace, *all* the people must be kept well informed." Furthermore, he argued that neglecting poor

Americans, especially white southerners, would have dangerous consequences, for "these are the folks who listen to anti-Semitic propaganda, who, if we leave them alone, follow the lead of Negro-baiters, and who are strongly influenced by Fascist rumors."[9] At a time that political leaders viewed national unity as critical for the war effort, Lomax advocated regional culture as instrumental for securing this lofty social goal.

Throughout the war years, Lomax sought to bring folk music into propaganda campaigns particularly designed to raise morale among different ethnic, racial, and regional groups. For example, he asserted that the mission for the AAFS during the war, and his work within it, was to "Preserve our heritage of pioneer democratic oral music while there still is time [and operate] in and through minorities and folk communities in the field of morale." During his trip to the Mississippi Delta in the summer of 1942, Lomax came to believe that "a sturdy and aggressive folk-lore program could become crucial for morale work," a view that resulted from his interactions with public school teachers, musicians, professors at Fisk, and "Negroes and people in the minority field" in general. T. E. Jones, the president of Fisk University, suggested incorporating black folk singers from Nashville into United Service Organizations (USO) camp programs as one way to accomplish this goal.[10]

Another of Lomax's suggestions entailed using AAFS materials to generate songbooks for military training camps. "These song books may be designed according to the needs of the regions in which the camps are located, according to the racial and occupational make-up of the camps," he wrote. "I feel, for example, that where any large group of second-generation Polish conscripts are located, Polish songs should be sung. The same for Negro, Mexican, Greek, Finnish, etc. conscript groups."[11] Like other regionalists, Lomax believed that reaching out to first-generation and naturalized American soldiers through musical traditions prevalent in their communities would make them feel more welcome in their military units and thus more willing go to war on behalf of the United States.

One problem with Lomax's approach was that he failed to recognize what many first-generation Americans actually wanted. Lomax's views in this instance aligned with those of liberals who sought to help assimilate ethnic children while bolstering their self-esteem by encouraging them to connect to their ethnic heritage. The hope was that they would see how America respected the traditions of their communities. One critic of this approach, the anthropologist Ruth Benedict, argued that forcing native-born ethnic Americans to identify with the folk traditions of a country with which they had no direct ties would neither help them to connect to American life nor enhance their self-esteem. After all, most wanted to become "American," not retain the practices of their parents.[12] Yet despite the fact that Lomax misunderstood the actual needs of first-generation citizens, his primary aim was to construct a democratic approach to wartime Americanism. It was, as the historian James Sparrow recognizes, a romanticized version of nationalism, but one predicated on pluralism and designed to include all groups of Americans, regardless of racial or ethnic lineage.[13]

To Lomax and other socially progressive revivalists, folk music was particularly helpful in rallying the nation under a banner of democracy because it was a participatory, grassroots cultural form. As products of oral tradition, folk songs were always open to revision. This indefinite revisability, coupled with its collaborative nature, set folk music in marked contrast to the commercial music that Tin Pan Alley concocted and sold to the masses. Many revivalists not only romanticized the allegedly democratic process of folk music but also idealized folk communities as microcosmic democratic societies. For example, in 1941 Lomax wrote, "The American Singer has been concerned with the themes close to his everyday experience. . . . His songs have been strongly rooted in his life and have functioned there as enzymes to assist in the digestion of hardship, solitude, violence, hunger, and honest comradeship of democracy."[14] If democratic unity was an important goal for which to strive, then folk music provided a way to achieve that goal, at least in the cultural arena.

To educate the public on the ideological issues embedded in the war and raise civilian morale, Lomax designed radio shows that used folk culture while he worked in wartime agencies. During his time in the Armed Forces Radio Service, Lomax wrote scripts for a morale-building series of radio dramas called *Singing America*. The series adopted a populist perspective by focusing on historically obscure figures who engaged in "heroic" acts.[15] In another scripted program that he wrote and produced for the BBC, Lomax "toured" the Lower East Side of New York City, narrating to the listeners what and whom he encountered along the way. The people he stopped to "interview" were mostly Italian and Jewish, and they explained their views on the war, the war effort, how they contributed to that effort, and how they felt about where they lived. At one point, a Mrs. Cucco explained, "Italians, Jewish, Irish, Negroes—all the same here. My name's Cucco, yours's Cohen, yours's Fennessy—we're all alike, 100 percent Americans." Later, a young woman named Sylvia, newly married with a baby, reflected on her life and the prospects for her daughter: "I can't wait for her to grow up, to see what she's gonna be like. I want her to have better things than I had—not money and clothes and stuff like that, but a feeling of security, of belonging. I'd like to see all the people I know or don't know with the same things." After this, Harold, a fast-talking local lawyer, drove home the point that America's strength lay in cultural diversity and the promise of pluralist democracy: "The different groups that came to America to escape persecution and take part in the growth of a new nation . . . [t]hey know they're free men, and that's why they make the best fighters in the world. . . . We've learned to live together down here, respect each other's rights and work for the good of the community. . . . After all [there are] no bars of race, nationality, class or creed down here. . . . Mark you, today, there's only one religion. The religion of freedom."[16] Here, Lomax chose one of the most ethnically diverse urban areas to illustrate the harmonious nature of the pluralist American society. American society, however, was hardly ever cohesive, especially during the war—as shown by the rise of race riots in urban centers such as Detroit and Los Angeles—but Lomax's wartime programs were designed to rally support for the war, not to provide a realistic portrayal of American life.

By employing the radio to unite Americans during the war, Lomax resorted to a tactic that had been used to generate national unity since the early 1930s. At the beginning of the Depression era, many civic and cultural leaders viewed radio as a "social space" that could bring Americans together during a period of economic and social instability. Anning S. Prall, the first chief commissioner of the Federal Communications Commission, announced in 1936 during a live radio broadcast that the medium had become a public forum that united Americans through common education, entertainment, music, and theater and thus served as a powerful determinant of national culture and identity. Public intellectuals, business leaders, and educators largely agreed.[17] Some commentators during the 1930s even claimed that the commercial nature of the national radio system served to protect American diversity and democracy. In 1939, David Sarnoff, the president of the Radio Corporation of America and chairman of the National Broadcasting Corporation (NBC), stated that American commercial radio ensured that "the broadcasting network shall serve the many and not cater only to the few, that its efforts shall always be directed to bring the greatest good to the greatest number." Radio was perhaps the most democratic media service in the United States because, according to Sarnoff, "Education of the masses—as well as of the leaders—is one of the bulwarks of our democracy. Radio is a mass medium. It reaches both the rich and the poor. . . . It brings the treasures of education to all alike. In fact, the richest man in the world cannot buy for himself what the poorest man gets free by radio."[18]

Although Sarnoff's assessment of the unifying potential of radio omitted any commentary regarding the gross social disparities that existed throughout the nation, others tried to harness the medium's potential particularly to combat exclusive conceptions of the national community. For example, in 1935 Harold Ickes created the Radio Education Project in the Office of Education to support programs that emphasized the racial and ethnic heterogeneity of the American people.[19] Even before his wartime radio work, Lomax combined these two views and used radio to both unify the American people and promote a culturally democratic Americanism inclusive of all citizens.

As the war escalated overseas, the Library of Congress (LOC) launched the Radio Research Project (RRP). Funded by the Rockefeller Foundation in conjunction with the LOC, the RRP consisted of a series of popular, educational radio broadcasts designed to thwart the spread of fascism in the United States. By weaving together snippets of local and national cultural material housed in the LOC into documentaries, the project leaders aimed "to exhibit to listeners the values inherent in the American tradition and way of life."[20] Of the many programs that the RRP generated, perhaps the most significant was the Regional Series, which featured episodes that chronicled the history of particular towns and regions. Writers for the program based their scripts on information found in the Local History Collection and in the Archive of American Folk Song and material that writers in the WPA gathered for the American Guide Series. Joseph Liss, the director, described the series as a collection of stories about different communities with the purpose of showing "in dramatic terms how these communities have contributed in the building of America." The program, he explained, "show[s] how specific industries, land, the way of live [*sic*] and the culture of the people contribute to democracy," with the intention to "show the real significance of big-concept words such as democracy, liberty, and America, by breaking them down into their everyday manifestations in communities and regions throughout the county."[21] Liss encouraged the writers for the Regional Series to "tell a simple story" using plain language and incorporating folklore and folk music that would help the nation to face the new challenges that the global war posed. He further instructed each writer to "tell the story of his own area as the story he earnestly believes to be a part of our growth as a democracy. If this is done we hope finally to have a documented story of the root of America which must sustain us." To get accurate depictions of American communities, the researchers recorded in both urban and rural areas, collecting the people's songs and stories that they then played to a national listening audience.[22]

Through radio documentaries and other programs, the RRP leaders attempted to introduce citizens to parts of the nation and its population that they most likely would not encounter in person. The RRP reflected the regionalism and pluralism of the era by celebrating cultural diversity and political democracy as the essence of the American identity. One of the RRP's leading officials, Alan Lomax, illustrated these ideas via cultural traditions found in folk communities. Lomax believed that commercial radio had failed "to draw on the rich background of regional speech, music, and history" found within folk communities. Unfortunately, "metropolitan" culture dominated the airwaves; when popular radio programs attempted to include regional aspects, the resulting "local color" segments were usually based on offensive regional stereotypes. The leaders of the RRP aimed to correct this misrepresentation by featuring ordinary Americans speaking and singing. Since live broadcasts were too expensive to produce, the RRP shows primarily relied on prerecorded material. Some of this material consisted of recordings taken during a carnival in rural Maryland; at a folk festival at an "Okie camp" for migrant workers in southern California; in a community in Georgia on the verge of being flooded for a Tennessee Valley Authority rural electrification project; and on the streets of Wilmington, North Carolina, a town that had become a wartime industrial center. By using the techniques of field recording, interviews, and "local sound" for the background music, the RRP helped to generate, according to Lomax, "a new function for radio: that of letting the people explain themselves and their lives to the entire nation."[23]

This is not to say that the project leaders did not use their programs to suit their agendas; they did. For example, the narrator at the end of the episode on the "Okie" camp articulated the message that the project leaders hoped to impart through the camp music festival: "It was good to find people who had music inside them, people who could dance to their own singing, their own hand-clapping, and their own laughter. Their festival, which gave them pride and belief in their own heritage; their camp council meeting expressed their native democratic instincts. Both together they meant one thing—the Okies and Arkies had found a home. . . . THERE IS a reason for singing and dancing now."[24] By choosing to highlight a population impoverished and displaced by the dust storms and agricultural crises of the previous decade, the RRP officials sustained the celebration of the marginal that had been prevalent in both the New Deal and Popular Front.

After Pearl Harbor, the RRP's emphasis that these shows could generate the national unity so crucial for the war effort reached a fever pitch. The anonymous author of an informational packet titled "Outline of Proposed Defense Activities for the Radio Research Project" wrote that the RRP "would acquaint the people of this country with their neighbors who are far away and about whose customs, traditions and problems they know very little, and it would help to bring about real unity as opposed to the talked about unity that now exists. In this program the people of America will show democracy in action rather than democracy dramatized."[25] Immediately following Pearl Harbor, Lomax sent telegrams to folklorists in several states requesting "recordings of reactions of four or five average men and women to Japanese aggression" within the next forty-eight hours. For good measure, he specified that they should "get colorful people who speak well."[26] Soon Lomax had enough material from many groups, including African Americans, Greeks, Poles, Italians, Chinese, and Germans, to broadcast a variety of American reactions to the war.

By the eve of America's entry into the World War II, the national identity that the revivalists had crafted during the Depression came to suit the kind of propaganda campaigns that characterized this war. Many revivalists employed in government agencies used their positions to ensure that propagandists incorporated folk music into various programs. This was especially true for Alan Lomax and other left-wing revivalists connected to the Library of Congress. Sparrow argues that after 1939, when the left-leaning Archibald MacLeish became head librarian, the Library of Congress became a haven for writers, folklorists, musicologists, and other left-leaning holdovers of the Popular Front. The programs produced through the RRP, such as the post–Pearl Harbor man-on-the-street interviews, particularly reflected the continued faith in both political equality and social justice that had characterized Popular Front Americanism.[27] While it is true that the message largely remained the same as it was in the prewar years, the *tone* changed. During the 1930s, folk revivalists had used folk music to help Americans withstand the daily drudgery of an economic depression. By the 1940s, especially after the United States entered the war, the revivalists' language became more urgent. Now folk music was a cultural weapon that could unite Americans, secure citizens' commitment to the democratic way of life, raise morale, and ultimately help defeat the enemy. This was a message that all leading revivalists espoused, regardless of their political leanings.

## Festivals Join the Fight

As the Washington folklorists pushed for the inclusion of folk music in government-sponsored propaganda, other revivalists contributed toward advancing the war effort through folk festivals and other types of pageants that featured ethnic and indigenously American musical traditions. Sarah Gertrude Knott's National Folk Festival (NFF) became the primary festival promoting the idea that folk music performance was instrumental in keeping the spirit of American democracy alive. While it remained a private event, the NFF promoted the same degree of pro-American patriotism as any governmental program during the World War II era.

In 1937, Knott moved the festival to Washington, D.C., where it would remain until 1942 under the sponsorship of the *Washington Post*. Although Knott did not have the same kind of political connections or positions as the Washington folklorists, she did manage to stage several successful programs during the festival's Washington stint and garnered the support of political figures such as Eleanor Roosevelt, who served as the honorary chair of the festival's general committee in 1938. As she did during her time in Dallas, Knott had to navigate the racial codes in Washington, D.C., another segregated city. During its stay, the NFF was held at Constitution Hall, a venue owned by the Daughters of the American Revolution (DAR). The hall became infamous in 1939 when the DAR refused to allow Marian Anderson, a renowned African American contralto, to perform. However, the NFF featured African Americans on the main stage both before and after the Anderson incident. How Knott was able to circumvent the DAR's racial policy is still unclear, but it does serve to illustrate the extent to which Knott adhered to a racially inclusive presentation of American folk traditions.

By 1940, Knott's festival had begun to adapt to the changing political conditions in light of the escalating war. The National Folk Festival Association (NFFA) adopted a more international perspective in addition to promoting a message of cultural tolerance that was increasingly coming into vogue. In a letter asking Teófilo Borunga, the mayor of the Mexican border city Juarez, to recommend a local mariachi band, Knott wrote, "Surely, there are no . . . stronger ties that bind Mexico to the United States than the traditional ties of song, music and dance that we have in common."[28] When she sent a similar request to the commissioner from Nova Scotia, requesting Canadian musicians, Knott further explained the NFF's response to current circumstances. Here, she broadened the emphasis on national unity to a continental level: "We feel that there has never been a time in the life of our country or yours, or any other for that matter, when it was so necessary for varied racial groups to understand each other. We know that the traditional expressions do more than any one thing to bring about that understanding."[29] Throughout January and February 1941, Knott sent letters to governors, ambassadors, and cultural officials in Canada, Mexico, Bolivia, Peru, the Virgin Islands, Haiti, Puerto Rico, and Panama asking them to send representatives for the eighth festival. Practically all of the letters stressed the need for understanding, tolerance, and unity among the nations of the Americas. Knott claimed that ethnic communities in the United States were sending their best musical groups to perform at the NFF because they recognized that "there has never been a time when there was such a need for better understanding, more tolerance, and a stronger national unity." She hoped to extend this effort and use the festival to generate a pan-American appreciation and exchange of folk music that would protect against the threat of fascism.[30]

After the United States entered the war, Knott situated the NFF within the context of wartime propaganda by inviting more immigrant groups to represent their cultural traditions, amplifying the festival's celebration of civic ideals through more references to "democracy" in the publicity for the festival, and designing the programs to raise public support for the war effort. Knott consistently argued that the festival contributed to a greater sense of national unity by bringing Americans from various ethnic backgrounds together in mutual appreciation. In an article promoting the 1942 festival, she explained, "As old and new Americans meet on common ground, there will be a practical demonstration of the democratic principles upon which our nation has been founded." The staging of the festival provided its own civic lesson: "The United States is one of the very few countries left today where people regardless of race, creed or nationality, can come together in their Nation's Capital to present their distinctive folk songs, music, and dances. The importance of encouraging this democratic attitude toward racial and national groups within our borders cannot be overestimated in these days of extreme nationalism." The ideals of democracy and cultural pluralism that the NFF promoted, Knott claimed, would help protect against the ideological threat that fascism posed.[31] Furthermore, she included choruses from the Army, Navy, and Marine Corps specifically to boost public morale.

Throughout the war years, the NFF presented an increasingly diverse array of ethnic music. The 1942 festival marked the first time the program featured Jewish performers. That same year, the NFFA staged a second festival at Madison Square Garden in New York City. (Knott estimated the audience at 22,000 for the entire duration of the NFF.) Now Knott's promotion of the festival was in full accordance with the wartime rhetoric, as she justified the NFF as a critical component of the war effort because it enhanced the cultural understanding and acceptance of the various groups in America.[32] In 1944, the festival highlighted Russian, Chinese, and Filipino performers, among others. The program noted that the emphasis on these traditions was no coincidence: "Since they are our allies in the world's struggle, and since we realize that the destiny of our country depends on the destiny of the world, and understanding must play an important part, we are more interested in their cultural expressions." Yet the author went beyond championing these groups as allies and commended them for contributing to the development of *American* culture: "We should, however, not be interested just for international reasons, but because these cultures are part of our own culture."[33] This emphasis marked a full reversal of the limited pluralism that characterized the initial festivals.

During this festival, the members of the NFFA became more introspective and started examining the NFF's purpose and how it related to festivals of the past. In a draft, the anonymous author of the article "A Glimpse of Folk Festivals in Other Lands through the Eleventh National Folk Festival" admitted that the initial festivals were ethnically myopic, focusing on only folk music of American Indians, southern blacks, and older ethnic groups such as the British, Spanish, French, and Germans, along with work songs of miners, sailors, lumberjacks, and cowboys. While the first programs represented "the attitude of our nation then," the author claimed, "it would not represent the feeling and thinking of our people today." The outbreak of war precipitated a dramatic shift in national mentality from xenophobic exclusivity to cultural inclusivity, and the NFF reflected this change: "A new America was speaking, one which recognized many of the folk heritages of the forty million and more new Americans who have come to make their homes here within the last sixty years, bringing a new store of vital expressions to add richness and color to the mosaic of our folk pattern."

The author acknowledged that prejudices still existed but argued that they were slowly eroding as people from various ethnic and regional backgrounds mingled in the Armed Forces and had new cultural encounters abroad. These experiences would most certainly break down prejudicial provincialism and create an impetus to make the nation more democratic in reality as much as in rhetoric, because when these people returned to the United States, "our petty national and racial prejudices in home communities will not be looked upon with favor. . . . When they come home they will not want to think of democracy in generalities but in specific application to their own lives." Furthermore, the author claimed not only that returning Americans would cease to maintain old prejudices but also that minority Americans, such as American Indians, would no longer stand for second-class citizenship: "[American Indians] will not be satisfied after this [war] to be 'just Indians' among neighbors who have been sitting on the sidelines while they faced gunfire." Those involved in the NFFA helped expedite this process by creating a microcosmic situation in which American democratic and pluralist principles were tried and triumphed: "We are testing one of the greatest experimentations in democracy, proving ourselves and showing others that people can live together in peace and harmony, without forgetting the manifestations of culture which makes each racial and national group distinctive."[34] With civic ideals keeping the peace, Americans could concentrate on cultivating cultural diversity through the festival. This view was in keeping with the pluralist form of nationalism that liberals emphasized during the war years. Burkholder argues that many pluralist liberals failed to recognize or comment on the complexity of racism in America even while they promoted cultural tolerance.[35] The author of the article, however, recognized the need for political and cultural democracy and called for an end to racial inequality, which illustrates a more nuanced version of wartime liberalism in the cultural arena.

The wartime rhetoric of democracy and cultural pluralism was so powerful that it even influenced the recreation industry. Many recreation activists, whose efforts at designing community leisure activities echoed the work of settlement house workers and playground advocates from the turn of the century, organized local events to generate grassroots support for this type of democratic Americanism. These recreationists often worked with Knott and the other members of the NFFA in designing and promoting programs such as patriotic celebrations and folk music festivals reminiscent of the cultural gifts approach. During World War II, the recreationists' mouthpiece, the magazine *Recreation*, featured several articles on how community folk festivals could aid in the fight for democracy abroad and at home, an effort that they continued even after the war. For example, the author of the article "Friends through Recreation" argued that folk festivals could foster American cultural pluralism and called for local recreation organizations to sponsor programs that would incorporate folk culture to make immigrants appreciate their native cultures and work to preserve their own traditions. The article's author feared that these unique contributions to American life were being lost as successive generations of immigrants became caught up in "the desperate human mob-need to 'be like everybody else.'" The best way to bridge intergenerational divides and the gap between immigrants and native-born citizens was to "emphasize the gifts the minority groups have brought with them to build our North American culture."

Much like the cultural gifts advocates, the author asserted that the ethnic cultures of immigrant communities must be made "an integral part of the whole pattern, not a brilliantly colored fringe stuck around the edge." She suggested that mainstream acceptance of cultural pluralism could be accomplished by including ethnic music in local patriotic celebrations of national holidays such as the Fourth of July and Memorial Day. Recognizing the contributions that immigrant cultures made in American life and commemorating the naturalized citizens who fought for the country in these celebrations "can do much to integrate nationality groups into the life of the community, to make them feel at home and proud of the special thing that they have to give to the whole country."[36] Recreation advocates believed that incorporating ethnic traditions into mainstream culture through folk festivals and patriotic celebrations would not only enhance American culture but also enable ethnic Americans to develop a sense of pride in their unique cultural forms.

Indeed, this was a view common among cultural leaders, pluralist educators, and even anthropologists such as Margaret Mead. Like Ruth Benedict,

Mead was a student of Franz Boas, but she advocated a less academic approach to the goal of ending ethnic and racial prejudice. Unlike Benedict, Mead strongly encouraged children from ethnic communities to identify with their cultural heritage and sought to use folk culture to overcome racial and ethnic prejudice.[37] Knott maintained a view similar to those of Mead and the recreation advocates. In one article published in *Recreation* during the war, she claimed that the NFF helped native-born Americans realize the pluralist nature of American cultural heritage. Like the pluralist recreation advocates, Knott stipulated that the cultures of ethnic minorities should be incorporated (but not assimilated) into mainstream American culture rather than remain isolated subcultures. She also believed that a key way to achieve this pluralism was through public performances of folk music. Citing the federal programs that used folk music to help establish international ties, Knott argued that these same programs could help with the domestic situation. "If a cultural relations program is of value in cementing friendships as the realization of common ideals internationally," she wrote, "it is reasonable to think that a practical, educational activity program applied to our own country, which utilizes in democratic fashion the traditional heritages of all our people, might serve a great purpose in the present and future development of our country."[38]

During a time of international upheaval, the NFF attempted to serve as an example of the strength of American democracy—cultural and political—in action. When reflecting on the festivals during the beginning of World War II Knott wrote, "We knew that we were living in one of the few nations left where groups, regardless of race, nationality or religious [*sic*] could come together for a friendly interchange of folk songs, music and dances which openly reflect our racial characteristics and national temperaments without interruption. We were proud to live in that country and we wanted to hold aloft this symbol of our democracy."[39] To Knott and the rest of the NFFA, the festival was that symbol.

As with the left-wing Washington revivalists, the rhetoric that Knott and other folk festival advocates used during the war years—their celebration of democracy and cultural pluralism—did not differ from the rhetoric they had used during the 1930s. What did change was the context of the message. Knott and her cohort of recreation advocates shifted their focus to accommodate their programs to the circumstances of war. They used folk music to illustrate the inherent plurality of the heterogeneous United States, which they contrasted with the forced homogeneity of fascist nations. Immediately before and after the United States entered the war, the pluralism of the National Folk Festival became much more inclusive, and some festival organizers even called for Americans to put the democratic principles that marked the wartime propaganda into practice after the war ended. Through folk music, these figures and other revivalists believed that they were educating citizens about their civic and cultural heritage, and they extended this effort to the citizens in training in American schools.

## Singing—and Teaching—Democracy

Folk music revivalists and their allies saw great potential in using folk music as a tool to educate children in American democracy, pluralism, and history, and they were not alone. For example, although Knott often received praise for her children's programs at the NFF, the Parent-Teacher Association specifically commended the festival in 1941 for teaching about American ethnic diversity on the eve of U.S. involvement in the war: "In today's confused world the young people especially need to learn something of our heritage. With understanding comes tolerance, and the Folk Festival, by bringing together groups from various sections of the United States with the characteristic folk expressions of each, should be a means of fostering a better understanding which should result in that greater unity for which we in America are striving."[40] Revivalists specifically argued that folk music instilled a democratic sensibility in American youth that stood in marked contrast to fascist and totalitarian mind-sets. In the midst of war, the composer and musicologist Henry Cowell moved the defense of folk music into the global arena by noting in 1944, "It is more urgently necessary than ever before for different democratic peoples to know each other more sympathetically and intimately." Through folk music—domestic and international—American students could gain a better understanding of, and compassion for, global peoples and thus continue the effort to make the world safe for democracy.[41]

Cowell's emphasis on internationalism reflected the views of political progressives who had participated in the Popular Front. Other revivalists shared his left-wing politics, specifically his emphasis on internationalism, and directed their efforts to presenting this view in American classrooms. Occasionally, these revivalists joined forces with educational experts in determining how music could best work in school curricula, particularly for civics classes. In the winter of 1945, a conference at Elizabeth Irwin High School sponsored by Camp Woodland, the progressive Catskill Mountain summer camp, gathered notable revivalists such as Pete and Charles Seeger, Alan Lomax, Benjamin Botkin, Harold Thompson (president of the New York Folklore Society), and the Columbia University anthropologist George Hertzog to discuss the implications of folklore for education in a democracy. It was hardly coincidental that these left-wing revivalists congregated at a summer camp, for Woodland, Wo-Chi-Ca (Workers Children's Camp), and other such camps were integral to the culture of the Communist Party, particularly during the 1930s and 1940s. Despite the attendees' leftist proclivities, the conference's focus on educating for the appreciation and protection of cultural difference was very much in line with a mainstream educational program that emphasized the importance of cultural differences labeled "intercultural education."

Schools involved in "intercultural" or "intergroup" educational initiatives incorporated curricula that provided information on different ethnic groups and their historical backgrounds, organized cultural assemblies, and banned books that demeaned ethnic and racial groups. These activities were predicated on the belief that the dissemination of information could successfully challenge negative stereotypes of ethnic and racial communities.[42] Theories of intercultural education were solidified in William Vickery and Stewart G. Cole's *Intercultural Education in American Schools* (1943). Guiding this program was the theory of cultural democracy, which entailed applying mainstream democratic principles to minority groups. They theorized that a set of basic civic ideals existed to which all Americans ought to adhere and that national unity should be built upon those ideals. Minority groups should not be forced to accept, or expected to separate themselves from, mainstream culture, but neither should they retain traditional practices that were undemocratic; in all other circumstances, the majority should respect their right to practice their own cultural traditions. Furthermore, these minorities would be granted full access to American culture while retaining their unique cultural characteristics. Essentially, "cultural democracy" advocated a type of nationalism that defined America as a composite of cultures connected by shared civic ideals. Emphasizing a unity-within-diversity view, Vickery and Cole sought to maintain a balance between forced conformity (and hyper-assimilationist programs) and a respect for cultural difference.[43]

Like the intercultural educators, many revivalists designed programs during the wartime and postwar years that not only encouraged tolerance of ethnic and racial cultural differences but also made those differences the root of American national identity. One of the first programs of this design was a children's show that Alan Lomax created for Columbia Broadcasting System (CBS) radio. In 1939, Lomax accepted an offer to take over hosting a weekly program of American folk music as a part of the American School of the Air (ASA) series.[44] Lomax's show was scheduled to run on Tuesday mornings from October through May. Although Lomax was not a professional educator, his show had several stamps of educators' approval; the Department of Education at CBS, the Music Educator's National Conference, and the National Education Association were all affiliated with the program. Throughout the program, Lomax emphasized the concept of applied learning. He prompted students to sing along to the songs that he presented, as well as to seek out music for themselves in their homes, schools, and communities. Lomax also encouraged students to attend music festivals, square dances, and other community gatherings that featured local folk music. The show championed folk music as a vital part of contemporary culture; therefore, as the teacher's manual mandated, "Wherever possible the interest of the class should center on the living oral tradition rather than on things to be found in books."[45] Officials at CBS estimated that more than 120,000 classrooms across the country would tune into the program. Lomax eagerly seized on this opportunity both to popularize folk music and to spread his gospel of the American democratic and pluralist heritage.

The ASA provided Lomax with the chance to design a radio program that would not only popularize folk music but also allow him to dictate what qualified as American folk music to a national listening audience. Before Lomax signed on to host the show, the ASA had aired a children's music program, *Music of America,* which featured both folk and popular songs grouped around historical periods. After Lomax took over, the show changed its name to *Folk Music of America* during the 1939–1940 season and then to *Wellsprings of Music* the following year, and it categorized folk music in the same way that Lomax and his father, John Lomax, did in their books of collected songs.[46]

Before World War II, Lomax emphasized work songs, dedicating episodes to such themes as railroad, teamster, lumberjack, forecastle, and "Negro work" songs. Occasionally, he designed a particular show around other, non-labor topics such as children's games, "nonsense," square dancing, and love songs. The show centered on performance—Lomax sang on most of the episodes, often with the assistance of different musical guests. The Golden Gate Quartet and Lead Belly (Huddie Ledbetter) performed on the "Negro Work Songs" and "Railroad Songs" episodes; Lomax's sister Bess accompanied him on love song duets; John M. "Sailor Dad" Hunt sang sea chanteys; and Woody Guthrie fittingly contributed to an episode on hobo or "vagabond minstrels" tunes. Most likely because of its focus on work songs, the show tended to be male-dominated. Apart from Bess Lomax, all of the guests were men who sang about the trials and tribulations of men's labor. Even though the show's themes were very specific—and somewhat narrow—the content was consistently national in scope. To emphasize this focus, during an episode that aired on February 20, 1940, the announcer Niles Welch requested that listeners send their favorite folk songs for the last two episodes, which were to be dedicated to listeners' submissions. Welch implored listeners across the United States to contribute their songs because, as he stated, "We want to have all parts of the country represented."[47]

Each episode of *Folk Music of America* followed the same format. After Welch's introduction, Lomax explained the day's topic and described the different aspects of the show's subject. He and the guests then sang songs pertinent to that theme. Lomax described his musical guests not as professionals but as authentic experts in their fields because they either *experienced* or had some intimate knowledge of the conditions depicted in the songs. "Sailor Dad" could sing sea chanteys because he came from a seafaring family; Lead Belly accurately sang field hollers and chain-gang songs because he had experienced the misery of both cotton sharecropping and convict labor. After Lomax and the guests bantered and sang a bit, the show dramatically shifted gears, and classical musicians replaced the folk singers. Every episode featured a particular song that Lomax first sang in a folk style, and afterward a professional orchestra performed a transposed version. Different composers took on the task of expressing the song's theme and tune through this orchestral version.

After this segment, Lomax closed the show by introducing the theme song of the next week's episode so children would be familiar with it and thus more likely to sing along; the ASA also provided a free classroom guidebook to enhance students' participation. Student engagement would help Lomax accomplish his goal, which he described in the introduction of one episode as an effort "to stimulate an appreciation of music as a part of our day to day living. The songs of unknown folk singers and the music of celebrated composers are human reactions to the world around us." He chose the topics and presented them via traditional singers and professional orchestras "to show this connection between music and the basic human needs and ideas from which it springs," an effort that clearly revealed Lomax's desire to use folk music to teach children his views of the culture, society, and national community in which they lived.[48]

Since *Folk Music of America* was a children's show that aired on commercial radio, Lomax did not have many opportunities to express his social and political views, but he did work to inject them into the episodes in various and subtle ways. For example, he conveyed his democratic, pluralist Americanism through the program's themes and music. Before delving into the national tradition that folk music illuminated, Lomax needed to establish that this music was indeed embedded in the American national heritage. This task was not so difficult with songs that had already been established as part of the American folk canon. Cowboy songs, Appalachian ballads, and older work songs such as lumberjack and seafaring songs were largely accepted as "traditional" folk music by the time *Folk Music of America* aired. In the program, however, Lomax also featured new music that people generated from their distinctly American experiences. For example, Lomax presented Woody Guthrie's "Do Re Mi" as a folk song (even though it was a topical song about the concerns of migrant families moving west) because it expressed a uniquely American situation. It also sent a clear message of support for an economically displaced population and illustrated the harsh treatment they continued to endure even after they reached their destination through lines such as "California is a garden of Eden, a paradise to live in or see / But believe it or not, you won't find it so hot / If you ain't got the do re mi."[49] Sometimes Lomax made sure to state explicitly that folk music that some listeners might regard as far from the mainstream, such as the blues, was as "natively American as cornbread, Kansas or Casey Jones."[50]

Once Lomax established that the music he aired was part of an authentic American folk identity—past and present—he then used it to define a particular view of the national culture and heritage. For him, folk songs represented the inherent diversity of American society, and one aspect of this diversity was an ethnic pluralism generated by waves of immigration. As Lomax wrote in a letter to the folk song collector Joanna Colcord in 1941, he wanted to begin a project recording the songs of ethnic minorities living in New York City because "America should make clear her concern for the cultural riches of the peoples whom she has welcomed into her borders."[51] Lomax expressed his commitment to crediting immigrants for contributing to the development of American culture by presenting their music in several *Folk Music of America* episodes. During one program on railroad songs, Lomax illustrated a romantic view of American pluralism through the construction of the national railroad system. The show began with the songs of Irish immigrant laborers in the North and then proceeded to the songs of African Americans laying down tracks in the South.[52]

This emphasis on cultural diversity as a defining feature of American strength and identity became even more pronounced as World War II escalated. For the episode "The Composer Looks Abroad" during the 1940–1941 season, the manual opened with a cosmopolitan assessment of American culture: "In the three hundred–odd years that a new American culture has been building, foreign influences from all over the world have gone into its make-up. Our folk music is complex, [with] influences from Africa, Spain, France, England, Ireland, [and] Scotland."[53] Lomax's script for the January 1, 1941, episode on British ballads took a more idealized view in light of current events: "America is the land where men from all over the world, speaking different languages, singing different songs, liking different kinds of cooking, have been able to meet and say, 'Hello stranger, where are you going? Stop a minute and let's have a talk. Where are you from? It's mighty good to know you.'" Again, he emphasized the pluralism of American folk music by recognizing that "Spanish, French, German, Russian, Armenian, Latvian, [and] Lithuanian" ballads and songs have helped shape the nation's folk music and, in an explicit attack against fascism, that "it is not against the law to sing in any language you happen to know here in America."[54]

As the U.S. government began gearing up for wartime mobilization, Lomax increasingly preached a dual message of American unity and antifascism. The growing popularity of the German Bund and pro–Mussolini Italian groups led public officials to fear the specter of violent division within American society. Therefore, many educational programs emphasized tolerance and diversity as part of a larger effort to sell an idealized view of American democracy.[55] Indeed, the teacher's manual for the first season of *Folk Music of America* situated the show within this trend. The author commended the growing appreciation of American folk music as an important part of the American heritage. This in itself was a noteworthy development, because "as one European nation after another has, in recent years, rejected democracy or compromised it, throughout America there has come the realization that our refuge and strength lies in the cultivation of our own democratic tradition." This tradition is best exemplified "at its musical core—American folk music."[56]

The antifascist commentaries that Lomax and other contributors wove throughout the series reflected the wartime celebration of American social and cultural diversity. Yet it is also important to recognize that Lomax was very sympathetic to the programs and ideas of the Popular Front, and many of the topics that he presented on the program reflected his political sympathies, as well. Besides inviting Charles Seeger, Woody Guthrie, and other leftists to be guests on the show, Lomax interpreted American folk music in ways that stressed aspects of the Popular Front platform—for example, by crediting common people for their contributions to the national cultural heritage. After all, as the manual explains, American folk music was "created and preserved by the common people, the pioneers, the farmers and the workers [and] these songs reflect the independence of spirit of the people who sing them."[57]

Lomax's political and social proclivities revealed themselves most clearly in the case of two of the show's main themes: labor and African American folk music. Labor issues were relatively easier to work with during the years of the New Deal and Congress of Industrial Organizations organizing. Although Lomax did not, and probably could not, call attention to specific labor problems during a children's radio program, his emphasis on *work* songs clearly indicated his political sympathies. Occasionally, he also managed to include comments directly pertaining to the plight of the American worker. The March 19, 1940, episode, for example, opened with a direct attack on poor working conditions, though safely referring to historical ones: "We have been singing songs and telling stories about the men who worked hard at dangerous jobs . . . pioneering men who blazed the trail for American industry. Their lives were harder than almost any worker's today: and they were often very poorly paid. . . . Still others revolted against the laws of society, grabbed a gun and fought back against a hard world."[58] Two weeks later, the episode "Poor Farming Songs" featured Woody Guthrie singing about the hardships that the American farmer had endured during the previous decade. The fact that the overwhelming majority of the episodes dealt with labor is further indicative of Lomax's left-wing political views. During the Popular Front years, leftist artists emphasized labor and working-class themes in film, literature, music, and art. The leftists involved in the front's cultural programs also enabled working-class citizens to become "artists" and generate works that depicted their own lives.[59] Even after the Popular Front technically ended in 1939, Lomax continued to promote this emphasis. Throughout the airing of *Folk Music of America,* he not only highlighted how American labor helped shape larger culture but also had the people who were part of these laboring traditions sing their own songs rather than feature big-name crooners singing Tin Pan Alley tunes that merely mused about the lives of the common folk.

Racial equality also remained a guiding principle for the American left that continued throughout the 1940s. From the outset of his career, Alan Lomax stressed the importance of black musical traditions for shaping larger folk music styles. Lomax's views of racial equality, however, were more subdued in *Folk Music of America.* By dedicating shows to specific African American themes such as spirituals and black work songs, he did emphasize their importance in shaping American musical traditions. In this respect, his show was akin to the federally sponsored *Freedom's People* (1941–1942) program, which also imparted messages of civil rights and racial justice. Each episode of that program recounted African American history and highlighted black advancements—one of which centered on black music, beginning with slave spirituals. The historian Barbara Savage argues that the writers of *Freedom's People* politicized the music by presenting slave songs as "acts of resistance" in addition to serving spiritual purposes. The program also featured work songs as sung by

Josh White, a frequent guest on Lomax's show and left-wing sympathizer, and depicted them as songs that had sprung from "the sweat of strong men building the strength of America," placing work songs within the civic nationalism of the World War II era.[60]

Although Lomax also sought to send a message of racial equality through *Folk Music of America,* many episodes dedicated to black folk culture tended to romanticize the circumstances from which the music developed. Rarely did Lomax comment on the poor living conditions, lack of civil rights, and lynch-law rule that most southern blacks endured. The closest that Lomax came to a direct commentary on American racial injustice, past and present, occurred at the beginning of an episode dedicated to blues music when he explained that "the blues arose as a direct expression of the suffering and sorrow of the Negro people in the South."[61] The strongest racial, and most controversial, statement that Lomax made with the show, however, was not in the music or the script but, rather, in the show's design. The program featured an integrated cast, a rare situation for the early 1940s. Most important, *Folk Music of America* was a show on commercial radio that featured black performers singing and reflecting on their own culture, and not white actors performing in oral blackface—a situation that barely existed anywhere in America at that time except in government-sponsored programs. This casting decision was a political act in and of itself, for, as Judith Smith argues, left progressives recognized the need for black performers on the radio as a crucial part of the fight to gain full citizenship.[62] Lomax argued that black traditions lay at the heart of American cultural identity because "without songs created or inspired by the American Negro, American music would have lost half its soul." Furthermore, black spirituals, generated by the combined "sorrows of slavery" and religious faith, were one of the nation's "noblest contributions to world music."[63] Although he could not state his position on civil rights explicitly on the air, through his presentation of American folk music Lomax did indeed make a powerful statement on the value of black culture and life in shaping the American experience, heritage, and overarching identity.

As much as Lomax believed in social and political equality, his beliefs were incompletely realized in the pluralist vision of American identity that he presented in *Folk Music of America.* Although he respected the cultural diversity of immigrant folk music, he never played songs in other languages, representing only traditions in English. Some immigrant groups were omitted altogether, particularly Asian ones—a noteworthy shortcoming as other educators of the era broadened their pluralism specifically to include Asian Americans.[64] Another group that did not fare well in the show was American Indians. Not only did Lomax fail to include their traditions in his musical portrait of America; when he did reference American Indians, he did so in a surprisingly derogatory manner. In a particular episode that focused on cowboys and pioneers in the West, Lomax referred to the Sioux Indians as a "real antagonist" who were "[a]-killing poor drivers and burning their trains," the trains belonging to the white pioneers, the "unsung heroes," according to Lomax. He did mention the government's encouragement of the buffalo slaughter but failed to reflect on it any more than to muse, "When the buffalo vanished, the power of the plains Indians was broken." The prairie was then open for industrious Americans to "conquer."[65]

Sometimes listeners noted the shortcomings in the diversity of folk traditions that Lomax presented. In one letter, the correspondence committee of Damascus High School in Maryland informed Lomax that the program introduced the fifty-one students in their seventh-grade music class to the vast cultural diversity of the American folk. However, one of the writers asked Lomax about two omissions in the show: first, the role of Spanish and Mexican traditions in shaping the music of the Southwest, and second, the role of American Indians, "the original Americans."[66] Most letters sent to Lomax, however, praised his *Folk Music of America*. Mrs. E. C. Ottoson of the folk music research department of the Pennsylvania Federation of Music Clubs commended Lomax for bringing folk music to the radio because the club members had "been trying for so many years to bring about an awakening among our musicians and friends of music to the amazing field of folk music lying unrecognized at our doorstep." A teacher from New Jersey informed Lomax that she used the show in her fifth-grade class for music education and to teach the social sciences.[67] This letter must have pleased Lomax, because, as he wrote to another teacher in Virginia, "My own interest in this field is in its social background and in the light that it throws on [the] American makeup."[68] Sometimes listeners wrote about how they were personally affected by the show. A listener from New York City, Peyton F. Anderson, complimented the episode "Negro Work Songs" and remarked, "In them one sees the courage and a rhythmic dignity even in adversity which makes me rather proud of my antecedents."[69] In addition to individual letters of support, Lomax often received packets of letters from different classes that had listened to the show. Some children wrote about the particular songs they enjoyed or submitted their own songs and games. The 1940–1941 Evaluation of School Broadcasts Research Project of Ohio State University informed Lomax that his show received positive feedback according to the weekly evaluations submitted by teachers who used the ASA series in their classes.

Lomax's program ended in 1942 after he began working for the OWI. For the duration of the show, Lomax used folk music to illustrate a distinctly national heritage and sought to teach children about American cultural diversity in a way that transcended mere tolerance of differences. Lomax's understanding of nationalism not only recognized social, economic, and cultural diversity but also used these distinctions to articulate what made the United States a unique nation. Despite myriad cultural, economic, and social differences, Lomax had faith that Americans were united through civic ideals and the promise of political democracy.

## *Conclusion*

As the nation moved from the Depression and New Deal years into the World War II era, the revival changed along with it. The "hard times" continued, resulting now from war rather than an economic depression. According to the revivalists, folk music served a specific purpose in this new climate. As a people's music, folk music could be an important cultural tool in a "people's war." Once the United Stated entered the war, the type of pluralist and democratic Americanism in which the revivalists believed came to define the rhetoric of the wartime propaganda campaigns. Therefore, the revivalists easily adapted their Americanism to accommodate the social, cultural, and political contexts of World War II. Now the revivalists argued that folk music could help secure Americans' commitment to their democratic national identity during a protracted fight against fascism.

However, by joining the propaganda industry, the revivalists became as guilty of both romanticizing America and exaggerating the unity of the American people as other wartime propagandists. In their effort to emphasize this unity, they largely failed to recognize citizens, such as Japanese Americans, who were cast out of the social and political systems, and those, like African Americans, who still suffered second-class citizenship. For many progressives, these grave failures of American democracy were overshadowed by the brutalities of the totalitarian regimes. Yet for activists who prided themselves on generating a culturally pluralist Americanism even before the war, the failure to acknowledge the full disjuncture between the wartime rhetoric of pluralism and the reality of American racism and prejudice was a significant shortcoming. This indicates that leftist revivalists such as Alan Lomax were willing to subordinate their earlier calls for social justice to promote the kind of pluralism that suited the government's propaganda campaigns.

Contrary to the rhetoric of the revivalists and other engineers of wartime culture and propaganda, the war did not unite all Americans. However, the war did unite the revivalists. While tensions did exist between some of the revivalists, most redirected their programs to accommodate the war effort. Both vaguely liberal revivalists like Sarah Gertrude Knott and political radicals like Alan Lomax endeavored to use folk music to champion American democracy. The need to stem the tide of fascism outweighed the social and political differences between the revivalists. Following the government's agenda was not difficult for political centrists like Knott, but leftist revivalists had to dull their political edge in order to become fully immersed in the mainstream war effort. However, they did not sustain their political concessions for long. After the Allied victory leftist revivalists resumed the political work that they began before the war. During the war, therefore, the revival experienced a brief period of unanimity; it was a level of unity that the revivalists would not reach again for the duration of the movement.

Perhaps the most ominous aspect of the kind of civic nationalism that American cultural and civic leaders championed during the war was its political exclusivity. When confronted with the policies of Nazism, liberal leaders and intellectuals began to return to examining racial and ethnic issues, issues that they had largely neglected during the Depression. By the middle of the 1940s, issues pertaining to religious and ethnic prejudice, civil rights, and immigration reform became part of the liberal intellectual agenda.[70] Nevertheless, while liberals generated a much more inclusive notion of nationalism than the racial nationalism of fascist nations, their civic consensus view of national identity—the idea that anyone could be considered an American if he or she adhered to certain political ideals—had its own limitations. As it turned out, those who did not believe in some national ideals, such as the faith in free enterprise that became increasingly significant in the postwar years, could be, and were, labeled un-American. Although the revivalists could not see it at the time, the civic consensus that they helped champion during the war would ultimately help lead to their own political ostracism by the following decade.

# 3

## ILLUSION AND
## DISILLUSIONMENT

The year 1939 may have marked the official end of the Popular Front, but it did not mean the end of the left-wing civic culture that members of the front initiated. These activists still pushed for social and economic justice to the extent that the Popular Front continued as a widespread social movement. The mid-1940s, in fact, marked two new periods in the history of the Popular Front, according to Michael Denning. The first, or "wartime Popular Front," ran in 1943–1944, and the second commenced the year immediately after V-J Day, stimulated by a surge of labor activism, including the campaign by the Congress of Industrial Organizations (CIO) to organize southern industries in "Operation Dixie" and a massive wildcat strike wave that ran through 1946. For many on the left, this was the heyday of the militant labor movement, when its "social-democratic laborism" appeared to be coming to fruition in American life.[1] Similarly, the years surrounding the war were a boon for many left-wing revivalists who remained active in the Popular Front movement. It was a time when their pro-democratic, pro-labor, and pro–civil rights stances closely aligned with the rhetoric of the left.

Throughout the World War II years, revivalists worked to secure a place for folk music in mainstream American culture. They did so largely by adapting their programs to suit the wartime propaganda campaigns. Having thrown themselves into the war to such an extent, the revivalists needed to learn how to readjust to a time of peace—and learn quickly to remain culturally and politically relevant. Just as major industries had to shift production to suit a postwar economy, the revivalists had to change their message for a postwar society in which fascism was no longer the enemy.

Several factors enabled revivalists on the left side of the political spectrum to segue from war to peace while remaining politically committed. The first was their prewar effort to make folk music socially relevant. During the 1930s, many communists had turned to folk music, particularly music from the rural South, as a way to connect to larger society because it was a distinctly American cultural tradition. Since many urban activists either came from immigrant families or were immigrants themselves, an appreciation of indigenous rural folk music provided a means to effectively become as "American" as old-stock citizens.[2] Those communists who championed the importance of folk music gravitated to a new group called the Almanac Singers, who used traditional and topical folk songs to advance left-wing social reforms. Although the Almanacs consisted of a small assortment of musicians, many left-wing enthusiasts, including public folklorists and writers, maintained affiliations with them. Together, these revivalists established a strong connection between folk music and political activism, especially in the realm of labor reform. It was a connection that many of these revivalists endeavored to strengthen soon after the war ended.

Another factor that helped the left-wing revivalists transition to peacetime was the political climate of postwar America. After the war, the United States experienced a surge of activism, and leftist revivalists sought to aid these struggles with their music. For a brief window in time, these revivalists had reason to believe that they were engendering permanent social and political reform in the United States. The labor movement gained a new sense of militancy after the numerous compromises that workers made during the war; the rise of wildcat strikes between 1945 and 1946 signified that a powerful grassroots drive was growing among the rank-and-file. The leftist musicians of the revival took full advantage of the labor movement's militant turn by forming close ties with left-leaning labor unions, participating in labor rallies, and singing on picket lines—thus bringing folk music into the fight for workers' rights once again. In this environment, leftist revivalists hoped to achieve their dream of generating a "singing labor movement."

The third component of the left-wing revivalists' success during this window lay in their understanding of national identity. These revivalists had crafted a version of Americanism grounded in the civic ideals of political democracy, cultural pluralism, and civil rights. This progressive view of nationalism was very much in line with the larger Popular Front Americanism that, according to Denning, appealed to a "popular *internationalism*" that resulted in a "pan-ethnic appeal to a federation of nationalities" in the domestic and global arenas.[3] To illustrate this argument, Denning cites the numerous ethnic and racial narratives that came out of Popular Front cultural products, and highlights the multiethnic "American" narrator in "Ballad for Americans" as particularly illustrative of this pluralist Americanism. While this emphasis on cultural heterogeneity was a key aspect of the nationalism that emerged from the racially and ethnically diverse Popular Front, it was also in keeping with the type of Americanism that followed from the Bournian tradition of "transnational"

Americanism that had influenced progressive revivalists since the beginning of the revival. Leftist revivalists involved in the Popular Front would work along-side other activists to sustain this Americanism during wartime and in the postwar years, when the larger political climate was sympathetic to such a view, and even during the late 1940s, when the escalating Cold War would sway public opinion in the opposite direction. The left-wing revivalists formed an important contingent of this Popular Front coalition, and, like the other cultural workers of the left, they would face increasing hostility to both their outlook and their music by the waning years of the decade.

Although labor activism was a primary cause for these revivalists, it was not the only one to which they dedicated their efforts. Through music, they fought for better housing conditions for low-income citizens, civil rights, and international peace. While some of these problems resulted from the postwar circumstances, most of them had deep roots. The leftist revivalists, along with other political progressives, had begun a concerted effort to change these conditions in the 1930s, and they continued their efforts into the 1940s. While many put their work on hold during the war—several served in the Armed Forces or worked in wartime government agencies—the leftist revivalists resumed their activism almost immediately after peace was declared. The story of the left-wing revivalists of the early postwar era is largely one of optimism, followed almost immediately with the disillusionment of political failure. At the same time, this story is also one of cultural success, for their combination of folk music and political activism would strongly influence popular perceptions of folk music in the succeeding decades. Their efforts during this brief window laid the groundwork for the cultural and political ideals that they would carry into the political activism spearheaded by a new generation of leftist activists.[4] It is for this reason that a closer exploration of the activity of the left-wing revivalists during the pre-and postwar years is a necessary chapter in the story of the folk music revival.

## *Radical Revivalists, Unite!*

Years after Lee Hays left the South, he recalled one of his experiences organizing in the region during the mid-1930s. He was in the backseat of a car with other organizers—a black man and a white woman—driving down a rural Arkansas road at night. Because they were breaking political, racial, and gender codes in a staunchly, and violently, conservative region, everyone was visibly scared. To help ease the fear that had gripped him and his companions, Hays started singing songs that they all presumably would know: church hymns. Soon, the other riders also began singing, which did have a calming effect. At one point, Hays remembered saying, "I wish we had as many labor songs as hymns and that folks sang them with the same feeling," to which a fellow organizer responded, "We will someday. And who do you think is going to make the new songs?" Hays replied, "Why, I guess we will."[5]

Indeed, that is exactly what Hays aimed to do when he came to New York City in 1939. Along with Millard Lampell, a journalist and leftist activist, and Pete Seeger, a son of Charles Seeger, who had recently worked with Alan Lomax at the Archive of American Folk Song and traveled around the country with Woody Guthrie, he started a musical group to promote social activism at home and rally support for the fight against fascism abroad. Pete Seeger explained that they chose the name Almanac Singers when he came across "almanac" while reading through Woody Guthrie's notes for his songbook, *Hard Hitting Songs.* Hays suggested that they use "almanac" because in rural homes there were always two books—the Bible and the almanac: "The [B]ible helps them to the next world and the almanac helps them through this world."[6] According to Lampell, the Almanacs' "creed" was a simple motto: "Our work is to be performed in the manner which best aids the working class in its struggle to claim its just heritage. We just stick to the old tunes working people have been singing for a long time—sing 'em easy, sing 'em straight, no holds barred. We're working men on the side of the working man and against the big boys."[7] Over the years Woody Guthrie, Pete and Butch Hawes, Bess Lomax, Agnes "Sis" Cunningham, Josh White, Arthur Stern, and others joined the Almanacs, trying to bring social and political reform to America, defeat fascism, and generate a singing labor movement.

Lampell's depiction of the Almanacs as "working men" was definitely an overstatement, for none of them held working-class jobs, but they were sympathetic to the needs of the American working people and sought to address their concerns in music. Arthur Stern described the group as a "scruffy lot" who at least tried to look like workers by affecting what they perceived as working-class dress, "feeling that to dress well was putting on airs and not part of the working-class décolletage." Although most of the members came from the middle or even upper classes, as "proletarian romantics" they consistently aligned themselves with working-class causes.[8] In so doing, the Almanacs embedded themselves in the Popular Front culture of the late 1930s and 1940s. As Denning argues, the Popular Front marked the beginning of "the *laboring* of American culture." Labor and working-class themes entered into American film, literature, music, and art; working-class people became "artists" who generated works depicting their own lives; and artists became laborers themselves, exemplified by strikes of cultural workers such as cartoonists employed at the Walt Disney Studios.[9] The Almanacs may not have been *of* the working-class, but they specifically sought to reach a working-class audience—with varying degrees of success. They often sang in working-class dialects, and their subject material—losing houses and farms to foreclosure, joining CIO unions, trying to feed families—were topics to which almost all working-class Americans could relate during the Depression years.

The Almanacs strongly sympathized with causes that Popular Front organizations championed, but, according to Lampell, at the beginning they lacked a clearly defined philosophy. Even though they all espoused "left-oriented feelings," those sentiments were "pretty vague and formless." The only original member to have clear political views *and* experience was Lee Hays because of his connection to Commonwealth College.[10] The labor school had a strong influence on the group; the Almanacs supported the same causes for which the college had advocated, and they based their living arrangements on the Commonwealth model. Most of the Almanacs at one time or another lived in the communal "Almanac house" in New York City. The location moved around a few lower Manhattan apartments, and members moved in and out, but in general terms, the Almanacs lived, worked, ate, and wrote songs communally. Hays explained that the communal songwriting was perhaps the most important aspect of the group. Drawing inspiration from the "Anonymous" literary movement in Paris during the 1920s, the Almanacs copyrighted their songs as a group so no one member would receive sole credit (unless a member wrote a song in its entirety). As Hays put it, this way the "emphasis was on the stuff itself" rather than the composer's reputation.[11]

The Almanacs released their first album, *Songs for John Doe,* in early 1941 while the United States, though still neutral, began gearing up for war. The album contained numerous antiwar songs, including "Ballad of October 16th," the notorious chorus of which excoriates Franklin D. Roosevelt as a warmonger who believes that "we won't be safe 'till everybody's dead." Comparing the draft to the Agricultural Adjustment Act's program of crop destruction, the chorus to another song, "Plow Under," simply states, "Plow the fourth one under / Plow under . . . every fourth American boy." *Songs for John Doe* revealed the Almanacs' ideological affiliation with the Soviet Union and support for the 1939 Nazi-Soviet Non-Aggression Pact the Soviets had with Germany (which ended the Popular Front). However, they quickly changed their tune as soon as the Germans changed theirs. In the album, *Dear Mr. President* (1942), they recanted their earlier position in the title song and declared their newfound support for U.S. intervention in such songs as "Round and Round Hitler's Grave."

In addition to drawing songwriting inspiration from international events, the Almanacs also focused on using music to reform domestic conditions. The members largely agreed on the causes their music supported, but they occasionally differed on how to get their messages across. Some, like Lampell, advocated an agitprop approach that dealt with larger issues and based lyrics on catchy slogans; others, like Guthrie, disdained slogan-based songs as empty and forgettable and rather sought to write personalized ballads that connected listeners to the songs' subjects.[12] Despite methodological differences, the Almanacs all agreed that their purpose was to use music to aid the fight for social, political, and economic change. Besides battling the forces of fascism, the Almanacs' priority was helping the labor movement. They operated at a time when the labor movement had reached a peak—buoyed by the success of CIO organizing drives that included many communist union organizers.[13] By composing songs such as "Union Maid," "Talking Union," and "Song for Harry Bridges," an ode to the

West Coast union organizer, which they performed at labor events, the Almanacs used music to rally for the cause.

The public reaction to the Almanac Singers was mixed. In 1941, *Life* magazine published a feature story about them, and they were invited to audition for a gig at the Rainbow Room in New York City. Yet at the venue, the group was treated more like a hillbilly novelty act than a source of legitimate political protest. The Almanacs did, however, become popular in many leftist circles, mostly in New York City. Bess Lomax Hawes recalled: "I think in other parts of the country, we would have had either a much more limited audience than we had in New York, or we would have had to develop a very different kind of repertoire, quite possibly not as outspokenly left. I think New York was a very special place at that time and when we toured, I think we more or less again sang to the converted."[14]

As they incorporated the leftist ethos prevalent in New York City, they often combined their political views with musical styles from other regions, particularly from the South. Lee Hays attributed their songwriting success to the fact that they drew inspiration from the people they encountered—striking tenant farmers, miners, steelworkers, textile workers, and any other group involved in the labor movement. Hays later reflected that they were able to "tap that root of the people's own culture—to mine out a particular vein. I think the Almanacs came closer to the mother lode than any other group before or since, because they were closer to the people, and from the people drew their wisdom and strength."[15] To other leftists, that was the quality that gave the Almanacs their unique character and made them more than simply a leftist agitprop group. The activist and social worker Harriet Magil praised the Almanacs for bringing something different to the movement in New York: "That's one of the things that was fresh about them. That they didn't just sit in the movement. They went out there where other people were. And while their point of view was gotten from the movement, their material was gotten from the people out there who had no connection to the movement."[16] By bringing songs that were from and about other regions in America, the Almanacs helped introduce urban activists to the plight of workers who were far removed from the union campaigns of the industrialized areas of the North.

Near the same time they formed the Almanacs, Pete Seeger and Woody Guthrie participated in a folk music radio show for adults called *Back Where I Come From* that Alan Lomax created and hosted for CBS Radio in 1940–1941. Similar to the Almanacs, *Back Where I Come From* introduced listeners to rural southern music, music that Lomax used to spread a politically progressive message that reflected the interethnic and interracial aspects of Popular Front Americanism. Through the music aired on the program, Lomax aimed to present "the seemingly incoherent diversity of American folk song as an expression of its democratic, inter-racial, international character, as a function of its inchoate and turbulent many-sided development."[17] Each episode focused on a theme, with different musicians singing and reflecting on that topic. Bringing then little-known singers like Guthrie and Seeger together with Burl Ives and Josh White, *Back Where I Come From* introduced listeners to musicians who would become major figures in the folk music scene during the 1950s and 1960s.

Lomax may have intended to illustrate American diversity in his program, but most episodes followed in the same vein as *Folk Music of America* by featuring an all-male cast reflecting on largely masculine activities, although this one emphasized agrarian life. As Woody Guthrie stated in one episode before breaking into the Populist anthem "The Farmer Is the Man That Feeds Them All," "You got to remember that there's still more corn than concrete in America." At times, the guests acknowledged that they tended to focus on "people from small towns, hilltops, and farm valleys" in discussing such topics as courting, tall-tale telling, and other aspects of small town life. Yet at least one show, on October 21, 1941, included urbanites discussing industrial labor. As Lomax remained committed to left-wing social views and employed singers openly sympathetic to the CPUSA, he masked his political leanings in folksy populism reminiscent of Norman Rockwell's America, often through sweeping narrations that opened each episode. For example, on February 10, 1941, the introduction declared, "Out of the heart of America come the songs and stories sung and told on *Back Where I Come From*. It's as American as the town hall, the picket fence, the country courthouse and ice cream sodas and prohibition."[18] Although his sympathies lay with the Popular Front, his program reflected the liberal populism of the Roosevelt administration.

Lomax maintained strong ties to the Almanacs: in addition to inviting individual members as guests on *Back Where I Come From*, he served as a "spiritual adviser" to the group as a whole. Lomax's interests in folk music at that time were rooted in rural music, especially traditions from the South. Many of his song-collecting expeditions focused on the South and Midwest, and his radio work reflected the rural regions where he traveled. He tried to lead the Almanacs in a more "countrified" direction that was reminiscent of his radio program, but the group members continued to prefer their musical eclecticism, which more strongly reflected their political outlook. While they did incorporate southern folk music that Lomax and Hays advocated, they also borrowed from other traditions, especially protest music that came from nineteenth-century British radicals and the American abolitionist movement. During their live performances in clubs, at labor rallies, and on picket lines, they often sang both traditional folk and topical songs, all of which served to advance progressive social and political reforms.[19] By combining traditional, topical, socially conscious, and even politically neutral songs and bringing them all into reform efforts, the Almanacs established a precedent that left-wing revivalists would continue into the 1950s and 1960s.

The Almanacs' musical diversity matched their group dynamic. They were a group that maintained a constellation of members who varied between part-time and full-time membership. By 1942, there were no clear leaders, and many of the group's early members had become involved in side projects. That same year, a group of members, including Bess Lomax and Agnes Cunningham, left New York City for Detroit to be at the epicenter of labor activism. Soon after, Seeger left for the army, Guthrie joined the U.S. Merchant Marine, and the group eventually disbanded. Yet the members would resume their efforts to use in political activism immediately after the war's end.

The merging of political activism with folk music that the Almanacs exemplified inspired many other young, left-wing folk music enthusiasts, especially the members of Folksay, a square-dance group that also began in New York City. Beginning in 1942 as an offshoot of the Victory Dance Committee, Folksay was an organization of young leftists who supported the war effort. In 1944, the troupe joined forces with American Youth for Democracy—a more broad-based and popular successor to the Young Communist League.[20] Folksay's mission was to merge folk music and political activism, but with a stronger emphasis on dance. Irwin Silber, a student and avid communist, became involved with Folksay shortly after it began. The group, as he described it, consisted of people who had a collective interest in "square dancing, folk music, and things like that, joined in a political framework." Folksay drew inspiration from the Almanac Singers, as many members had attended rallies where the Almanacs performed and followed their path of fusing traditional music with messages of political change. The Almanacs provided an example of how to be politically radical and still connected to American culture, Silber explained, "We wanted something that was America. . . . It wasn't just the Almanacs, it was Woody [Guthrie], Lead Belly, and Pete [Seeger] and so on, pulling it together that made a connection to the music and political values that made a lot of sense to us."[21] Although, as Silber recognized, there was nothing overtly political about square dancing, the Folksay members believed that they made a political statement just by engaging in this tradition: "We were really interested in square dancing. We felt, in that sense, that we were, in reviving the authentic folk music, we were making a political statement." The statement that they made was a rejection of popular commercial culture, and Folksay members expressed this rejection by creating a performance style that combined traditional dancing with topical songs and themes.[22]

Folksay members viewed rural Anglo-American folk music as illustrative of an indigenously American radicalism that could easily be used to spread a political message, and they were not alone. For instance, the same year that Folksay formed, the dancer Sophie Maslow created a performance, also titled "Folksay," based on Carl Sandburg's *The People, Yes* that incorporated music by Woody Guthrie and Earl Robinson. These political dancers turned Sandburg's democratic Americanism into a call for political action. Through their dances, these political enthusiasts generated a community of politically like-minded New Yorkers who also had a penchant for rural music.[23] By the end of the war, this community would grow both in numbers and in geographical range.

With the Almanacs, *Back Where I Come From,* and Folksay, left-wing revivalists rooted themselves and their political positions firmly in the American cultural heritage. These revivalists were all sympathizers with the Americanism that the CPUSA espoused during the Popular Front, and they sustained the rhetoric that had characterized Popular Front civic culture even after the Soviet Union halted the official mandate. Not only does this reveal that left-wing revivalists maintained a degree of autonomy from the party, but it also indicates that their political affiliations were predicated on something more than just an interest in following the party line. Rather, the leftist revivalists were primarily interested in using the musical cultural heritage of the American people both to fight fascism abroad and to bring about political reform at home.

## A Time to Gain

Shortly before Folksay formed, the CPUSA experienced sweeping changes. The antifascist ethos that marked the Popular Front resumed after the Soviet Union formed the Grand Alliance with the United States and Britain. In the midst of this, Earl Browder completed the Americanization of the CPUSA by dissolving it as a party and turning it into a political organization called the Communist Political Association (CPA) in 1944. The CPA still followed the communist precedent of emphasizing the significance of the working class, but it selected such mainstream political figures as Washington, Jefferson, and Lincoln as leaders to emulate. Unfortunately for Browder, dissolving the CPUSA as a *party* went too far for the Soviets' taste, and he served as the CPA's first and last president.

Browder's failure had much to do with the shifting political climate of postwar America. After the war ended, communists and left-wing progressives experienced a short-lived euphoria; the Allied forces had defeated fascism, and a new spirit of labor radicalism coursed through the working class. By the end of 1946, more than five million workers in the electrical, steel, coal, auto, oil, railroad, and packinghouse industries had gone on strike. The number of people joining left-wing causes swelled, and Browder's moderate, reformist views no longer suited the increasingly militant milieu. In 1945, Moscow reestablished the CPUSA and placed the hard-line William Z. Foster at the helm.[24]

As the revived party galvanized card-carrying members, the general spirit of activism that characterized the immediate postwar years—spurring wildcat strikes and initiating a new phase of the Civil Rights Movement—rallied leftist sympathizers and fellow travelers. Many leftist revivalists, especially those connected to groups like Folksay, rode this wave of optimism and offered their musical talents to aid the struggles. The founders of the Almanacs and other musical activists spearheaded this drive and formed a new organization with the purpose of bringing music and musicians into social activism. In late 1945, Pete Seeger and Lee Hays convened several of their musical and political associates in Seeger's apartment. The point of the meeting was to pick up where the

Almanacs had left off: to generate music to support labor, civil rights, and peace movements, as well as the general drive for social and economic justice. Forming People's Songs, the organizers planned to establish a newsletter and expand from their New York City center to the rest of the country; eventually, branches emerged in Los Angeles, Chicago, Detroit, and on various college campuses.[25]

Mario "Boots" Cassetta, a member of the West Coast branch of the organization, described how the members combined a love of folk music with a zeal for activism: "It wasn't a political organization in that sense of the word. . . . We were there because each of us somehow were freaks about folk music and its application to whatever a struggle we might think was worthwhile struggling against or for."[26] Cassetta's view that People's Songs was not a political organization in a narrow sense was correct. The members were united by a shared interpretation of American democracy as a means toward social justice, and they used folk music in efforts to secure that justice—whether it was economic justice for working-class Americans or political justice for marginalized and disfranchised citizens. While this interpretation of democracy served as a guiding principle for the group, People's Songs members did not have a common political platform: some were communists while others were progressive-liberal holdovers from the New Deal era. Their political affiliations may have differed, but they had the same goals for domestic reform. Some commentators lauded People's Songs for bringing folk music back into political activism. In the winter of 1946, Mike Gold declared in the communist newspaper *Daily Worker* that the new organization was bringing "songs of, by and for the people" back into people's struggles, an effort indicating the "spirit had not died—it has only been unemployed."[27] Although Gold made this statement shortly after People's Songs formed, his assessment proved correct; the organization soon became a primary outlet for left-wing revivalists, and other political activists, who still believed in the democratic ideals that were embodied in Popular Front Americanism.

In assessing the place of People's Songs in both the narrative of the folk music revival and the larger history of the American left in the twentieth century, two concepts in the sociology of social movements help to contextualize the group and its significance: Aldon Morris's theory of movement "halfway houses" and Thomas Rochon's theory of movement "critical communities." Morris explains that a halfway house within a social movement "is an established group or organization that is only partially integrated into larger society because its participants are actively involved in efforts to bring about a desired change in society." Because of such a group's emphasis on altering the status quo, it is often isolated from dominant culture and society and does not generate a "mass base." It therefore is unable to produce widespread political or social change because it does not generate a large audience through which it can disseminate the group's views. However, the importance of the halfway house is that, through its members' efforts to generate change, it amasses "a battery of social change resources" that become significant tools in the larger movement.[28]

In the case of People's Songs, its significance lay in the songs its members found, altered, or wrote to use on picket lines, in rallies, and to inform a wider public of contemporary political struggles.

By carrying the spirit of New Deal/Popular Front era Americanism into the postwar era, People's Songs also became a "critical community" for the left side of the revival during the mid-1940s. According to Rochon, movements turn the critical community's ideas into action and work to diffuse their values throughout larger society. The left-wing revivalists who formed People's Songs included the folklorists Charles Seeger, Alan Lomax, and Benjamin Botkin; the musicians Woody Guthrie, Betty Sanders, Tom Glazer, and Agnes Cunningham; and the lyricists and writers Gordon Friesen, Waldemar Hille, and Irwin Silber. Rochon explains that once a critical community becomes established, it begins to generate its own means of communication.[29] These methods of communication serve to reaffirm the ideological convictions of the group, connect members of the movement, and keep the activists informed on developments within the movement. The key form of communication for People's Songs, as the critical community for left-wing revivalists, was the *People's Songs* bulletin, a magazine through which the group promoted its vision of Americanism and informed readers about new songs. The group's Americanism had what Michael Denning calls a "radical edge," illustrated by its celebration of traditional icons such as Abraham Lincoln and more radical, but nonetheless American, figures such as John Brown.[30] By adopting these articulations of Americanism, the revivalists of People's Songs ensured that the nationalism they promoted was rooted in both an American and a *radical* context.

Although the members of People's Songs were interested in folk music, they did not focus exclusively on traditional white and black music from the rural South or ethnic enclaves in urban centers. Instead, they continued to expand the definitional boundaries that the Almanacs had begun to stretch during the early years of the decade. In the first edition of *People's Songs,* they explained their approach to music by describing the organization's goals:

> The people are on the march and must have songs to sing. Now, in 1946, the truth must reassert itself in many singing voices. There are thousands of unions, people's organizations, singers, and choruses who would gladly use more songs. There are many songwriters, amateur and professional, who are writing these songs [and] it is clear that there must be an organization to make and send songs of labor and the American people through the land. To do this job, we have formed PEOPLE'S SONGS, INC. We invite you to join.[31]

Many of the questions regarding People's Songs' understanding of folk music were answered through the group's name. The organizers encouraged members to write topical songs and parodies of popular songs and to change the words of old folk songs and use traditional songs in new ways to support political activism. In so doing, People's Songs followed the course that labor radicals like the Wobblies charted during the early years of the century and that the left continued to follow during the 1930s. However, it also broadened the communist definition of "the people" from that of the working class and its supporters to include almost anyone—even the bourgeoisie—because the group believed that "the people" meant anyone whom its members could reach with their political message.[32]

The members of People's Songs devoted much of their efforts to writing topical songs, which they spread to other musical social activists through the bulletin. According to the editors of the inaugural issue in February 1946, People's Songs published the bulletin "to create, promote and distribute songs of labor and the American people." The editors encouraged readers to submit any song that would "suit America's varied traditions": traditional songs, new songs with a steady beat, and cantatas were all considered relevant.[33] Despite this open call for any kind of music, folk music enthusiasts and folk singers formed the core of People's Songs. Throughout the first several issues of the bulletin, People's Songs grappled with its musical identity, trying to figure out what music best suited its programs. By the fifth issue, the editors found common ground: "People's Songs is interested in folk songs, work songs, and the best in the song traditions. But not to the exclusion of new songs. It works not as a folk-lore society, but as an organization serving the cultural needs of the people—in songs."[34]

Distinguishing themselves from a folklore society did not mean that the members of People's Songs rejected older traditions. Rather, they maintained that folk songs, the music of the people, were part of a vibrant, living tradition. In their view, even traditional songs had a political dimension in 1940s America. Benjamin Botkin explained that People's Songs was steeped in "the rich and democratic traditions of American folk music" and that the members believed "that the whole American Folk tradition is a progressive people's tradition. For that reason our comments, our new songs, our activities are, in great measure, rooted in the fertile soil of American folk music."[35] The organization clearly helped to keep the political spirit of progressive political reform alive during the 1940s, a spirit that the editors of the bulletin reaffirmed every month.

In each issue, the bulletin requested that readers subscribe to the magazine and join local People's Songs branches. People's Songs described itself as designed "to spread these songs around, to bring to as many people of this country as possible, the true, democratic message that comes with the music—to make these songs which the people created, go to work for the people at last."[36] People's Songsters spread these messages by singing for political causes and by printing songs of and for the people in the bulletin. The editors particularly encouraged readers to submit parodies of traditional songs because, as they explained, "By taking a familiar folk song and writing new 'socially significant' words for it . . . you can create a potent weapon."[37] People's Songsters hoped to use these musical weapons in reform movements that would secure political and economic rights for all Americans. The editors pushed this message by printing songs that emphasized American democratic values, such as "The House I Live In" (1943), by Abel Meeropol (writing under the pen name Lewis Allen), which depicts an America that adheres to civic ideals. In his lyrics, Meeropol describes his ideal America as a nation that practices "the same for black and white" and provides "a home where all are equal."[38] Although the song mainly reflects the celebration of cultural pluralism that characterized pro-American propaganda campaigns from the war, Meeropol reveals his political views by identifying racial equality as a characteristic of his idealized America, which was omitted when the song was turned into a short film in 1945 starring Frank Sinatra.[39]

The writers even couched their political views in well-known patriotic songs. In the foreword to *A People's Songs Workbook,* an edited compilation of songs printed in the bulletin, Pete Seeger, Waldemar Hille, and Earl Robinson describe the collection as a representative body of American music: "There are old American ballads here, songs of the Negro people, songs that helped build America, international songs (such as those of the Spanish Loyalists), union songs and more recent topical-political songs. They tell your American history." The *Workbook* commences with "The Star Spangled Banner," whose tune, they explain, came from an English drinking song, which "merely goes to prove that it came from the people and shall forever belong, flag and song both, to the people." Continuing in that vein, they include the song "Jefferson and Liberty" to illustrate how music "helped to spread the promise of a new democracy during Thomas Jefferson's campaign."[40] Politically inclusive democracy was one ideal for which the members of People's Songs strove, and they presented ways to bring marginalized Americans into the political process through specific reform efforts.

The movements the *People's Songs* bulletin supported reflected the ideals of the American left during the immediate postwar era. Silber explained that at the beginning, People's Songs had a very close relationship with the CIO, when the CIO unions were still on friendly terms with the left. Members of People's Songs often sang at labor rallies and strikes; the left-wing National Maritime Union was especially fond of bringing People's Songsters onto their picket lines.[41] Indeed, the organization's emphasis on labor is evident in the very first issue of the bulletin, which opens with the Wobbly anthem "Solidarity Forever." In their call for song submissions in the following issue, the editors provide a list of topics for which songs were "IMMEDIATELY NEEDED," including such issues as "the high cost of living, picket lines, [and] labor unity." Lest readers think that this was all they needed, the editors add, "Not to be neglected are [songs about] the people's concern about atomic power, about labor's role in peace, and our concern for suffering minority peoples everywhere."[42] In addition to songs, the bulletin included pro-labor square dance calls for anyone who wanted to hold a socially conscious dance. In the piece "Union Square Dance," calls such as "Break the ring and add two more / Six in the union is better than four" and the concluding call, "That's all, but before you're through / All make sure to pay your dues," clearly indicated People's Songsters' desire to generate an audience that was sympathetic to the American labor movement.[43]

People's Songs may have been primarily interested in aiding the labor movement, but that was far from the group's only concern. In calling for songs that reflected the needs of "minority peoples" and printing songs and square dances that encouraged racial egalitarianism, the leaders of People's Songs used the bulletin to push for an end to racial and ethnic discrimination. Silber, who succeeded Pete Seeger as the executive director in 1947, commented that in addition to white, rural folk music, the members of People's Songs were particularly interested in blues and jazz, something that he attributed to both musical appreciation and the organization's support for the growing Civil Rights Movement. Celebrating jazz and blues enabled People's Songs to demonstrate "an expression of concern for [the] black democratic struggle; an association of the movement with the culture of black people." Among the members whom Silber cited as civil rights advocates, Alan Lomax ranked the highest.[44]

From the New Deal era through People's Songs, liberal and left-wing revivalists supported civil rights, and they disseminated this message among a public audience through various media outlets. The Almanacs provided an example of how musicians could use their trade to raise awareness of the fight against discrimination, a precedent that People's Songs closely followed. The Almanacs wrote antidiscrimination songs such as "Jim Crow" (1941). Set to the tune of the traditional song "Groundhog," "Jim Crow" explained, "This is a Land of Democracy / Why isn't everybody free? / Jim Crow!" Furthermore, notable black and politically left-leaning musicians, including Josh White, Sonny Terry, and Brownie McGhee, lent their musical talents to the group. These musicians, and other black folk singers, including Lead Belly, wrote several songs that decried American racism, and they accompanied the other Almanacs into People's Songs after the war.

In the mid-1940s, Woody Guthrie encouraged Moses Asch, a record producer and affiliate of People's Songs, to release an album of songs that Guthrie wrote about contemporary circumstances through his company, Disc. Guthrie hoped that songs about recent incidents of violence against black veterans, such as "Blinding of Isaac Woodward" and "Killing of the Ferguson Brothers," would call attention to the "lynchings, hangings, tarrings, featherings, and blindings" that blacks suffered throughout the country. Furthermore, Guthrie informed Asch that by showing what "is happening right and left all up and down the country . . . Disc could win the friendship of not only 13 million Negroes, but with many other Nationalities and colors."[45] Others, while sharing Guthrie's sentiment, were not as militant and couched their views in more measured language. In 1947, Botkin explained that "Negro songs of protest" fit in the long heritage of American freedom songs that spoke to "liberating or being liberated from bondage and oppression." He wrote, "The final lesson of the freedom songs of the Negro is the lesson of all freedom songs in America. . . . [O]ur songs of freedom from the American Revolution on down, are a part of our folk bill of

Rights, hymning eternal and basic concepts of social justice."[46] If there was an American political ideology, in Botkin's estimation, it was rooted in the dual concepts of freedom and social justice for all citizens.

Sometimes the songs that musicians wrote after becoming involved in left-wing circles became controversial. The affiliations rural musicians had with urban leftists provided them with new rhetoric that they incorporated into their songs, rhetoric that included a vocabulary that was a far cry from their backgrounds. One of the most infamous cases of this is Lead Belly's song "Bourgeois Blues," which he wrote after encountering racial discrimination in Washington, D.C. Some scholars of the revival interpret this song as a case of the left co-opting a rural southerner and forcing its ideas and vocabulary on him; Lead Belly had experienced far worse treatment in the Deep South, which makes his outrage at segregation in Washington and his repeated refrain that the racist policies rendered the city a "bourgeois town" rather suspect. However, this interpretation not only patronizes the performer but also implies an inability on his part to adopt new political positions. It discounts the fact that, perhaps through their encounters with northern leftists, southern musicians learned a new political vocabulary that encapsulated what they felt and experienced. As the folklorist John Greenway argued, incorporating political rhetoric into a folk song "does not lift the singer out of the folk" or negate the folk qualities of the song.[47] The important issue in this case is not whether Lead Belly was fully aware of the nuances of Marxist ideology or whether his song was musically "authentic." Rather, it provides an example of how left-wing revivalists encouraged folk singers to highlight American racism in their music and thus to bring folk music into efforts to eradicate racial discrimination.

The members of People's Songs also followed the Almanacs' precedent by composing new songs about racial injustice. Occasionally *People's Songs* featured songs that called for a universal brotherhood that denied racial distinction, as with the song "God Made Us All," by calypso singer Lord Invader, which calls for people to "unite" across national boundaries whether "you are a Jew or an Italian / A Negro or a subject of Great Britain."[48] Most of the songs, however, dealt specifically with the American racial situation. Norma and Paul Preston contributed "Mister KKK," which includes the lyrics "You can preach about white supremacy / But it's got no place in a democracy." In the same issue of the bulletin that featured "Mister KKK," the editors printed "Hallelujah, I'm A-Travelin'," a song composed by a southern black farmer (whose name was omitted for security) commending the Supreme Court's ruling in *Morgan v. Virginia*, which desegregated interstate buses.[49]

Many People's Songsters contributed songs that specifically attacked racist political figures. The leading members Lee Hays and Bob and Adrienne Claiborne protested the notoriously racist and anti-Semitic Senator Theodore Bilbo and the racist Congressman John Rankin, both from Mississippi. The Claibornes' "Listen Mr. Bilbo" provides a history lesson on the important roles that members of ethnic and racial groups played in national development and refers to Bilbo's own immigrant ancestors. The song directly addresses the senator, and the authors note how Bilbo disdains "Negroes," "Jews," "Poles, Italians, Catholics, too," which they follow with "Is it any wonder, Bilbo / That we don't like you?"[50] Other readers submitted songs that called attention to specific racial incidents. Harold Preece and Celia Kraft contributed "Columbia Town," about the lynching of black war veterans. In the introduction, they explained that they decided to write the song "because they [were] angry, as good southerners, about the way Negro citizens are treated in the enlightened democracy of the South."[51]

In addition to featuring songs that protested racial discrimination, the bulletin kept the People's Songs community apprised of other efforts—both internal and external to the organization—to fight American racism. In the September 1946 issue, the bulletin informed readers about a concert that People's Songs had arranged at the Town Hall theater in New York City called "Sing to Kill Jim Crow," the proceeds of which would be donated to the Civil Rights Congress. The following June, the magazine featured an article, "Singing Uncommercials," that praised a new ad campaign on the New York City radio station WNEW. According to the writer, "Instead of plugging soap and mouthwash, they are plugging brotherhood—between all mankind. Yes, no matter what the color of your skin or what church you go to." The station aired a series of four one-minute songs that Hy Zaret and Lou Singer composed as public service messages. The December 1947 issue posted one of these pieces, "Brown Skinned Cow," which addresses racial prejudice through the lines "You can get good milk from a brown-skinned cow / The color of the skin doesn't matter no how."[52] Even though Zaret and Singer were Tin Pan Alley songwriters—the scourge of American music, many revivalists believed—their songs became acceptable when they supported the same causes that the left-wing revivalists advocated.

The bulletin soon became the primary means for spreading both topical and traditional songs of protest to members across the country. To help more specific, or local, causes, the editors of the bulletin published smaller pamphlets based on the material featured in the magazine. The topics of these pamphlets varied from explaining how to establish a regional People's Songs branch and how to stage a hootenanny to how to secure the printing of a publicity release. Some of these pamphlets addressed regional projects, as in the case of "Housing Action Songbook: On to Sacramento" that the California branch of People's Songs issued during its participation in the campaign for better housing conditions. Included in that publication are several songs that also appeared in the bulletin, such as the Almanac Singers' "Jim Crow," which, the editors explain, would help in the effort to "sing out against restrictive covenants," and "On to Sacramento," which a songwriter composed specifically for the event.[53] The author of another pamphlet, "Organize a People's Songs Branch," describes the organization's general aims and beliefs this way: "We believe that the songs of any people most truly express their life, their struggles, and highest aspirations. . . . [W]e extend a welcoming hand to anyone, no matter what religion or creed, or race, or nation, who believes with us that songs can bring about a stronger unity between all people, and that songs can thus fight for peace, for a better life for all, and for the brotherhood of man."[54] Indeed, this was a message that the editors of the bulletin reinforced through every song they printed. Supporting people's struggles was the driving purpose behind People's Songs, and through the bulletin, the leaders spread this message to a listening, singing, and reading audience.

In 1947, the members of People's Songs entered the national political arena: Henry Wallace announced his candidacy for the presidency, and People's Songs threw almost everything they had into his campaign. Wallace had served as the secretary of agriculture and then as vice-president under Roosevelt. As an advocate for peace, for a more conciliatory relationship with the Soviet Union, and for extending civil rights to African Americans, Wallace was certainly an unusual national political figure. In a move that only added to his unconventionality, Wallace selected Glen Taylor, a senator from Idaho who was also a cowboy musician, as his running mate on the Progressive Party ticket. Shortly after Wallace announced his candidacy, several People's Songsters, including Paul Robeson, Bernie Asbell, and Pete Seeger, began traveling on his campaign tour. Alan Lomax signed up as the musical director for the campaign, and various members composed campaign songs that People's Songs sold individually and in bound collections such as *Songs for Wallace*.

The primary vehicles for spreading these songs were the "Wallace Caravans," groups of actors and musicians that performed in traveling musical and theater troupes. Working with sympathetic unions and other progressive organizations, the caravans crisscrossed the country, traveling by car to perform shows modeled after the agitprop productions of the 1930s. Through dances, skits, and songs, the Wallace Caravans illustrated specific issues of concern to the Progressive Party, which included "jobs and labor unity, racial equality, lower prices, decent housing, health care for all, and peace," according to the Caravan member Marianne "Jolly" Robinson. The Caravan leaders were headquartered in New York City, but they collaborated with unions, other labor organizations, and regional branches of the Progressive Party in many parts of the country. Among the labor groups with which they worked was the International Workers Order, a radical group primarily composed of recent immigrants.[55]

In addition to leading the Wallace Caravans, People's Songs ran the music at the party convention in Philadelphia and organized a mass rally at Yankee Stadium. When People's Songs began to suffer hard times after the passage of the Taft-Hartley Act in 1947 (which dealt a irreparable blow to both communists and organized labor) and in light of the growing anticommunist sentiment, which led to the ouster of communists and fellow travelers from the labor movement, the Wallace campaign gave them a shot of hope, according to Silber. "It was a very, very exciting kind of thing, and it had enormous significance," he said. "It was a people's movement."[56] Regardless of their entry into national politics, People's Songs remained a halfway house for the Popular Front holdouts and left-leaning former New Dealers because the Progressive Party remained far afield from mainstream political trends. In the end, Wallace failed miserably in the polls, coming in fourth behind the Dixiecrat Strom Thurmond. Despite the excitement that surrounded him, Wallace remained aloof and disconnected from even the largest group he courted: the labor movement. Stylistically, he painted himself more as an agrarian populist than an urban workingman. Wallace even followed Alan Lomax's suggestion that he travel around the South with Pete Seeger on the assumption that Seeger's banjo playing would endear him to rural southerners. However, no matter how much Seeger played, it would not have overshadowed the fact that Wallace ran an interracial campaign to white southerners who supported racial segregation. Ultimately, rising conservatism and anticommunism, the concessions Harry Truman made to win over voters who potentially would have sided with Wallace, and the fact that Wallace was a lousy politician all help to explain this crushing defeat.

Despite Wallace's personal failures as a presidential candidate, his campaign, at least initially, represented the fruition of the Popular Front dream. Even though the Communist Party had denounced Browder's Americanization efforts by the mid-1940s, it did not follow that all of those affiliated with the left renounced what those efforts stood for—especially for those involved with People's Songs. While it is true that Wallace, a political independent, had ties or at the very least sympathies with the Communist Party, it took more than this connection alone to excite his supporters to the extent that Silber described. Rather, by seeking to end segregation and other discriminatory practices based on race and by supporting the labor movement, Wallace stood for downtrodden Americans—the same citizens that leftists had supported since the 1930s. In Wallace, the members of People's Songs saw a politician who aimed to include all citizens, regardless of race or economic status, in the American body politic. By supporting a presidential candidate, People's Songs members did not seek to bring the revolution to America; nor did they think they were going to undermine the American system by placing a "communist stooge" in power (few believed that Wallace would win, anyway). Rather, they viewed Wallace as a national politician who shared their interests in radical social and economic reform; stumping with Wallace enabled them to spread this message across the country.

## A Time to Lose

The failure of the Progressive Party at the national level devastated People's Songs because the members had invested so much time, energy, and money in the campaign. Yet political failure was not the only source of their disillusionment. After the war, left-wing revivalists had experienced a surge of optimism, a wave that continued for the next few years. However, in the midst of what seemed to be the era of left-wing progressivism, conservative opposition steadily grew, erupting by the end of the decade. Now these political revivalists had to contend with another political shift, which jeopardized both their vision of Americanism and their musical careers.

As the nation took a decidedly conservative turn in 1947 and 1948, People's Songs' ties to the left ultimately led to the group's demise. During this period, the CIO began to expunge left-wing unions from its ranks. Singing for progressive labor unions had been a primary source of income for the organization, and after the labor movement adopted the politics of anticommunism, the number of gigs for People's Songs members declined significantly. The debts the organization accrued led it into worse financial straits and forced it to close its doors in 1949. The specter of anticommunism, however, was not new. People's Songs' political proclivities had riled conservative critics even before the Cold War began to heat up. Attacks from newspaper columnists associated with the far right came as early as 1946. These voices were in the minority at this point, but they would not be for long. In fact, this was only the beginning of the influential role that right-wing figures would play in American society and politics. The collaboration of Republicans and conservative southern Democrats rolled back New Deal programs and sentiments, with the Office of Price Administration and the federal government's open support of labor unions as the initial casualties. Meanwhile, the Federal Bureau of Investigation increased its surveillance of suspected subversives, and the House Un-American Activities Committee (HUAC) continued to investigate suspected communist conspirators. As a left-wing organization, People's Songs was a prime target for the antiradical crusaders.[57]

The actual relationship that People's Songsters had with the Communist Party, however, was laced with ambiguities. While People's Songs did have affiliations with the party, with members such as Silber acting as conduits between the two, the relationship was rather one-sided. The party often failed to recognize what People's Songs was doing, or could do, to help the communist cause in America. Despite his indefatigable efforts to bring the party and People's Songs closer, Silber remembered, "It was usually a constant struggle to get the Party to pay attention." Contrary to anticommunists' arguments that the party manipulated folk music to indoctrinate the minds of American youth, Silber explained, "All this nonsense about the Party pulling strings and creating folk music images and so forth, it's all bullshit. . . . If anyone did it, I did it, and I was not a master puppeteer."[58] On the whole, People's Songsters ignored the controversies that preoccupied party leaders and did not participate in wider debates regarding the role of culture in the party.[59] This situation, however, did not cause left-wing revivalists to discontinue working with the CPUSA in reform efforts such as labor activism, civil rights, and global peace. Although some sought affiliations with the Communist Party under Foster, the revivalists associated with People's Songs mainly took up Browder's emphasis on reforming America rather than initiating a worldwide communist revolution. According to other accounts, the relationship between People's Songs and the party was "symbiotic": the singers found employment by singing for radical organizations, and those organizations used the singers to publicize their causes.[60] In any event, the depth of the relationship that People's Songs had with the party became a moot issue as the American public began to turn against anything and anyone that had *any* relationship to the left.

By the end of the 1940s, pessimism had replaced the earlier optimism of the left. Rather than bemoan their failures, however, the left-wing folk revivalists called for a return to their first principles: reestablishing some understanding of what America stood for, what the national identity entailed, and how to resume the fight for an inclusive, democratic United States. For these progressive revivalists, the rhetoric of the Popular Front—democracy, unity, and equality—was all they had to go on, and they carried this message through their fights for peace, labor rights, and civil rights during the Cold War years.[61]

Most of the songs that members composed stressed the need to fix national problems rather than reflected the changing party line. Initially, they focused primarily on supporting the labor movement, but their interests expanded as the decade progressed. Pete Seeger explained the shift from exclusively fighting for labor to more generally reforming American society as a whole through music: "In 1946 if somebody asked me, 'what's your purpose Pete?' I said that I'd like to make a singing labor movement, like the Wobblies had. . . . But as the labor movement kicked out the radicals, I settled for 'let's get America singing.' Maybe the basic democratic philosophy in these songs will filter out subliminally to the American people."[62] Seeger sustained this view even after People's Songs ended. Although it may appear that he relinquished his radical beliefs by trying to spread a somewhat vague "democratic message" to a wider audience through his music, this effort was actually in keeping with the type of radicalism that brought revivalists like him to the left in the first place.

Despite its short duration, People's Songs did have a significant impact on the folk music revival. Within the three years that the group was active, People's Songs deepened the relationship between folk music and political and social activism. Whether People's Songsters sang for the labor movement, to end racial discrimination in America, or to warn about atomic weapons, they worked to change American life. In addition to jump-starting the careers of many people who would become active in the folk music world in the following decades, the organization introduced politically inclined people to the utility of folk music. Guy Carawan, a singer from California who became active in the Civil Rights Movement through the Highlander Folk School, credits the Almanacs and People's Songs for getting him excited about politically charged folk music. When he first developed an interest in folk music, Carawan had dismissed political songs as musically trite. In time, however, he realized that many good songs came out of politics, channeled through such outlets as the Almanacs and People's Songs. At the end of the 1950s, Carawan looked back to those groups as an inspiration and commended them for spreading "the idea that folk songs can and should express the present as well as the past."[63] By publishing songs that addressed different social and political problems in the bulletin, People's Songs used traditional songs, parodies of traditional songs, and topical pieces as aids for political and social protest. In so doing, the *People's Songs* bulletin helped to secure a place for protest songs in a popular conception of folk music, which set the stage for the close relationship that the folk music revival developed with a new generation of political activists in the 1960s.

For the first two decades of the movement, the founding folk music revival-ists had had a relatively easy time crafting and disseminating their version of Americanism because the national political, social, and cultural climates were receptive to both their music and their message. The rhetoric of democracy that permeated New Deal and Popular Front politics gave the revivalists political support, and the cultural pluralism of the Roosevelt administration and World War II propaganda created a receptive atmosphere. The new generation of re-vivalists who came of age during the late 1940s—the younger, left-wing mem-bers of People's Songs—did not have the same base. Domestic circumstances had changed to the extent that the channels that previously connected political revivalists to a public audience had largely closed. Even before the defeat of the Wallace campaign, organized labor's conservative turn severed the ties that left-wing folksingers had made with most unions; no longer could they perform at large-scale union rallies or rally striking workers on picket lines through song. The termination of these relationships signified the end of the revivalists' dream of a singing labor movement. The late 1940s thus signaled the beginning of a difficult era for left-wing revivalists. They continued to promote their cultur-ally and politically democratic version of Americanism, but in the new political climate, their message reached a much smaller audience.

As the 1940s drew to a close, the euphoria over the successful defeat of fas-cism faded as America prepared for a (renewed) fight against communism. Battling communism both at home and abroad was nothing new to the United States; the country had sent troops to overthrow the Bolsheviks in 1919 and had attempted to root out suspected communists (and other radical subver-sives) in the years following World War I. The establishment of the Truman Doctrine in 1947 again signified America's commitment to fighting the spread of communism on the global stage, a fight that turned into military action in 1950 when American troops returned to the battlefield in Korea. While foreign policy emphasized stemming the tide of communism abroad, American politi-cians sharply curtailed the rights of suspected communists on U.S. soil. The year 1947 also signified the passage of the antilabor Taft-Hartley Act, which forced union leaders to sign loyalty oaths and disavow association with the Communist Party. This fate also befell leftists working in the federal govern-ment with the passage of Executive Order 9835 that same year, which estab-lished the Federal Employee Loyalty Program. By the end of Truman's tenure in office, anticommunism had officially enveloped both the federal and state governments, as thirty-nine states had enacted loyalty programs and HUAC conducted hearings on suspected communism in the government and entertainment industry, while Pat McCarran led a similar effort in the Senate. The ideological war against communism abroad and communist influences at home made political, and even cultural, dissent dangerous endeavors—a situation that gave the Cold War era during the 1950s its appearance of political acquiescence and social conformity.

## Conclusion

The 1940s encompassed periods of extreme optimism and bitter disillusionment for the leftist revivalists. The lingering effects of the pro-democracy campaigns of wartime propaganda, combined with the spirit of radicalism that coursed through American society during the immediate postwar years, spurred the politically progressive revivalists to return to their prewar political and social activism and use folk music as an aid in programs that pushed political democracy, economic equality, and cultural pluralism. Yet the optimism that propelled these revivalists—and other like-minded citizens—did not even last to the end of the decade. The labor movement, along with the rest of American society, grew increasingly conservative as the postwar years turned into the Cold War era. The failure of the Wallace campaign to win a fraction of the number of votes that it had projected destroyed the left-wing revivalists' hope for national political reform. The rise of anticommunism and public support for the political oppression that it engendered during the early Cold War era defeated many of their efforts at social and economic reform, as well.

Yet rather than being a story of failure, the 1940s proved to be a defining phase of the revival. Despite the setbacks that Popular Front revivalists suffered by the end of the decade, the members of People's Songs secured a place for folk music within social and political activism. The connection between folk music and activism became one of the defining aspects of the revival, as folk music became a common feature in political activism up through the early 1960s and then again even after the end of the revival. Folk music therefore became an important cultural tool for political protest, a tool that the Almanacs and the People's Songs "halfway house" introduced to the revival and other social movements of the postwar generation. The connection between folk music and politics that drew activists to folk music, and many folk music fans to activism, also came with a price, shown by the political backlash that many revivalists of the Popular Front era suffered during the era of the second Red Scare.

While the early Cold War era is commonly regarded as a period of political consensus and sociocultural conformity, precisely because of this political backlash, this interpretation omits sectors of society that refused to submit to the status quo. This was particularly true for many people who participated in the folk music revival, especially the former members of People's Songs. Although these were difficult years for many leftist revivalists, the revival continued to move forward, operating sometimes above and sometimes below the national radar. These revivalists, like many progressive Americans, still believed in a politically democratic and culturally pluralist Americanism, and they continued their efforts to bring this view to a public audience. The Cold War political landscape did take a toll on the size of the audience, but it did not dampen many leftist revivalists' efforts. Through booking agencies, periodicals, and progressive schools, these revivalists continued to use folk music to illuminate American civic ideals and challenge policies they viewed as antidemocratic. Through records and performances, they rebelled against cultural conformity by showing that American culture and heritage was steeped in diversity. The musical programs in which the leftist revivalists participated provided outlets through which they voiced their cultural and political dissent, reaffirmed their faith in democracy, and fought to make civic ideals applicable to citizens who were still denied access to the political system. The period immediately following the end of People's Songs marked a time when revivalists—liberal and leftist—largely stepped off the national stage that they had enjoyed during the New Deal and World War II eras. They used this time to both regroup and reassess their motivations and tactics. Rather than kill the folk revival, the challenges of the early Cold War years enabled the revivalists, even those disconnected from the left, to refine their messages and their music, and paved the way for their reemergence on the cultural—and political—stage by the end of the 1950s.

# 4

## KEEPING THE TORCH LIT

The Cold War took a heavy toll on the revival programs that developed during the World War II years and their immediate aftermath, with several not surviving the political backlash. Much as they had in the past, the revivalists adapted to the new circumstances through experimentation and by diverging into different interest groups. In doing so, they managed to retain some control over the type of music that was brought to the public and the ways in which the music was disseminated to a listening audience. The sheer fact that they largely kept hold of the reins of the revival and that they managed to survive the era lent a positive quality to what was otherwise a socially difficult and politically dangerous time.

Shortly after the war, folk music began to enter the realm of popular, commercial culture. By the early 1950s, folk music appeared in popular literary anthologies, in school curricula, on college concert stages, and on the radio.[1] One group of revivalists used the growing commercial popularity of folk music to move into the musical mainstream. In the process, they stripped from their music and on-stage personalities any overt references to political platforms or ideologies. At the same time, a second group, now organized under the name People's Artists, remained unabashedly radical during a time in which even being a reformer meant political censure. In 1947, the same year that Congress passed the Taft-Hartley Act and President Harry Truman established the Federal Employee Loyalty Program, the U.S. Attorney-General compiled the official List of Subversive Organizations. The House Un-American Activities Committee (HUAC) had been investigating suspected communists since it formed under Martin Dies in 1938, and by 1950, the anticommunist crusaders in the House of Representatives were joined by their counterparts in the Senate with the establishment of the Senate Internal Security Subcommittee. The heightened vigilance, combined with Nikita Khrushchev's revelations about Stalin, caused the number of left-wing revivalists to dwindle significantly, as fellow travelers jumped ship, leaving behind only the committed core. This core, however, remained as politically active as it has been during the Popular Front and World War II eras, if not more so. This, of course, had its consequences, and these revivalists struggled to keep their programs and music afloat amid the weight of federal investigations and congressional hearings.

As the radicals continued to use folk music to express political dissent, a third group turned to folk music to voice their personal dissent from the cultural conformity of mainstream America. These cultural nonconformists—many of whom were college-age—grew interested in folk music because it was far removed from what they saw as the banality of 1950s popular culture. Forming their own subcommunity within the growing revival, these enthusiasts used particular types of folk music, especially old "hillbilly" and "race" recordings from the 1920s and 1930s, to develop their own cultural identity. By the end of the 1950s, this wing of the movement began attracting a segment of the baby boom generation, an audience that grew exponentially in the following decade.

The fourth element of the increasingly fragmented revival was represented by a company and an individual rather than a group. Moses Asch, the head of Disc Records and then Folkways Records, produced albums of traditional and contemporary folk music throughout the decade. As a record producer who specialized in folk music throughout the 1940s and 1950s, Asch connected many segments of the revival, ranging from the political activists to the college enthusiasts. Beyond merely supplying the market with folk music recordings, Asch brought folk music into junior high and high school civics and history classes. Through his educational albums, Asch continued to uphold a faith in political democracy, "popular internationalism," and American cultural pluralism and spread this view to a new generation of schoolchildren, echoing the radio work of Alan Lomax during the 1940s. However, unlike Lomax, Asch operated through his own business, which gave him greater leeway in projecting his political ideals. Although clearly sympathetic to the left, Asch somehow managed to escape anticommunist censure. Many of his cohort were not so fortunate.

While disparate, these groups were united through a shared commitment to use folk music to envision a different kind of America—whether through cultural, political, and educational reform or by empowering the members of a new generation to develop identities that reflected their place in American life. Furthermore, each group challenged some aspect of Cold War America, from presenting an internationalist Americanism that contrasted sharply from the insular nationalism of the cold warriors to challenging the political status quo by supporting the growing Civil Rights Movement or simply rejecting mainstream cultural norms. On the one hand, the fragmentation of the revival enabled several of these groups to fly under the censors' radar and thus keep the movement alive in a difficult social and political environment. On the other hand, the fragmentation of the 1950s caused the movement to lose the cohesiveness that it had maintained in the 1930s and 1940s. The revivalists of this era continued to share a belief in a pluralist and democratic America, but their means to achieve that end began to vary significantly.

## Negotiating the Cultural and Political Terrain

The cultural and political climate of the 1950s affected the revival in different ways. Some revivalists, such as Sarah Gertrude Knott, consistently maintained political neutrality during the heyday of the Popular Front.[2] The apolitical nature of the National Folk Festival (NFF) allowed her to escape the political scrutiny that People's Songs faced. While Knott managed to circumvent the political difficulties of the era, she was not so successful in navigating the cultural shifts. Throughout the decade, Knott continued to promote the festival as an important representation of the nation's cultural heritage. Furthermore, she still argued that the festival served a key role in promoting American cultural diversity and intercultural understanding, a message that she crafted during the World War II years and tried to adapt to the changing circumstances of the Cold War era. In 1953, Knott affirmed that if Americans could still gather "to present the folksongs and dances of their choice or inheritance, regardless of race, nationality, or creed, we can rest assured that cultural freedom, now denied many peoples of the world, is still our precious heritage."[3] Now was not the time for Americans to sit back and bask in their freedom; the world was still rife with ethnic, racial, and political tensions that could threaten national security at any moment. Knott explained this fear in the opening to the program book for the twenty-first festival in 1955, writing that the nation, and the world, faced "a highly uncertain future of a highly developed, scientific age," and the need for international peace was still strong. While looking to the military to keep the peace, Knott also argued that "cultural and spiritual activities must be given consideration, for they are forces that must eventually bind nations together in a universal community of peace." The way to achieve this peace was through mutual understanding, and folk music provided the means to attain this because "rich folk heritages from all parts of the world" had integrated into American culture, and these cultural heritages "furnish a golden key with which we may unlock the doors to mutual understanding of many peoples of the world."[4] The festival of that year illustrated this global emphasis by broadening its pluralism even further, now including Lithuanian, Indian, New Zealand, and Yugoslavian music and dance, along with a group from Jordan studying at Southern Illinois University who presented Middle Eastern songs.

Knott maintained political neutrality even as she highlighted ethnic traditions in her festival, which could have been interpreted as indicating an affiliation with the left. One of the effects of Cold War Americanism was a hyper-nationalism that eschewed any traces of globalism. For example, Mary

Tallmadge, wife of the governor of Georgia, had Frank Magruder's well-respected textbook *American Government* removed from classrooms on the grounds that it emphasized "internationalism" rather than "nationalism" in 1951.[5] Anticommunist activists often used one's advocacy of internationalism to determine whether citizens were sympathetic to communism—whether they supported world peace or simply enjoyed foreign films. This conclusion was not too far off the mark, because supporting internationalism was one way that left-wing Americans continued to uphold a faith in their Popular Front ideals. In fact, maintaining a cosmopolitan outlook became a defining feature of leftist revivalists throughout the early 1950s. Yet Knott continued to keep her distance from left-wing politics, even as her international festival challenged the cultural insularity that often characterized Cold War Americanism.

Despite Knott's efforts to reach a broad audience, the attendance estimates for the festival fell as the decade progressed, but this had more to do with the proliferation of new folk music venues than with declining interest in the genre.[6] New festivals, organized by younger revivalists, catered to the interests of a growing and increasingly diverse community of folk music fans. By the end of the decade, these types of programs had siphoned much of the new generation of revivalists from programs like the NFF, which largely resisted incorporating the types of music and musicians that were growing in popularity among young folk enthusiasts.

Increasingly, folk music moved in the realm of 1950s pop culture. Perhaps this popularity was a reaction to the rise of technology and urbanization, aspects of modernization that generated nostalgia for an "American heritage" located in local history and regional folk culture.[7] Or perhaps it resulted from the general vogue of do-it-yourself (DIY) activities during the postwar era, as Pete Seeger argued. Since amateur musicians could easily pick up a guitar or other "folk" instrument and learn the rudiments of many songs, folk music was well suited to the contemporary trend of leisure hobbies. Seeger even wrote and mimeographed his own guide to playing the banjo to encourage people to start singing and playing folk music for themselves. Although the exact cause is debatable, the effect was that folk music became a hot commodity, and many individual folk musicians, including Josh White and Burl Ives, became musical celebrities, as did folk groups such as the Weavers.

Consisting of the People's Songs veterans Pete Seeger, Lee Hays, Fred Hellerman, and Ronnie Gilbert, the Weavers formed in the late 1940s. As a more polished iteration of the Almanac Singers, the Weavers initially played for primarily left-wing audiences but broke into the musical mainstream in 1950 with their recordings "Tzena, Tzena," which peaked at number two on the pop charts, and "Goodnight, Irene," which reached number one, selling more than a half-million records. Despite their growing commercial success, the Weavers maintained connections to the left by performing at functions and fundraisers for left-wing causes and hiring Harold Leventhal, a musical and political kindred spirit, as their manager.

The ties between the Weavers and the left grew strained, however, as the Weavers gained popularity. Pete Kameron, the Weavers' second manager, spurred the group's turn away from the political by curtailing their political engagements and dropping overt political messages from their music. Kameron also solidified the Weavers' place in popular music by securing a record contract with Decca Records. This arrangement included the accompaniment of a professional orchestra—a situation that irked many Weavers fans, who favored a more traditional, stripped-down style.[8] The more hard-line political revivalists believed that by recording commercially popular albums, the Weavers had abandoned their musical and political integrity. They not only altered songs to appease a commercial audience—removing lyrics about the Dust Bowl from Woody Guthrie's "So Long, It's Been Good to Know You" and a reference to suicide by a morphine overdose from "Goodnight, Irene"—but also replaced the "folk" sound of fiddles and guitars with xylophones and professional string arrangements on their records. The Weavers themselves, however, liked their new sound. Ronnie Gilbert had always been a fan of pop music, and Lee Hays celebrated the fact that they had broken the popular barrier and gotten traditional folk songs on the Hit Parade.[9] By adapting to popular preferences, the Weavers had more success than any other folk music group in bringing traditional songs, as well as the music of traditional folk singers such as Lead Belly and Woody Guthrie, to mainstream audiences.

The Weavers, moreover, still hoped to bring the music and message that began with People's Songs to a wider audience. Often their songs had a political undercurrent, especially in the context of the Cold War. Pete Seeger recalled, "We wanted to see if we [could] get some healthy music out in this very decadent time, to counteract." Yet he acknowledged that the Weavers were also limited in how far they could go. For instance, they could not sing "The Hammer Song," a song that he and Lee Hays wrote, because "the words freedom and justice, only Commies talked about things like that. The word peace was also something only Commies talked about." However, they were able to insert a pro-peace message into a Christmas song, in which they sang, "Peace, frite, pace, pakoi, shalom / the words mean the same, whatever your home."[10] Furthermore, they revealed their political views by featuring international songs in their repertoire, which illustrated their hope for world peace and challenged the insularity of Cold War nationalism.[11]

Some political progressives recognized the underlying political message in the Weavers' music. Myles Horton, a co-founder of Highlander Folk School, praised the Weavers for making this message more mainstream, saying, "I remember very clearly the early days of the Weavers when the people [began] to use singing as a protest thing, politically. They were the first group to catch the imagination of their country."[12] Anticommunists also took note of the Weavers' political side. In 1950, the publication *Red Channels: The Report of Communist Influence in Radio and Television* listed Pete Seeger as a subversive. Soon the Weavers lost their sponsorship from Van Camp Beans and suffered a wave of cancellations for concerts and television appearances. As some revivalists renounced their political pasts to save their careers, the members of the Weavers did not and were blacklisted as a result.[13]

The repression that the political revivalists faced peaked in the mid-1950s. In 1955, HUAC subpoenaed Seeger to testify about his activities with the Communist Party; two years later, Hays, Hellerman, and Earl Robinson were also called to testify. When asked to name names, all refused to do so. Hays and Hellerman appealed to the Fifth Amendment to explain their refusals to answer questions; Seeger pled the First Amendment; and when asked why he refused to answer questions, Robinson cited "all the amendments, all the Constitution; every one."[14] Even as the political investigations of the McCarthy era took a toll on the number of political revivalists, it did not dampen these revivalists' efforts to make the nation live up to its democratic principles.

## Sharpening the Political Edge

Anticommunism and the accompanying blacklists did not stop the revivalists who sought to use folk music to bring economically and politically marginalized groups into the national fold. In *American Folksongs of Protest,* originally published in 1953, for example, the folklorist John Greenway compiled songs from tenant farmers and sharecroppers, striking textile workers, coal miners, populists, Wobblies, and southern African Americans and situated them in their historical contexts to illustrate an American radical heritage. Greenway was not the first to publish these songs, but his collection is noteworthy because it openly challenged the Cold War ethos of the early 1950s. Greenway stipulated that "folksongs are songs of the folk; [the songs'] qualifications should be seen as nothing more than tests to which full folk possession can be determined," meaning that folk songs come from a people's perspective.

Weighing in on the debates over the authenticity of folk songs, Greenway argued that they can have identifiable authors, but they have to represent themes, conditions, beliefs, or values with which the rest of a folk community can identify. The folk song composer's "function is not that of a consciously creative artist, but that of a spokesman for the community, an amanuensis for the illiterate, or, to put it more precisely, for the inarticulate."[15] Although Greenway maintained a broad definition of folk songs, he espoused a narrow understanding of who could be classified as a member of the "folk." Greenway cited the economically marginalized, such as the unskilled workers of the Congress of Industrial Organizations, as "the only folk we have," although miners, textile workers, and some agricultural workers could also bear the folk label. Furthermore, contemporary political songwriters such as Woody Guthrie and Aunt Molly Jackson were to be understood as folk singers because they spoke *for* different folk communities; if they were not recognized as such, according to Greenway, "then we have no folk, and we have no living folksong."[16] By using American folk songs to illustrate a heritage of dissent, Greenway carried forward the People's Songs tradition of using folk songs to challenge the political status quo.

Another group that followed this tradition was People's Artists, a booking agency for left-wing musicians, which began shortly after People's Songs folded. Former members Paul Robeson, Betty Sanders, Pete Seeger, Irwin Silber, and Bob Wolf figured prominently in the leadership of People's Artists. In 1950, the organization began publishing the magazine *Sing Out!* after a line from the Pete Seeger and Lee Hays song "If I Had a Hammer." According to Silber, "People's Artists and *Sing Out!* started with a more self-conscious theoretical perspective, more consciously left" than its parent organization, People's Songs. Their overt leftism limited their appeal, but they nevertheless did a great deal to keep folk and politically topical songs alive during a difficult time.[17]

*Sing Out!* went through several stages during its career. When the magazine began, its political/musical approach reflected the concerns of the left during the escalating Cold War: peace, civil rights, constitutional rights, and fending off anticommunist attacks. Silber, who edited the magazine for sixteen years, remembered the early years as difficult but exhilarating, as young leftists like himself believed that they were "keeping the torch lit," that through *Sing Out!* they protected and maintained a tradition that had begun with the International Workers of the World balladeers and had carried through the Almanacs and People's Songs. "We were continuing that tradition of trying to make music that would enhance people's self-empowerment and work on behalf of causes that were in the interests of working people," Silber explained in 1999.[18] Throughout the 1950s, the editorial staff of *Sing Out!* endeavored to use "the music of the people" to fight for the people—on domestic matters such as political and cultural inclusion for marginalized groups and economic rights for the working class, and on such international issues as world peace and an end to nuclear armaments.

From the outset of the Cold War, Communist Party (CPUSA) members and Popular Front holdovers opposed America's entry into a new war, fearing that the escalating tensions would lead to nuclear destruction. In his study of the American left, the historian Maurice Isserman challenges the historical interpretation that casts the 1950s as an apolitical decade ruled by consensus politics by arguing that activists of the decade served as a bridge between the Old Left and the New Left by becoming a source of inspiration for latter. One of the main ideological precursors to 1960s radicalism that Isserman cites was the type of pacifism that developed during the 1950s.[19] Indeed, pacifism was a strong current among the few remaining members of the Old Left during the 1950s, and the left-wing writers and contributors to *Sing Out!* often advocated for international peace during the escalation of the Cold War. Songs such as "Peace, It's Wonderful" and "Song for Peace," both featured in the first issue of the second volume, are indicative of the antiwar attitude that the leftists of *Sing Out!* espoused. The editors also printed songs criticizing nuclear weapons and policies, such as Lawrence Gellert's "Atom Bomb Blues," Vern Parlow's "Talking Atomic Blues," and Leo Cooper's "Alvin the Adamant Atom." Cooper's song depicts atoms as resisting being used as tools for nuclear destruction and ultimately deciding that only "when the people win their fight to let peace shed its light / When all nations unite, we'll divide."[20] Evidently, antiwar holdovers from the Popular Front had found a home in politically driven revival outlets such as *Sing Out!*

In the domestic realm, the contributors and writers of *Sing Out!* continued to advocate for political and social justice in prose and lyrics. In keeping with a tradition that began with the *People's Songs* bulletin, *Sing Out!* informed socially progressive folk enthusiasts about activities that combined music and activism. An article from the December 1951 issue, "The Unity Chorus—Democracy at Work," highlights a community chorus, consisting of workers, students, housewives, and other musical amateurs from New York City, that "in its form of organization, its selection of repertoire, and the relationship among its members is democratic to the core." The author further notes how the "accomplishments of the chorus have proven, once again, that a group democratically run with a sound approach to music for the people can make a lasting contribution to the people's struggles." Choruses like this were notable for using music to further progressive causes and to teach about the importance of social justice in song. For these reasons, the magazine hoped to continue to spotlight "people's choruses" in future issues.[21] By the mid-1950s, when several members of the folk revival community—and a few staff members of *Sing Out!*—faced subpoenas from HUAC, the call for local musical groups that sang about justice became especially urgent. The author of an article about the rise of folk singing in Canada emphasizes this point: "There is a need today, as there has never been before, for the basic sentiments of the American people for peace and in defense of our democratic heritage to be expressed. Singing groups of all kinds can be an extremely important outlet for that expression."[22]

In addition to noting musical activities that epitomized democracy in action, the magazine began running a section called "Heritage—U.S.A.," which taught readers about the American democratic heritage as found in folk song. Debuting in the third volume, each "Heritage—U.S.A" column featured "some song from our American musical tradition, which, in the opinion of our staff, helps us to understand the democratic history of our country." The staff writers designed the column to display the struggle for social justice as a key aspect of American democracy, as illustrated via two main themes: the first, under the heading "Who Built America," focusing on "the songs of the working people"; and the second, called "Hard-Hitting Songs," featuring "songs of struggle from the mighty democratic movements in our country's history." The second category included such causes as "the Abolitionist Movement, Populist and Socialist songs, union songs, and protest songs of the Negro people and other national minorities."[23] The series opened with "The Erie Canal," followed by Joe Hill's "The Tramp," Woody Guthrie's "The Great Dust Storm," "Just Take a Seat" (from the General Motors sit-down strike of 1936), and traditional African

American songs such as "Go Tell It on the Mountain" and "Wade in the Water." Songs from specific types of labor were also important in the grassroots development of the American democratic heritage. For instance, cowboy songs, according to the writers of "Heritage—U.S.A." column, "provide a most significant page in our democratic folk heritage" because workers composed them to address the unique conditions of labor that they endured. The writers used other historical topics, such as the Gold Rush, to illustrate the evolution of American political democracy. While the promise of gold lured poor Americans westward in the hopes of quick riches, the editors used the scenario as a teaching moment: "In this process of movement and dis-location, a new kind of democracy began to grow, a comradeship and kinship born of suffering and search."[24]

Although the contributors to *Sing Out!* were rather vague about how they defined "democracy," they clearly articulated what living in a democratic society entailed: political and economic justice for all citizens. *Sing Out!* amassed a collection of folk songs from readers' submissions and from the library of People's Songs, songs that were applicable "in the people's struggles of today for peace, for equal rights, for rent control—and an inspiration for new works of every kind."[25] Added to the roster of people's struggles that *Sing Out!* promoted through song was equal rights for women. One "Heritage—U.S.A." section that focused on the Lawrence Textile Strike of 1912, featured James Oppenheim's poem "Bread and Roses," in which he articulated the demands of the striking female workers. The poem and subsequent song focus primarily on labor problems, but *Sing Out!* emphasized the feminist perspective. According to the author of the column, "Bread and Roses" is still "a song for today, for the complete emancipation of women."[26]

Several issues later, Silber contributed an article examining the musical subjugation of women. In "Male Supremacy and Folk Song," Silber investigated how male supremacy—an ideology that he claimed had been used to divide workers, lower the standard of living, and "cripple all struggles for peace and for human rights"—had affected American music. Popular music from the 1950s would lead one to conclude that "women are only concerned with some esoteric romance—usually unfulfilled—and that life is one long series of sexual thrill, lonely heartbreak, infidelity, and eternal reminiscence." Silber did concede that male chauvinism appeared in some folk songs but emphasized that those songs "represent only a small portion of our country's folk heritage which is, by and large, a part of the democratic expression of our proud history of struggle for equal rights." But Silber did encourage folk singers to eliminate those rare examples of sexist folk songs from their repertoires, because anything that "undermine[s] the emerging role of women and leaders and participants in the battle for human rights and peace ha[s] no place today."[27] Years before the second wave of feminism, the *Sing Out!* community advocated for women's rights as a part of the overall struggle to generate an Americanism that respected the rights of all citizens, regardless of gender.

In a tradition that began in the *People's Songs* bulletin, *Sing Out!* also featured numerous songs and articles in support of the escalating Civil Rights Movement. Each year, the magazine celebrated Negro History Week because, as the editors explained in the third annual issue, "The annual celebration of Negro History Week has helped millions of Americans to know more about the democratic heritage of their country than almost any other commemoration. For a knowledge and understanding of Negro History unmistakeably [sic] shows the rich heritage of democratic struggle which belongs to our people today."[28] *Sing Out!* advocated civil rights activism by frequently including songs that decried Jim Crow practices. The magazine also kept readers informed about other activities (plays and concerts) that dramatized the struggle and commended musicians, especially African American performers, who worked to advance the cause. The second article on "people's choruses" that *Sing Out!* ran, for example, featured an interracial chorus from St. Louis. The article's author stipulates that a "prerequisite" for people's choruses should be to "reflect the inter-racial character of the people's movement for peace and civil rights," then provides a step-by-step guide for establishing an interracial chorus, emphasizing the importance of singing black and white songs, of having black singers take the lead not just in spirituals but also in white songs such as English ballads, of having blacks and whites serve in leadership roles, and of encouraging black and white singers to socialize outside the chorus.[29] The writers at *Sing Out!* often stressed that groups and demonstrations against racist practices had to be interracial. In an article that serves as a how-to guide for people campaigning for the Progressive Party in 1952, the staff at *Sing Out!* recommended forming interracial singing groups because they could "demonstrate physically this unity much more graphically than an all-white group singing songs to end Jim Crow."[30]

The songs and articles of the early issues of *Sing Out!* consistently decried American racism, particularly practices that excluded African Americans from participating in the dominant culture and society. In his article "Racism, Chauvinism, Keynote U.S. Music," Silber explained that racism was prevalent in American culture, especially in music, as shown by segregated audiences, discrimination against black musicians, and the general "debasement of Negro culture in the United States." He even attacked the Musicians' Union for tacitly encouraging this discrimination through its segregated unions, noting that the black unions were generally small and financially weak.

Throughout the article, Silber noted that these discriminatory practices not only affected the black community but also extended to ethnic minorities. "One of the greatest crimes of Jim Crow America in the cultural field has been the consistent debasement of the folk cultures of national minorities," he wrote. Negative stereotypes of "Jewish, Italian, Mexican, Irish, Slavic, Chinese, and German culture[s]" have been featured in "American 'popular' culture for decades."[31] The staff of *Sing Out!* sought to counteract this cultural discrimination by spreading folk songs that illustrated the ideals of political and cultural democracy: topical songs that championed rights for minority groups and ethnic folk songs that naturalized citizens brought into American culture. Several "Heritage—U.S.A." sections highlighted ethnic traditions. In the issue dated September 1952, the column focused on Jewish songs and the cultural contributions of Jewish immigrants and refugees, because "the heritage of the Jewish people is one of struggle for freedom. Their songs, many of which have appeared in *Sing Out!* . . . like the one presented here, are a vital part of our HERITAGE— U.S.A." Similarly, a few months later the column focused on Mexican American songs, which, according to the author, "are a much-neglected portion of the democratic cultural heritage of the United States."[32]

*Sing Out!* also printed topical songs that protested discriminatory practices against ethnic citizens. In the spring of 1957, the magazine debuted "The Ballad of Sherman Wu." Set to the tune of "The Streets of Laredo," the song dramatized an incident at Northwestern University in which a fraternity refused to allow a student to pledge because of his Chinese lineage. Yet rather than focus on songs that people composed *for* minority communities, *Sing Out!* also printed protest songs that were written within these communities. As Silber wrote in 1957, "Today's folksongs are being written by southern sharecroppers, both Negro and white; auto, garment and smelter worker; GIs in every branch of the armed forces; Mexican and Puerto Rican Americans; and many, many more kinds of people who feel the need for their own expression."[33] Indeed they were, and the staff at *Sing Out!* made a point to highlight these and the songs of a new generation of folk composers.

While the revivalists of People's Artists and *Sing Out!* continued to articulate a view of American identity that had been intrinsic to the revival since its inception, this group took a more militant stance in calling for the protection of ethnic and racial minorities' cultural rights and demanding political and economic rights for them, as well. For this reason, these revivalists supported programs of social activism, such as a new phase of the Civil Rights Movement—a cause that, by the early 1960s, had become central for many revivalists. These revivalists believed that if underrepresented groups achieved both cultural and political rights, they would be able to secure their inclusion in the American national community.

At the same time that the writers at *Sing Out!* were fighting for the rights of minority groups during the 1950s, they also had to fight for their own rights. *Sing Out!* recognized the anticommunist pressures in 1951 with an article on the trial of the communist leader Victor J. Jerome, who was "accused of plotting to overthrow the government of the United States by voicing his views on culture." This, the article's author wrote, "is only one step away from total censorship of all cultural expression."[34] Shortly thereafter, *Sing Out!* reported to its readers that its editors Irwin Silber and Betty Sanders had been called to testify before HUAC. Rather than bemoan their suffering, Silber and Sanders used this as a rallying cry, urging readers to "support the movements and organizations which are fighting for a free and decent America. Make these songs even more powerful weapons."[35]

As more members of the folk community were called to testify and forced to defend their political views, affiliations, and musical programs, the tone of *Sing Out!* became more urgent, attacking the hearings as violations of American civil liberties. The author of the appropriately titled article "The Time of the Lists" declared, "Many citizens and organizations concerned with preserving our democratic rights have dared to defy the McCarthy 'know-nothings' and have spoken against the arbitrary 'listing' process as being opposed to the principles inherent in our constitution and Bill of Rights."[36] As with all of the causes for which they fought, the writers and contributors at *Sing Out!* defended themselves from the witch hunts and blacklists by appealing to American democratic principles. The magazine showed readers that these principles not only were sanctified in the U.S. Constitution but also were an intrinsic aspect of the nation's cultural heritage—a position that they defended through songs, articles, and regular columns such as "Heritage—U.S.A." In the opening of the sixth anniversary issue, the editors reaffirmed this mission, stating, "If our songs and articles have helped the American people in any way in their search for peace, in their defense of our democratic liberties, in enriching their lives with the best of our American song tradition, then we think that we have served our country—and our people—well."[37] From the perspective of American history and cultural heritage that the writers of *Sing Out!* held, it was HUAC, the editors of *Counterattack,* and other anticommunist organizations that were being "un-American."

For much of the 1950s, *Sing Out!* circulated among a small core of left-wing revivalists. Because of its limited audience, the magazine was forced to miss some issues between the spring and fall of 1954, and at that point officially it turned from a monthly into a quarterly publication. In an editorial, Silber pointedly explained that the magazine reached "about 1,000 people every month—and according to the experts who are supposed to know about such things, that's not enough to warrant a monthly visit."[38] Although *Sing Out!* may not have been a commercial success, in many ways it was a cultural success for revivalists who remained committed to Popular Front Americanism. In this respect, it is similar to the Popular Front magazine *Friday,* which lasted from 1940 to 1941. Michael Denning explains that while *Friday* was a failure according to publishing standards, it was a cultural success because for a brief moment in time it spoke to and represented the young members of the Popular Front—it was a product of and for that community. This indeed was how *Sing Out!* operated: it was perhaps the only outlet for politically committed revivalists who remained true to the vision of the America that they hoped to generate during the heyday of People's Songs.

Another way to illustrate the magazine's larger political and cultural significance is through Verta Taylor's concept of social movement "abeyance mechanisms." Taylor explains that certain abeyance mechanisms that exist within social movements enable the movements to continue through politically hostile periods and therefore provide continuity between periods of heightened activism. When movements lose public support, thus entering a period of abeyance, the members who retain their commitment to the cause tend to become marginalized and are forced to carve their own space. While these groups may not have an impact on the sociopolitical conditions of their era, their significance lies in their ability to provide "a legitimating base to challenge the status quo" and, thus, become potent sources for protest.[39] *Sing Out!* became an abeyance mechanism for the left side of the revival, championing the ideas of peace, democracy, and social justice that had been at the center of the Popular Front and ideas that would become the ideological crux of the New Left that emerged in the following decade.

The work of the politically radical folk revivalists of the 1950s challenges the view that a veil of political consensus completely enveloped the nation during the era of blacklists and anticommunist witch hunts. Although the domestic situation, along with Khrushchev's revelations about Stalin and the Soviets' brutal suppression of the Hungarian uprising, decimated the ranks of the CPUSA, it did not crush all political activity on the left. The revivalists at *Sing Out!* sustained the left side of the revival, and they undertook their efforts in public. As several communist leaders went underground, the political revivalists continued to publish their views for anyone who was willing to listen or read. These efforts had consequences: they could destroy careers, lead to imprisonment, or even become physically dangerous.[40]

A key revivalist who risked all of these consequences and yet continued to use folk music to enhance political reform and a culturally pluralist and politically democratic Americanism was Pete Seeger. Harold Leventhal recognized that Seeger became a "spokesman" during this era for people who still believed in progressive reform; the folklorist Roger Abrahams credits Seeger with sending college folk music fans down a progressive path. Even when Seeger could not find much commercial work because of the blacklist, he was well received on college campuses and launched his first tour at Oberlin College in 1954. While he may have tamed his overtly political language, Seeger never hid his political and social views. Seeger became the "Pied Piper" for young fans of folk music and progressive politics in the 1950s. They viewed him, according to Abrahams, as a "very clear-headed individual who represented exactly what we felt, politically and spiritually." Through his activism for peace, labor unions, and civil rights, he showed them "how music could fit into such a life agenda."[41] Silber described Seeger during the 1950s almost as an icon of the revival, staying that he "came to realize that he stood for something, that he represented something [and] that he was helping to keep a movement and a spirit alive. [T]he 1950s . . . was probably his greatest period, because he did what nobody else was able to do. I think plenty of other people did what Pete was doing in the 1960s. . . . But, that decade, he bridged the gap in many ways."[42] Seeger was especially effective at reaching children at summer camps. Left-wing camps such as Camp Kinderland, Unity, Woodland, and Wo-Chi-Ca played a significant role in introducing children to progressive politics and social views, as well as to folk music; the revivalist Irwin Silber and the musician John Cohen served as counselors in the 1940s into the 1950s.

During the 1950s, these camps became one of the last remaining sources of employment for blacklisted folk musicians. Seeger was often a guest at these camps, particularly at Norman Studer's interracial Woodland.[43] Seeger himself noted that he helped keep the progressive side of folk music alive during the escalation of the Cold War. He believed then, and in retrospect, that the 1950s was a politically frightening time and that fascism was alive in America under the guise of McCarthyism. Echoing Silber's assessment, Seeger likened his role during this era to that of a link in a chain of political activism. "I am very fortunate to have been able to be [a link] between people like Woody [Guthrie] and Lead Belly, as well as what I learned from Alan Lomax and my parent [Charles Seeger] and [a lot] of others," he said. "In the 1950s and the 1960s, when Lead Belly and Woody weren't around, I really felt that I wanted people to learn the lessons they had taught me."[44] Seeger continued to play this role even after the demand for social justice reentered political discourse in the following decade.

Seeger and the staff at *Sing Out!* did keep the political "torch lit" during the dark days of the second Red Scare. Those who remained true to the democratic vision embedded in Popular Front Americanism took pride in their sustained efforts to use folk music to bring about political reform. In interviews conducted over the course of the 1970s, Silber sounded a self-congratulatory note on his, and others', ability to remain politically committed in the face of extreme adversity.[45] It is probable, however, that during the 1970s political revivalists like Silber looked back on the 1950s with nostalgia. In 1957, he viewed his actions during the early years of the decade in a much different light, admitting to the folklorist Archie Green that his staunch leftism caused errors in judgment regarding international communism. Silber noted that the "one-sided" and "sectarian" views he developed had blocked his ability to critically evaluate communist positions and policies. At the same time, however, he wrote that even as he regretted the "left-wing dogma" that the staff expressed in the editorial page of *Sing Out!* during the early 1950s, "a lot of good work was accomplished, and there is much to be proud of in those early pages."[46] Despite the soul-searching that left-wing revivalists such as Silber had to do by the end of the decade regarding their views on party politics at home and abroad, they did not question the *domestic* political reforms for which they fought. Throughout the 1950s, they remained committed to their key causes: civil rights, racial and gender equality, and an end to nuclear weapons.

## The Cultural Rebellion

Despite the outward appearance of conformity in 1950s America, rebellion against the sociocultural status quo was gathering strength in pockets around the country. The Beats of the early 1950s formed one of the original and, eventually, most famous counterculture movements of the era. Rejecting middle-class

American values, the Beats scorned affluence and consumerism in favor of "voluntary poverty," avant-garde expressionist art, sexual liberation, drugs, and jazz.[47] Shortly after the Beats emerged in the New York City neighborhoods of Morningside Heights and Greenwich Village, the counterculture revivalists began to form communities that shared many of the Beats' cultural and physical spaces. These folk enthusiasts did not look to folk music as a political tool or as a way to define the nation; rather, they used it to define themselves. They rejected the popular folk music the Weavers and Burl Ives sang on the radio and eschewed the political language and activism of the People's Artists cohort. With them, the personal became political. Listening to folk music became a way to rebel against packaged popular culture that dominated the suburban communities from which many of them came. As with the "beatnik" counterculturalists, the young "folkniks" emerged from urban and suburban areas; congregated in bohemian enclaves; and adopted mannerisms, dress, and lifestyles that challenged dominant culture. They also frequented the same music clubs, bought records from the same record companies (companies that produced both jazz and folk music), and are often mentioned side by side with the Beats in memoirs and novels about the counterculture of the 1950s.[48]

One strong connection between the two groups was a mutual interest in African American music. The types of music these groups favored, however, differed widely. The Beats generally enjoyed the more free-form, fast-paced sounds of contemporary bebop, whereas the folk music fans turned to blues and the early commercial "race" records of the 1920s and 1930s and hunted for recordings from that era. Eventually, they began to seek out the musicians, many of whom were still living, including Son House, Skip James, Sleepy John Estes, and Mississippi John Hurt, who would play a major role in the blues revival of the 1960s. Some scholars have argued that the Beats' interest in African American music stemmed from their "romantic primitivism," meaning that they idolized black artists for allegedly embodying traits that were absent in white culture, such as earthiness, "wisdom," and "nobility," that resulted from their history of oppression and marginalization. To the Beats, African Americans' outsider status is exactly what made black culture interesting and imbued it with an air of authenticity—a view with remarkable parallels to John Lomax and other early folk song collectors. It would be difficult to attribute this same attitude to the revivalists, however, because their interest in rural music did not focus exclusively on black traditions. In fact, the young revivalists often prized recordings of rural white music—Anglo-Saxon ballads and "hillbilly" songs—just as much as their "race" counterparts. Rural folk music therefore provided the same type of respite from mainstream music and mainstream society that urban jazz did.[49]

Common interests led some outside observers to lump the Beats and the folk fans into one counterculture. Yet as Abrahams has observed, the relationship between them was a "friendly unfriendliness." While they often frequented the same parties and functions, they showed visible differences and even tensions. For instance, the folk enthusiasts tended to be more politically aware than the

Beats. Abrahams also notes that Beats tended to be more interested in narcotics and other controlled substances than the folk fans.[50] One figure who managed to bridge the gap between these groups was Harry Smith, who organized the *Anthology of American Folk Music* in 1952. Issued on Folkways Records, the *Anthology* consisted of six albums of commercially recorded folk music that Smith selected from his enormous personal collection of 78s. Grouping his songs into three vague categories—"Ballads," "Social Music," and "Songs"—Smith did not rely on a scholarly system to categorize the music; nor did he employ the traditional commercial method of labeling white country music "hillbilly" and black music "race." Rather, he deliberately broke from prior definitional categories by omitting any racial indications and following his own method of organization. Smith openly admitted that he selected the songs for the *Anthology* because they sounded odd or were interesting versions of significant traditional songs. In this way, Smith believed that the *Anthology* would appeal to "musicologists, or possibly [to] people who would want to sing them and maybe would improve the version."[51] Through his unique musical categorization, cryptic liner notes, and bohemian persona, Smith affixed an air of oddity to both himself and his music.

The *Anthology* had a profound effect on young revivalists in particular. The collection provided an alternative to the mainstream culture of the 1950s, and the new LP format made these recording accessible to a larger audience. While it was sometimes difficult to find in record stores, the *Anthology* became the communal "document" for a "generation of urban youth who began to seek their truer America in its vernacular musics," according to the music critic Jon Pankake. By featuring Delta blues, traditional Cajun music, mountain string-band music, Fa So La shape-note singing, spirituals, jug band songs, bad man ballads, and many more examples of early American music, the collection introduced listeners to music that sounded worlds away from their current surroundings.[52]

While attending Swarthmore College in the early 1950s, the folk revivalist Ralph Rinzler became one of the early fans of the *Anthology*. Although many of the recordings were only twenty years old at the time, to him they sounded "like something that had come out of another time and place entirely, from another world, they seemed so distant and miraculously exotic. . . . The whole thing was wondrous to me, it was thrilling." The *Anthology* made it possible for people to understand that there was "an enormous range of stuff" out there and that the task at hand entailed finding out exactly how wide that range was. Through the *Anthology,* Rinzler and other young enthusiasts learned that there was a whole other world of music that they never knew existed while growing up.[53]

Rinzler was part of the growing coterie of college students who became interested in folk music in the early 1950s. Located largely in progressive liberal arts schools such as Swarthmore, Bennington, and Oberlin, the young folk fans began forming a community based on a shared interest in folk music sung by traditional performers, most of whom came from the rural South. The *Anthol-*

*ogy,* and Folkways Records, became a de facto meeting ground for many of these students. For example, Stephen Lee Taller, a student from Oberlin, wrote to Moses Asch, the head of Folkways, in 1954 informing him that he had been hosting *Folk Song Festival,* a popular show on the college radio station for the previous two years, and that he mostly played songs from the *Anthology* and other Folkways records. At Oberlin, he wrote, many students were interested in folk music, and they particularly favored these more obscure recordings to the more popular, mainstream folk music.[54]

By developing an interest in folk music, the college revivalists followed the path of using music to craft an identity apart from the cultural mainstream. Like those of the early Beats and political revivalists, their community was small. Lawrence Block, a member of this cohort, explained, "The great majority of collegians were still gray-flannel members of the Silent Generation, ready to sign on for a corporate job with a good pension plan. Those of us who didn't fit that mold, those of us who'd always sort of figured there was something wrong with us, sat around the fountain in Washington Square singing 'Michael Row the Boat Ashore' and feeling very proud of ourselves for being there."[55] Yet at the same time that they stood apart from mainstream America, they also differed from the first generation of folk enthusiasts. They grew up in urban and suburban communities and mostly learned about this music from one another; many were introduced to traditional folk music via word of mouth, records produced by Folkways and other small labels, radio shows such as Oscar Brand's *Folk Song Festival* on WNYC, and campus folk song clubs. Another member of this cohort, the musician Dave Van Ronk, explained a generational difference emerged at this time wherein the young enthusiasts began to reject the music of their forebears and created their own musical niche within the movement.[56]

Roger Abrahams was a year ahead of Rinzler at Swarthmore and also very active in the campus folk music scene. Like Rinzler, Abrahams came from a Jewish family. His parents were German, and he grew up in a highly political household that was secular but culturally Jewish. This phenomenon of Jewish teenagers adopting a love of anachronistic, rural American folk music during the 1950s was not unusual. Ronald Cohen notes that many children of Jewish immigrants developed an interest in folk music and began playing traditional instruments such as banjos, fiddles and guitars because it "connected them to American history and culture, legitimizing their search for belonging, and at the same time serving as an outlet for their alienation from the political status quo."[57] Indeed, Abrahams echoes this sentiment, arguing that it was "central, absolutely central" that the music in which he and other college students were interested was inherently American. Interestingly, although the children of Jewish families saw old, rural folk music as a way to connect to America, it also disconnected them from their contemporary culture and society. The music from the *Anthology* and other recordings from the 1920s and 1930s was a far cry from the popular songs of the 1950s.

## The Personal, the Educational, and the Political

While Harry Smith is credited with compiling the *Anthology,* it is quite possible that he would never have completed the task—or have been able to release the collection—if Moses Asch had not been involved. Born into a literary Eastern European Jewish family, Asch was the son of Sholem Asch, one of the most famous Yiddish authors of the twentieth century. In 1914, Moses Asch came to the United States to escape war in Europe. He returned to Europe in 1923 to study electronics in Germany, and during that time he began to develop an interest in American folk music. Asch recalled being chided by his European friends that the United States had no folklore of its own and thus no national culture. However, while vacationing in Paris in 1923, he discovered the American folk tradition when he came across John Lomax's *Cowboy Songs.* According to Asch, the book "guided me through life because there he [Lomax] said that folklore and folk songs were the real expression of a people's culture." Furthermore, the collection showed that "there was a uniqueness in our [American] culture. It was not just a 'melting pot.' Lomax showed that there was folklore in America." Asch commended Lomax for loosening the scholarly grip on folk music and credited Smith with doing the same almost forty years later.[58]

Asch entered the recording industry in 1939 and through his company, Disc, released Jewish folk music, jazz, and educational material throughout the 1940s. After an ill-fated venture with a record of Christmas songs by Nat King Cole that missed the holiday season, Asch landed in dire financial straits and was forced to declare bankruptcy. However, with the help of his assistant, Marion Distler, he got back on his feet and formed Folkways Records in 1949. In many ways, Disc Records foreshadowed the musical eclecticism that came to characterize Folkways. From the Disc releases of Lead Belly's *Negro Folk Songs,* Frank Warner's *Hudson Valley Songs,* the Palestinian String Quartet's *Hebrew and Palestinian Folk Tunes,* and an album of calypso music by Lord Invader, Asch's concept of folk music was always inclusive, and he often balanced between liberal pluralism and left-wing internationalism. On the one hand, he adhered to the pluralists' assertion that American folk music included ethnic traditions, while on the other hand, he sustained the leftists' international emphasis through his extensive series of global folk music.[59]

The left-wing side of Asch's social and political views significantly influenced his work in the music industry. Despite his persistent claims that he was not a political activist, Asch came from a political family; one of his closet relatives was an aunt, Basha, who was a communist revolutionary and had served as an educational consultant under Lenin. Besides his lineage, Asch had several childhood experiences that permanently shaped his worldview. When Asch traveled to the United States to reunite with his parents during World War I, he crossed paths with injured soldiers returning from the front. As he told Tony Schwartz, seeing the mangled bodies was his "first experience of what man does to man," and it left a lasting impression. When he reached the United States,

Asch was forced to remain at Ellis Island for a week because his father had mis-spelled his name and stated his birthday incorrectly on official forms. Again, he recounted to Schwartz that this experience affected him deeply. "And so, the rest of my family went, [and] there I was a kid [alone]," he said. "I saw what was happening and I saw these immigrants like myself. They were shut off." In an-other interview, Asch stated that this experience made him recognize "the need of the people to express themselves some way against this injustice." As Asch recollected, both of these events forever shaped his commitment to helping those who were socially, economically, and politically dispossessed to speak out against their conditions.[60]

The Depression years also had a profound impact on Asch's social views, and he, like many leftist sympathizers, became acutely interested in the plight of the "common man." According to his son, Michael, Asch was a New Deal Democrat who was connected to a coterie of political progressives—a network of "democrats, socialists, communists, and anarchists" who believed that they must work to generate a society that would eliminate inequality. This was the ideology that lay behind the founding of Folkways Records: to fight against fas-cism, racism, and economic exploitation and create a world of "peace, brother-hood, and equality." Michael Asch maintains that Folkways was his father's (and Marion Distler's) response to the times; it was a place where social equality could thrive, "if not in real life, then at least, symbolically."[61] As with Alan Lomax, Asch's social views coincided with the ethos of the Popular Front dur-ing the late 1930s, and this outlook shaped much of his work in the recording industry.

Asch regarded Folkways not simply as a record company but as a medium for the higher mission of documenting critical aspects of the people's culture. This is what led him to enter the educational market during the Disc Records era. The mid-1940s marked the beginning of Asch's two most notable tenden-cies: recording socially progressive music and attempting to fill holes in the re-cording market. These two traits worked in tandem. Rather than simply producing music to fit different market niches, Asch consistently recorded music that he believed was culturally or politically significant and marketed it to specific groups. For example, Asch marketed his early Lead Belly records by distributing flyers for the recordings to black history teachers with the claim that "they are of undoubted educational, cultural, and entertainment value not only to the whole Negro race, but to every American as well."[62] Disc even had a Children's Department, with Beatrice Landeck, a music educator and freelance columnist for parenting magazines, serving as its "counselor."[63]

In 1949, Folkways released its first educational record, *Who Built America: American History through Its Folksongs*, performed by Bill Bonyun. Beatrice Landeck's liner notes describe the songs as "the spontaneous expression" of the early immigrants and pioneers "whose experiences are the substance of histo-ry." She explains that the album was particularly suitable for young children because "the simple words, without scholarly pretension and full of laughter, reveal the deeper meaning of history as no written record can possibly reveal it." "Green Mountain Boys," "Erie Canal," "Auction Block," "Jesse James," "Mi Chicara," "So Long, It's Been Good to Know You," and the Navajo song "Happiness" do indeed span American history and include both traditional and relatively contemporary folk songs. The album adheres to the concept of cultural democracy by including Hispanic, American Indian, and African American songs and grouping them together under the umbrella of American civic ideals. Landeck's liner notes summarized the album this way: "Here are the songs that define our democracy—all the nationalities, races and creeds living together in one peaceful community—striving for similar goals, maintaining through its law and common desires the kind of peace the world is longing for. These are the people who built America and are still building America—they are the bones of our democracy."[64] In one sweeping statement, Landeck thus set the stage for future albums that stressed political democracy, cultural diversity, and a people's perspective on historical events that Folkways Records sold to American schools.

During the mid-1950s, Folkways Records began issuing albums of songs dedicated to particular historical periods and events. In 1954, Asch and Distler released *Frontier Ballads* (featuring Pete Seeger) and *The War of 1812* (featuring Wallace House). Asch wrote the liner notes for both albums to provide a historical context for the songs—a historical view that contrasted from the dominant historical interpretations during the 1950s. Rather than emphasizing the unity of the American people, Asch's view of U.S. history focused on a native radical tradition, and he noted the nation's cultural diversity and the freedoms inherent—though not always practiced—in American democracy. Referring to the pioneers of the nineteenth century as "the freedom seekers, the adventurers, the non-conformists, [and] the naturalists," Asch describes their westward trek as a search for freedom in the "democratic" frontier. In Asch's view, the U.S. West was a bucolic escape for marginalized Americans, including persecuted Mormons, oppressed urban immigrants, and economically displaced tradesmen. However, he also depicts the injustices American Indians endured through forced removals and the "No Irish Need Apply" phenomenon as examples of the nation failing to practice its democratic proclamations.[65]

When Asch released *Frontier Ballads,* the United States was fully immersed in the Cold War, a war in which all citizens were expected to participate. While many factors have led historians to conclude that political consensus dominated American society, a key aspect of this assessment pertains to the forms that patriotic expression took during the decade. The praise that politicians and businessmen heaped on the modern corporation for heralding an era of consumption provided the final nail in the coffin of the producerist and antimonopolist nationalism that had characterized popular Americanism through the New Deal era. Now the qualities that constituted the American way turned from a broad populism and faith in "the people" to a faith in "free enterprise" and a focus on domesticity and middle-class affluence.[66] Textbooks reflected this shift in mainstream Americanism, as shown by a changing definition of democracy. The historian Stephen Whitfield explains that during the 1930s, democracy became a "call for social action"; in the 1950s, it stood for the "status quo" and something vaguely understood as the opposite of the equally ill-defined terms "fascism" and "communism." Furthermore, these textbooks presented American ideals synchronically rather than as evolving over time. Besides painting a static view of American identity, textbook authors paid scant attention to explaining the intricacies of the U.S. economic system; overlooked any economic, political, or racial discrimination and disparities; and focused almost exclusively on extolling the virtues of capitalism rather than emphasizing the political guarantees of the Bill of Rights.[67] Fear of political reprisal put teachers and administrators on the defensive, forcing them to excise any curricula and remain silent on any topic that could be deemed remotely controversial to protect their jobs and reputations. Yet it was precisely at this time that Asch began to market his own politically progressive version of U.S. history to schools and libraries. Although his first foray into this area was through musical records, by the end of the decade he had begun releasing albums of songs and historical texts, whose liner notes featured lesson plans for guided discussions and homework assignments. Through these albums, Asch revealed his version of Americanism, which differed sharply from the Cold War interpretation of the nation's past and present.

Asch released the first of these albums in 1958. *The Patriot Plan,* written by Charles Edward Smith and narrated by Wallace House, used historical documents to trace the development of American democratic principles during a time in which education as a whole no longer stressed such a view. In the introductory notes, Smith describes the album as an exploration of the diachronic character of American democratic thought: "Combining the written and spoken word, this book-and-record project re-creates the dynamic growth of civil and human rights in Colonial America and seeks to bring into perspective the far-reaching changes in democratic concepts that occurred during that period." Through speeches and written material, the album taught students about the "evolution of Democracy," beginning with the Mayflower Compact and continuing through the years leading up to the American Revolution. However, instead of relegating this story to the past, Smith's liner notes clearly stated its contemporary relevance: "Whether we are new or old Americans or, more typically, a mixture of the two, the past has the concreteness of home and heritage. Inevitably it holds hope for the future."[68]

Beyond broadly declaring the album's importance for documenting the trajectory of the American democratic character, Smith situates each recording in its historical context and explains how and why it contributed to the development of American democracy. Early documents, such as the Puritan piece "A Body of Liberties," serve either to foreshadow future developments or to highlight emblematic individuals who set a democratic course. For the track "Roger Williams: A Letter to the People of Providence" (1648), Smith describes Williams as "one of those individuals, rare in any land, whose tolerance was deep-rooted in a sense of humanity." According to Smith's text, Williams's virtues, such as his belief in the separation of church and state and "freedom of conscience," and his advocacy for the humane treatment of American Indians, rendered him "one of the greatest of Americans." Other documents are included to show the development of the American conception of rights that was eventually codified in the Constitution. Excerpts of the Maryland Toleration Acts are explained as expressions of religious toleration that foreshadowed aspects of the Bill of Rights. Smith commends Samuel Adams's "Letter of Correspondence from the Town of Boston" for emphasizing a concern for civil rights and for describing an early version of checks and balances that "contributed to the blueprint for our representative form of government." Yet Smith attributes the most significant contribution to American political thought to James Otis's 1764 statement on the rights of British Colonists, which, he explains, "relates to many aspects of our contributions to human rights. . . . [I]t reflects evils of colonialism not altogether eradicated in some areas of the world and . . . emphasizes, in a most clear-cut manner, the right of all, regardless of race, to equality."[69] By weaving together an appreciation for diversity and civil rights and citing them as the foundation of American development, Smith and Asch clearly point to the concept of cultural pluralism and political rights as the crux of American national identity.

The following year, in 1959, Asch released another album with text again written by Smith as a part of a series of documents and speeches called "Heritage, U.S.A." Smith introduced the album, *The Coming Age of Freedom,* with a succinct statement of the purpose behind the series: "In this series of documents and speeches you will, we hope, arrive at least at a nodding acquaintance with the significant facets of our national life, the continuing maturation of democracy itself, the gradual realization of the principles inherent in the Declaration of Independence, and the consummation of national unity."[70] Again, the album reverts back to the ideals on which Asch believed that the United States was founded, and he issued the records to explain how those ideals serve as the cornerstone of the American heritage. They also fit in well with the fascination with national sacred texts such as the Declaration of Independence and icons such as the Founding Fathers that permeated the educational and cultural context of Cold War America.

Yet there was also a strong note of subversion. The albums recast the "sacred texts," imbuing them with new meaning by rooting American political identity in democratic rights for all citizens, even for those who were being denied those rights. During this period, school curricula emphasized unquestioning patriotism. This entailed teaching children not to question the political and social status quo, which included segregation and the disfranchisement of African Americans in the South.[71] In fact, by the end of the 1940s, most teachers had virtually ceased acknowledging race altogether, opting instead for the term "culture" when referring to racial minorities. "Race" continued to remain absent from classrooms throughout the 1950s, precisely as the Civil Rights Movement began to accelerate. The Red Scare was largely responsible for this shift, as supporting or even discussing civil rights activism could cause one to be suspected of communist sympathies.[72] During a time of Federal Bureau of Investigation (FBI) activity and HUAC hearings, when displaying sympathy for racial egalitarianism was enough to secure a branding of "subversive," these albums rooted American political identity in democratic rights and called for the extension of those rights to *all* Americans. Thus, Asch simultaneously endorsed civil rights activism and challenged the trend of teaching children not to question the political and social status quo by emphasizing diversity *and* demanding that the civil rights of all citizens, irrespective of race, be upheld.

Like Alan Lomax, Asch was not a certified educator; he therefore employed those in the education field to produce (and sell) the records. In 1955, he produced the pamphlet "The Recording as a Teaching Tool: A Bulletin for Parents and Teachers," edited by Florence B. Freedman and Esther L. Berg. The booklet contains numerous passages written by primary and secondary school teachers, as well as by college professors, all stressing the importance of music in education. Several of the educational experts argue that teaching through music allows young children to engage actively with material, and others maintain that music provides social and cultural views that traditional school texts tend to omit. Richard E. Du Wors and William B. Weist of the Department of Sociology at Bucknell University praised Tony Schwartz's *New York 19* (1954), a Folkways record of the sounds of street life in New York City, because the album "creates an awareness in the student of the multi-cultured nature of city life" and teachers could use it "to show cultural diffusion, acceptance, and transformation . . . [and] demonstrate universal values from their local expressions."

This belief that music could instill appreciation of American cultural diversity is the underlying message of the entire pamphlet. Marguerite Cartwright of Hunter College explains in her article "The Use of Records in Intercultural Education" that teachers could effectively teach "unity within diversity" through recorded material, an argument that Angelica W. Cass of the New York State Department of Education further develops in "Using Records of Folk Music in Adult Education." Cass asserts that music, especially folk music, helps students to generate informed opinions, understand historical events, and recognize "the international character of our nation." The comprehension of American cultural pluralism that folk music provides could also help students from immigrant backgrounds understand their role in American culture and society, according to Esther Brown of the Colorado State College of Education. Using ethnic folk music in classrooms is especially important for urban schools, where, in Brown's view, "foreign students are often made to feel ashamed of their culture, where the pressure to become 'Americanized' as quickly as possible is strong." Folk music combats this tendency and allows students to accept their cultural heritage as a component of American culture, a "self-knowledge and self-respect without which democracy is impossible."[73] While American intellectuals lamented the increasing homogenization of American culture and society during the era of (alleged) consensus and gray flannel suits, Asch and other folk revivalists used folk music to define an American past and present rooted in political dissent, diversity, and civil rights.

A dual emphasis on internationalism and American cultural diversity was particularly strong throughout Asch's tenure at Folkways Records, even for records not specifically produced for classroom use. One of the aspects of American life that Asch sought to expose was the difficulty the nation faced in encouraging citizens to welcome ethnic and racial minorities into the American community. In 1955, Folkways released *Nueva York,* a documentary album about Puerto Rican migrants living in New York City that was a brainchild of Tony Schwartz. It contained interviews with migrants, their neighbors, public school teachers, and other New York City residents that Schwartz recorded over an eight-year span. Although Schwartz presents a variety of voices in *Nueva York,* he is clearly sympathetic toward the migrants, people whose hardships were similar to those of his immigrant parents. Some of the stories he includes are explanations of why people left their homes for New York and what they encountered after they arrived—notably, difficulties navigating the city, overcoming language barriers, facing housing discrimination, and suffering from poverty. In 1959, Robert Shelton commended the album in the *New York Times* for publicizing the social and economic issues that accompanied the postwar wave of Puerto Rican migration to New York City.[74] *Nueva York* suggests that, despite the decline of interest in Popular Front Americanism, Asch managed to keep the spirit of democratic, pluralist nationalism alive in the albums he continued to produce throughout the decade and into the 1960s, skirting the political pressures of the 1950s in the process.

Ultimately, although he remained politically nonsectarian, Asch can be classified as a progressive revivalist who shared many sympathies with the left-wing members of his cohort. Asch's political views were grounded in faith in the promise of an inclusive democracy, and he imbued most of the albums that he released with this view. While it was a view that many Popular Front communists espoused, to Asch it was just the essence of the American identity, and he did not hesitate to criticize those who tried to hamper the democratic process, even if it meant challenging the nation's political status quo. The liner notes for *The Coming Age of Freedom,* for example, present a searing indictment of the current political state: "Within a democracy we want . . . a constant intermingling and recapitulation of forces and beliefs, a situation (never in actual balance) that we maintain only with the utmost tolerance and devotion, not mere lip-service, to the principles of the Declaration of Independence and the Bill of Rights. . . . A healthy democracy, as Jefferson reminds us, is a turbulence."[75]

Comments like this were enough to get a record producer such as Asch into political trouble. During the late 1940s, another progressive record company, Young People's Records (YPR), produced albums of folk music for children.

YPR had its own folk music and American history series, "Fact and Folklore." With a format based on Alan Lomax's shows for CBS Radio, the records arranged the music historically, with topics that ranged from Columbus and Daniel Boone to cowboy, maritime, logging, and railroad songs. The albums also included Native American songs and mentioned that white men had cheated the American Indians and stolen their land. Even though the YPR albums did not contain overt political messages, in 1950 the American Legion accused the company of having communist sympathies, and YPR landed in *Red Channels*. School districts followed suit by banning YPR albums from their libraries.[76]

Folkways, by contrast, survived the period largely unscathed. Perhaps the company managed to fly under the political radar because, as Michael Asch claims, his father could argue that he was simply a businessman trying to succeed in a capitalist society, and "what could be more American than that?"[77] It is more likely that Folkways survived because it was a small enterprise, unlike YPR, which was widely popular, and because it was a commercial company that marketed albums largely to individual teachers (rather than to whole school districts) and libraries. In many respects, Folkways operated in a manner similar to that of children's trade book sellers in the 1950s and early 1960s. According to the historian Julia Mickenberg, trade books were rarely blacklisted because, unlike textbooks that were sold in mass quantities and subject to local, state, and federal scrutiny, schools and libraries carried a limited number of each title. In addition, since publishers released multiple titles every year, anticommunist groups could not feasibly scrutinize each one. Likewise, the educational albums that Folkways released represented only a fraction of the company's catalogue—a catalogue from which teachers and librarians could select various titles for educational use. Furthermore, as Mickenberg explains, librarians had more leeway and were able to maintain progressive sympathies even as anticommunists bore down on teachers. Therefore, certain materials continued to appear in libraries even as they were banished from classrooms.[78] Perhaps, then, Asch was able to save his company by devising a business strategy that specifically targeted librarians and the occasional progressive teacher, as well as by keeping a low profile.

In 1955, the FBI briefly put Asch under surveillance, citing suspicious albums such as *China Reconstructs* and six records of Polish folk music. Yet the file ultimately concluded in 1956 that Folkways was a "legitimate business enterprise" and that there was "no reason to question the integrity and loyalty of its president, Marion Distler."[79] Despite his relatively unproblematic experience during the Red Scare, Moses Asch made an obvious jab at the years of fear and political intimidation in his opening dedication of *Gazette* (1958), an album of topical political songs performed by Pete Seeger: "I have always believed that it is the duty and privilege of publishers of materials that reach a wide audience to make available to the general public as great a variety of points of view and opinions as possible—without the heavy hand of censorship or the imposition of the publishers' editorial view. . . . To those who believe in the free and uncensored expression of not only their own beliefs, but the opinions and ideas of others, I dedicate this album."[80] Although McCarthy had died the previous year, his death had not signaled the end of McCarthyism. Through the close of the 1950s and well into the 1960s, musicians, filmmakers, labor leaders, and other professionals, along with members of immigrant and minority groups, suffered the lingering effects of the Red Scare, especially from private groups such as the John Birch Society.[81] In this atmosphere, Asch's commentary in *Gazette* was still politically risky, yet Folkways continued to evade political censure.

Asch not only avoided the blacklists but also remained a popular figure in educational circles throughout the decade. During the early 1950s, he received invitations from the National Catholic Music Educators Conference, the Catholic Library Association meeting, the Association for Supervision and Curriculum Development conference, the American Association of School Administrators (a department of the National Educational Association), and the Music Educators National Conference to market Folkways albums.[82] He also traveled extensively to conventions for the Anthropological Association, the Modern Library Association, and the Society for Ethnomusicology and even became a "fixture" at the Music Library Association. As early as 1952, he realized that libraries would be his chief clients and that he could potentially reach both music and social studies educators, as well. Occasionally, other record distributors even contacted Folkways, as Mario Piriano of Knight Education did in 1960, requesting catalogues of educational material that they would then distribute through their companies.[83]

Near the end of the 1950s, the schoolchildren who had learned about folk music through Folkways records had come of age and were on the verge of becoming the new rank of college-age folk music enthusiasts. This generation both witnessed and contributed to the folk music boom of the 1960s. By 1958, the folk music revival was poised to become one of the defining cultural phenomena of the 1960s. Asch had played a pivotal role in making this possible.

## Setting the Stage

While popular interest in folk music had begun earlier in the decade, the commercial folk music boom took off in 1958 when the Kingston Trio hit the airwaves with their rendition of the Appalachian murder ballad "Tom Dooley." Neatly dressed in matching clothes, with well-coiffed hair, the Kingston Trio consisted of Bob Shane, Dave Guard, and Nick Reynolds, who formed the band in California. The trio became widely popular soon after releasing their first album.[84] Yet they did not hold on to their musical monopoly for long. Soon groups based on their model mushroomed across the country.

Many revival programs began to adapt to the fact that folk music was rising up the Billboard charts. The political views in *Sing Out!* began to subside as the magazine became preoccupied with discussing the implications of folk music's newfound popularity. Pete Seeger initiated this self-examination in 1956 in his regular column, "Johnny Appleseed, Jr," noting, a bit prematurely, that the revival was already in "full force." In another column a few months later, he reiterated the connection between folk music and a DIY ethos, writing, "The revival of interest in folk music . . . is simply part and parcel of a gigantic counter-trend in American life. (The main trend is, of course, mass production and mass media.)"[85] *Sing Out!* contributed to the growing musical DIY interest by printing folk songs that readers wrote and submitted to the magazine in the regular feature "The Folk Process." Debuting in 1955, the section featured new versions of traditional songs, new verses added to old songs, or new songs set to familiar tunes. The purpose of the section was to show that folk music was a dynamic art form while also reaffirming the genre's usefulness in challenging the sociopolitical status quo. The first feature was a song titled "Greenfeather." Set to the tune of "Greensleeves," the song lauded the anti–McCarthy "Green Feather" groups on college campuses. Over the course of the late 1950s and early 1960s, the column regularly featured songs that pertained to college life, atomic fears, freedom rides, and the sit-in movement—issues that revealed that much of its readership consisted of young, college-age folkies.

As those at *Sing Out!* rejoiced at the increasing number of folk music fans learning to play instruments and write their own songs that formed the new ranks of folk revivalists, they also grew weary of another feature that increasingly characterized the folk boom: commercialism. While many performers realized that to get folk music into the mainstream they would have to become "commercial," and others recognized that by performing on record labels and in major concert venues they had already become "commercial," still other revivalists strongly distrusted commercial outlets and mainstream media precisely as folk music became a key feature of popular culture. Most of all, they disdained popular versions of folk songs because most were watered-down versions of traditional songs.[86] Many left-wing revivalists particularly feared that commercial versions of folk songs would omit references to political or cultural dissent. In 1956, *Sing Out!* ran an article about the rise of interest in folk music, as shown by the newfound popularity of songs such as "Sixteen Tons," "John Henry," and "This Land Is Your Land." Already suspicious of mainstream music outlets, the writer lauded the growing interest in folk music while still criticizing the music industry: "While the commercial publishers and arrangers frequently distort both music and words of these songs—this development of interest in folk song must be heartily welcomed. Our American music can only be made healthier by it."[87] As long as the music, and the message behind it, remained in the contemporary versions of traditional songs, as well as in the new compositions, then the revival would remain on track.

Groups like the Kingston Trio were but one component of the vast commercialization of folk music. Producers, record labels, concert venue managers, and others helped push folk music onto the public scene. As Folkways continued to produce largely esoteric material aimed at educators and folk purists, other companies grew eager to ride the popular folk music wave. Jack

Holtzman, the founder of Elektra Records, for example, entered the recording business in 1950 and went to New York City specifically to record folk music. Unlike Asch, he focused almost exclusively on English-language music and largely left the ethnic market to his competitor. Seeking to bring "the directness and honesty and poetry, especially of the Anglo-American ballads to a whole new audience," Holtzman marketed his recordings to college-educated people who read books and frequented art galleries, people much like him. He and Asch had catered to the same market niche in the early 1950s, but near the middle of the decade, their paths diverged. By the end of the 1950s, Holtzman primarily recorded popular musicians such as Josh White (who had lost his folk credibility by becoming commercially mainstream) and even some ethnic singers such as Theodore Bikel and Cynthia Gooding.[88] Elektra and other record companies would largely determine the direction the revival would take at the height of its popularity.

In 1958, amid the escalating popularity of folk music, Alan Lomax returned home from an eight-year song-collecting trip around Britain, Italy, and Spain. Although he had dedicated much of his career to getting a public audience for folk music, he was unnerved by the direction in which folk music was moving as it gained popularity. The year after his return, Lomax published the essay "The Folkniks and the Songs They Sing" in *Sing Out!* in which he criticized not only the commercial outlets but also the popular "folk" singers for not taking the time to learn singing styles of the communities from which these songs came or the music's "emotional content." The revival, according to Lomax, began in the 1930s "as a cultural movement with overtones of social reform." Eventually, the "amusement industry" turned the "cultural movement" into the popular "boom." A negative side effect to this new phase of the revival was that the "city-billy" singers had more access to the entertainment industry and thus were able to quickly generate a devoted following. To keep their following, Lomax claimed, "they translate folk music in ways that make it more understandable and acceptable to their market—an urban middleclass group, with a college background," thus taking folk music away from the tradition-bearers.[89] Clearly, the conflicts over the commercialization of folk music ran deep. Even though folk music had been commercialized ever since the rise of the recording industry, to the older revivalists the new folk music craze threatened to pervert the music they cherished. If this is what it took to make folk music part of mainstream American culture, then maybe it was time to rethink the revival.

## Conclusion

While the end of the 1950s is notable for setting the stage for the emergence of the folk boom, the importance of the decade lay just as much in the revival's struggle for survival. For the majority of revivalists, most of whom were political progressives, the decade was one of uncertainty, fear, repression, and betrayal; even the revival had its share of friendly witnesses who testified before

HUAC. In his assessment of the termination and lasting legacy of the culture of the Popular Front, Michael Denning describes all constituents of the left after 1948—from the hard-line party members to the peripheral fellow travelers—as "repressed and expelled from public culture; it became a beleaguered subculture whose emblems were the Weavers, the Rosenbergs and Paul Robeson," all of whom fell victim to the Red Scare.[90]

Contrary to this grim picture, not all left-wing revivalists suffered irreparable defeat. Some—like the revivalists connected to Folkways, progressive schools, and *Sing Out!*—continued to push their political agenda, despite the risks. As Denning argues, the cultural formation of the left in the 1930s and 1940s was a powerful current that transcended the Communist Party and progressive political forces from which it emerged. Therefore, some left-wing sympathizers managed to retain enough autonomy from the party to survive the political repression of McCarthyism, albeit with bruises. Moses Asch and certain members of the *Sing Out!* community are examples of such figures. Even some revivalists who had sought affiliations with the Communist Party—people like Silber and Sanders—managed to continue their work throughout the decade. Perhaps it was precisely *because* the party ignored the revivalists in the 1940s and 1950s that they were able to remain standing for the duration of the Red Scare. Not only did these revivalists sustain the pluralist version of American democracy that had emerged during the Popular Front, but they also did it largely on their own. Much of the left was gone; so was the broad coalition that had come together during the Popular Front.

Denning describes the legacy of the Popular Front during the 1950s as a residual cultural awareness, the *spirit* of the movement continuing aesthetically through novels and movies. In arguing this way, he appeals to Stuart Hall's assessment that, even when "social forces" are defeated in the larger political or social landscape, they do not disappear entirely. Even though the Popular Front had faded from the mainstream, the revivalists sustained the emphasis on the people and the democratic ideals embedded in the movement, which became the guiding principles of many of their cultural programs. The writers, editors, and musicians of People's Artists, Folkways Records, and *Sing Out!* spelled out what needed to be done to achieve lasting political reform and provided ways to challenge the social and political status quo by bringing music into programs of social activism. Even the products that appeared to lack any overt political message—such as popular "folk" anthems like "This Land Is Your Land" and "The Hammer Song"—proclaimed the very ideals of Popular Front Americanism. The messages that America "was made for you and me" and that one could "sing out love between my brothers (and my sisters) all over this land" were grounded in the democratic ideals that emerged during the Popular Front, ideals that the revivalists continued to rely on to reform the nation throughout the 1950s. The significance of these revivalists lay not in the size of their audience, which was small, but in their challenges to the social, political, and cultural norms. By looking beyond institutional politics, we see that many activists worked to keep the political torch lit by continuing the fight for social justice and political rights.

Ultimately, then, rather than being the nadir of folk music activities, these years bridged the gap between the Old Left generation of folk music enthusiasts and the baby boom generation. During this decade, pluralists such as Knott used folk music to emphasize American cultural heterogeneity; political and cultural radicals used music to protest or escape the strictures of the era; and young enthusiasts used folk music to define themselves and the type of America of which they sought to become a part. It was also during this time that the definition of folk music began to stretch to a breaking point, however. If Lomax was right in his assertion that the new generation of folk music fans did not understand the meaning behind the music, was that meaning lost? Indeed, that question soon became a major source of contention during the folk boom.

# 5

## THE BOOM

The late 1950s was a rather bleak time for suburban youth culture. Rock-and-roll, the former outlet for teenage angst, had been co-opted by commercial forces, which effectively rendered the music safe and bland. Jazz, the music of choice for culturally alternative teenagers, grew increasingly avant-garde, and "Crow Jim" attitudes (i.e., Jim Crow in reverse) among hard bop musicians rendered jazz a black music scene that restricted whites from gaining access. The world of pop music offered little hope. According to the musician Dave Van Ronk, the pop music of the late 1950s was so vapid and "insipid" that he and his college-age cohort were forced to "seek out alternatives," and folk music became their genre of choice. Such was the case for many high school kids, to the extent that folk music filled the musical void for much of America's white, middle-class youth.[1] Whereas the older members of the baby boom generation focused more on traditional groups, younger enthusiasts gravitated to the young, popular folk interpreters. Groups like the Kingston Trio looked and sounded like the rest of the white middle class, making them accessible to white teenagers. Yet at the same time they represented something different: they sang songs like "Tom Dooley" that, while being old, were new to the children of suburbia. The Trio differed from their commercial predecessors, such as the Weavers, not only because they lacked a political history but also because they tailored their music to the youth market. Their stripped-down, acoustic sound contrasted with the Weaver's orchestral arrangements; to many teenage fans, this was not their parents' music. The newfound popularity of folk music groups such as the Trio led mainstream media outlets to adapt to the times. Robert Shelton, who joined the *New York Times* staff as the folk music critic, observed that by the early 1960s, folk music had become a definite part of the musical mainstream. "A longer perspective may revise this view," he wrote, "but it appears from a distance of a few months that 1962 was the year when the folk-music revival outlived its period as a fad and became an established staple in the popular-music diet of this country's listeners."[2]

Shelton's observation was correct. By 1962, folk music had officially hit the big time. In popular culture, the years between 1960 and 1965 are viewed as the era of the folk boom. Much of the audience during this period were holdovers from the previous decade—the folk music fans who gathered in urban coffee houses, small music clubs, colleges, and parks—but soon hordes of young, baby boom enthusiasts overwhelmed them. The enormous popularity of folk music during these years would seem to indicate that the revivalists had succeeded in making folk music part of mainstream American culture. The revivalists, however, were not the vanguard of the folk boom. Rather, commercial outlets and mainstream media largely dictated the type of folk music sold to a mass listening audience. Motivated by economic gain rather than political and social idealism, music entrepreneurs, television producers, and some musicians sought to cash in on the folk music craze that they were in the process of creating.

As folk music peaked in popularity during the first half of the 1960s, the revival as a whole experienced a structural sea change. During this period, two generations of revivalists controlled the movement. The first had emerged during the 1930s and the People's Songs era, and the second consisted of the oldest baby boomers who had come of age. The baby boomers generally divided into two camps marked by their divergent views regarding folk music: musical traditionalists, on the one hand, and members and sympathizers of the emerging New Left on the other. The former helped to complicate the boom years, while the latter played a critical role in perpetuating the politically infused Americanism that the older revivalists had carried through the 1950s and adapting it to a new era of political activism, thus forging links between the Old Left and the New Left.

In their effort to cope with the rampant commercialization of folk music, the first generation of revivalists operated through the various outlets that they had formed before the boom. *Sing Out!* continued through the early years of the 1960s in much the same vein as it had in the late 1950s, examining the growing popularity of folk music and what it meant for both the revival and American culture as a whole. The members of the *Sing Out!* community did not necessarily condemn the widespread popularity of folk music, but they did try to retain some level of control to ensure that traditional and topical folk music did not become obsolete. At the same time, other revivalists—many of whom contributed to *Sing Out!*—hoped to tap into the fad to advance the causes that they had pursued in the past. Many took their interest in cultural preservation a step further by initiating a music festival designed to feature contemporary popular musicians and traditional players on the same stage. The organizers of the Newport Folk Festival hoped to attract young people to listen to their favorite singers from the radio and stay to hear traditional musicians. Similarly, some revivalists used

the widespread popularity of folk music as an opportunity to incorporate this
music into school curricula. Moses Asch spearheaded this effort, as he had done
in the previous decade, and the end of McCarthyism enabled him to amplify his
political views. Through entertainment and education, these revivalists hoped to
steer the popular wing of the revival back to its cultural—and social—roots.

Among the baby boom generation emerged a coterie of folk enthusiasts who
focused primarily on the music itself. Instead of advocating a social agenda,
they promoted a cultural one. Rejecting the Kingston Trio and other popular
folk acts, these enthusiasts returned to the source: traditional music. They
worked literally to *revive* this music—either by painstakingly studying the musical techniques from recordings of the 1920s and 1930s or by seeking to discover, or rediscover, musicians who were steeped in these traditions and bring
them back into recording studios and on concert stages. These "neo-ethnics," to
use Van Ronk's term, appreciated traditional music in much the same way that
older revivalists such as Alan Lomax did, but they began to form their own
trajectory somewhat independently from the revival. Yet in the midst of carving
their own niche within the world of folk music, they had to contend with the
fact that the genre had become a teenage fad. They responded by shunning any
connection to the mainstream aspects of folk music and focusing exclusively on
rural, regional music. Rather than relying on mass media outlets and the commercial record industry, these revivalists created their own programs: college
folk clubs, festivals, and student-run magazines that catered to their interests.

The other wing of baby boom enthusiasts, those who participated in left-
wing activism, moved beyond the purely musical realm and initiated new efforts that incorporated folk music into social and political reform. These figures'
political views and interpretation of Americanism showed remarkable parallels
to the ideals and activism of the Old Left from the Popular Front era. Both political movements were predicated on the belief that America could still be reformed to achieve democratic goals and become inclusive of marginalized
groups. While the New Left largely emerged from the baby boom generation
that had now come of age, many revivalists from the People's Songs era aided in
the revival of political activism. This established a period of cooperation wherein activists from these two generations shared a belief that folk music promoted
a pluralist democratic Americanism that in turn would help generate the kind
of political reform that the nation so desperately needed. Thus, the 1960s
marked a critical new phase in the revival wherein the revivalists worked to
sustain the political and social message of the movement amid a national folk
music craze.

## Commercialism and the Revival

In delineating a theory of music revivals, the ethnomusicologist Tamara Livingston argues that the final stage of a revival is marked by the development of
a revival industry: nonprofit and for-profit ventures that include concerts and

festivals, magazines, record companies, and music education material that cater to the revival community. These media outlets not only keep the community informed (ideologically as well as musically) but also help maintain the community of folk music fans as they spread across the country.[3] Following Livingston's argument, the late 1950s through the early 1960s marked the culmination of the revival, for during this period a plethora of folk groups sprouted, as did radio shows, music venues, and magazines that catered to the revival community. As for periodicals that spoke to the folk community, *Sing Out!* remained a key forum for exploring and discussing all aspects of the folk revival and, increasingly, the folk boom, as well.

In 1961, during the rapidly accelerating folk boom, *Sing Out!* continued to evaluate the positive and negative consequences of the growing popularity of folk music. In his regular column on folk music happenings, "Frets and Frails," Izzy (Israel) Young looked at the positive implications of the commercialization of folk music, noting that the more that record companies released folk albums, the more folk music would become a key part of American culture. Folk music would move out of its niche market when "night clubs, radio and TV" started featuring more folk artists. As this happened with increasing frequency, Young argued, "the important singers will not have to languish and play only in occasional benefit concerts or for a few devoted followers. When the folksinger can make a living, folkmusic [sic] will have arrived."[4] By 1962, folk music *had* arrived, and who held the reins of the boom was anyone's guess.

As the folk boom continued to pick up steam, folk music became—revivalists believed—increasingly compromised in the realm of popular culture. In an editorial on the state of folk music in 1963, Irwin Silber commented that, while there were many positive aspects regarding the popularity of folk music, he was troubled by the over-commercialization of the music and iconography: "Now, folk music, like the quiz shows before it, has become a device to sell soap, hair tonic, soft drinks, [and] cigarettes. In an age where the sweetest music of all is played on the cash register, folk music has become a commodity, an object of the marketplace, to be judged, weighed and sold by the Lootenanny of 1963." In the same issue, Bob West from Fairborn, Ohio, echoed Silber's sentiment, exclaiming in his letter to the editor, "What they heck has happened? I was sitting in front of the television when, by God, Oscar Brand started singing. When I started to listen [I realized] it was a DOG FOOD COMMERCIAL!!!"[5] Yet in the middle of the commercial morass, some revivalists found hope. Benjamin Botkin contributed an article in which he examined the folk boom, ultimately concluding that it was a good thing for American culture. "What is being revived, in other words, or rediscovered, is not so much American folk music as the musical past of America," he wrote.[6]

The accelerating popularity of folk music led *Sing Out!* to feature a symposium, "Folk Music and the Top 40," that addressed the relationship among commercialism, popularization, and folk music in early 1966. Interestingly, the overall tone of the symposium was positive: the folklorist Roger Abrahams recounted his initial disgust at hearing a "pop" singer cover a traditional ballad, but then realized "that this sort of popularization of folksongs had been going on for hundreds of years." The bluegrass banjo extraordinaire Earl Scruggs noted that, with the arrival of folk in the Top 40, "the general public has become increasingly aware of the value of folksongs." Others, while still praising the widespread interest in folk music, sounded a note of caution. Pete Seeger commented that revivalists "should strive to see that local people are not ashamed of their local traditions and different national and racial groups are not ashamed of their national and racial traditions." Botkin continued his call for cultural diversity, noting, "If the folk song revival is to survive, it must, as an urban movement, continue to ally itself with the egalitarian 'urban majority,' on the side of the dynamic, creative forces of cultural pluralism and equality against the forces of conformity and reaction."[7] As long as traditional artists continued to be respected and traditional music did not become too adulterated, then the revivalists could take pride in the success of folk music as it reached a national listening audience.

Commercial folk music, however, overwhelmingly dominated the boom. One of the symposium themes was the effect that the nontraditional musicians of the boom had on the public image of folk music. Although they belonged to the same "scene," commercial folk acts were a varied lot.[8] All-male groups such as the Kingston Trio, the Chad Mitchell Trio, the Limeliters, and the Brothers Four were of the more clean-cut variety and often sang traditional songs and material written by other songwriters in addition to their own compositions. Some, like the Chad Mitchell Trio, added satirical and even political songs to their repertoires as the decade progressed. Other popular performers included the folk "queens" Joan Baez, Carolyn Hester, Judy Collins, and Odetta, whose musical selections also consisted of traditional and topical songs. Still other acts included mixed-gender groups such as the Rooftop Singers and Peter, Paul, and Mary, the latter of which became one of the most popular acts during the boom. Peter, Paul, and Mary, along with Baez and Collins, became especially notable for bringing the music of other songwriters of the revival (such as Bob Dylan, Tom Paxton, and Shel Silverstein) to a wider audience. Many of the albums that these singers and groups recorded landed in the Top 40 during the first three years of the 1960s. In the spring of 1960, the Kingston Trio's *Here We Go Again* was the best-selling album. During the same year, the debut album by the Brothers Four reached number two and spent twenty weeks in the Top 40. In 1962, the satirist Allan Sherman's album *My Son the Folk Singer* remained in the Top 40 for six weeks, and an illustration of Joan Baez was featured on the cover of *Time*. The following year, fifty radio stations featured a folk music radio show (usually with the word "hootenanny" in the title), and in August, WCPO in Cincinnati dedicated all of its airtime to folk music.[8]

Of all the programs that emerged during the early 1960s, none encapsulated the commercialism of the boom quite like *Hootenanny,* a folk music television show on ABC. Aired on Saturday nights beginning in April 1963, *Hootenanny* featured a variety of popular folk acts and soon became one of the most watched shows on the station. Richard Lewine and Jack Linkletter, the show's producers, filmed each episode on a different college campus and specifically tailored the program to the youth market. Many folk musicians criticized the show, not only because it glorified the faddish aspects of the folk boom, but also because it blacklisted Pete Seeger and the Weavers from performing. The producers claimed that they did not include Seeger because he was not popular among college students. However, many believed that they based their decision on Seeger's political reputation. Since Seeger could not play, several musicians, including Joan Baez, Bob Dylan, Tom Paxton, and Peter, Paul and Mary, refused to perform, as well. Yet Seeger encouraged these singers to appear on the show in the hope that they would help introduce good folk music to the young audience; even his half-brother Mike Seeger performed with his group the New Lost City Ramblers.[9]

By staging folk music concerts on college campuses, *Hootenanny* tapped into what had been a common feature of the revival long before the advent of the boom: folk music festivals. Throughout the 1950s, progressive colleges such as Swarthmore and Oberlin hosted folk festivals. Even the schools that did not have full-scale festivals often invited folk music performers to give individual concerts. When the Kingston Trio emerged on the music scene in 1958, they first became popular among a college audience. That same year, George Wein invited the Kingston Trio to perform at his annual summer jazz festival in Newport, Rhode Island. Wein, a music promoter, had begun the Newport Jazz Festival in 1954. The success of the Kingston Trio in 1958 led him to organize a separate Newport Folk Festival the following year. Hiring Albert Grossman, a music manager and owner of the popular Chicago folk music club Gate of Horn, as the festival organizer and commissioning Studs Terkel to serve as the emcee, Wein launched the first Newport Folk Festival on July 11, 1959.[10]

As an annual event, the Newport Folk Festival appeared more akin to the National Folk Festival (NFF) than the smaller college festivals. The fact that the Newport board included many advocates of jazz and blues music, however, set the festival on a very different path from that of the NFF, since the latter took years to incorporate blues music and ignored anything that was nontraditional. In the introduction of the program book for the 1959 Newport festival, the organizers set parameters for the music that they believed should be included under the rubric of American folk music. Unlike the NFF and most regional festivals, Newport included both traditional and contemporary performers. The organizers celebrated this musical pluralism, stating in the program, "The Scholars, the City-bred folksingers, and the 'authentic' singers are here to give to you what is probably the very first representative picture of American Folk Music ever held on the concert stage."[11] Opening with Pete Seeger, the first festival was a two-day event that included Sonny Terry and Brownie McGee, John Jacob Niles, the Viennese singer Martha Schlamme, the New Lost City Ramblers, Memphis Slim, Cynthia Gooding, Frank Warner, Odetta, the country singer Jimmy Driftwood, Oscar Brand, Barbara Dane, Jean Ritchie, the Kingston Trio, and more. The festival program includes brief biographical sketches of each performer, but, as Ralph Rinzler, one of its writers, noted in retrospect, no distinction was made between traditional and nontraditional musicians.[12] Unlike the NFF planners, the Newport organizers did not bathe their program in the rhetoric of patriotism and democracy, although they did note the contributions that the festival performers made to "the cause of American music and our democratic way of life."[13] Thus, Newport quietly advocated the Americanism of the revival—an advocacy that would become increasingly overt as the decade progressed.

The following year, the Newport Folk Festival added a new host of performers, including singers and musicians such as the Brothers Four, Peggy Seeger, Ewan McColl, the flamenco group Sabicas, the Ducorans African Trio, John Lee Hooker, Lester Flatt, the Abyssinian Baptist Choir, and Cisco Houston, among others. In the festival program, Pete Seeger reflected on the revival and the growing folk boom. Explaining to readers that the revival dated back to the 1930s, he commended public folklorists such as Alan Lomax for initiating the movement and then credited musical groups of the 1940s and 1950s, such as the Weavers and the Kingston Trio, for augmenting the current groundswell of interest. The new folk music enthusiasts were more interested in creative entertainment outlets and believed that folk music would contribute to their worldliness: "The great range of different kinds of folk music indicates that here is a new kind of cosmopolitan citizen: one who can listen to an Israeli hora one minute and the next minute to an unaccompanied English sea chantey, or a gutty deep south blues."[14] Indeed, the Newport Folk Festival aimed to enhance that appreciation of cultural diversity. It therefore was not restricted to traditional music in an effort to uphold standards of authenticity, as were many of the other folk festivals. Rather, it embraced the popularity of folk music and committed itself to bringing both new and traditional artists, foreign and domestic, to the same stage. Eventually, this pluralism became both the festival's strength and its weakness.

In the midst of the 1960 jazz festival, a skirmish broke out between students and police in downtown Newport, an incident that prompted the city to ban both festivals. The hiatus for the folk festival lasted for the next three years. In the interim, a new festival emerged just down the coast. The Philadelphia Folksong Society, in conjunction with local folk music fans, organized the first Philadelphia Folk Festival, which debuted in September 1962. Kenneth Goldstein, a record producer and folklorist, helped direct the program, which shared Newport's eclectic approach of combining popular and traditional performers—many of whom had appeared on the Newport stage—and addressing the social and cultural issues embedded in the folk boom.[15]

During Newport's suspension, Albert Grossman left the festival to manage Bob Dylan and Peter, Paul, and Mary. Pete and Toshi Seeger deftly filled his place. Together with Wein; his wife, Joyce; and the singer Theodore Bikel, they established the nonprofit Newport Folk Festival Foundation (NFFF). Run primarily by musicians, the NFFF overhauled the organization and execution of the festival. As Pete Seeger and Ralph Rinzler recalled, the first two Newport programs featured major acts in the popular folk music scene but tended to neglect actual "folks." Seeger was dismayed that the people from whom he had learned traditional music were not included to the extent that he believed they should be, and he, along with Toshi, his half-sister Peggy Seeger, and British the musician Ewan McColl pushed to incorporate even more traditional singers, alternating their performances with those of the urban revivalists. Through this arrangement, they hoped that the festival would connect disparate folk groups within the folk music community. They recognized that Newport still needed to include urban performers to attract an audience but decided to pay all musicians, regardless of fame, $50 per diem (in addition to living expenses) to appear at the festival. Any additional profits that the festival garnered would go back to the foundation to be redistributed among cultural conservation programs that worked to protect and present local traditional culture. Pete Seeger believed that through this arrangement, the Newport festival was "in effect, giving wide publicity to something that had been going on for at least twenty years."[16]

Because of Seeger's prodding, Newport fell in step with the revival after 1963, for it now brought traditional music to the stage and raised social and political awareness through topical singers. By combining traditional musicians, popular urban singers, and topical singer-songwriters, the Newport Folk Festival also reflected the Zeitgeist of the folk boom era. Its audience numbers rose with the tide of interest in folk music, both traditional and contemporary. The festival soon included new musical categories that were becoming incorporated under the ever expanding umbrella of folk music. The festival also grew more interactive and initiated small afternoon sessions, or musical workshops, dedicated to bluegrass and topical protest songs, as well as to traditional folk music. Initially, the program appeared to lack a strong social or political agenda, calling instead for the protection of regional traditions. Yet this emphasis broadened the politics of the revival—in seeking to protect cultural traditions, the Newport organizers brought cultural advocacy under the umbrella of social and political justice.

As Seeger and the rest of the NFFF continued to bring traditional and topical folk music to a popular audience, Moses Asch sustained his efforts to bring folk music to an educational audience. With the onset of the folk boom, the educational value of folk music became a cause célèbre among core revivalists; contributors to the *New York Folklore Quarterly* became particularly engaged with this topic. In 1962, John Anthony Scott argued that folklore and folk music should be taught in primary and secondary schools, not as a separate subfield but as an intrinsic part of American history classes. Folk music could provide students with a deeper understanding of their own heritage and the cultures of people around the world, thus making them aware of their place in the national and international communities. Articulating the international position, Scott claimed that because folk music transcended national boundaries, it could give schoolchildren the ability to attain a "whole sense of the unity of our world, the unity of its peoples and even the brotherhood of man."[17] In his article "The Place of Folklore in Education" in the following issue, Norman Studer reaffirmed the pluralist Americanism of the revival, commenting that folk culture would also help children of minority groups connect to their cultural heritage and thus allow them to fully participate "in this vast and varied crazy quilt pattern of peoples, called by sociologists a pluralistic society." By incorporating folk music into primary school curricula, Americans could combat the ill effects of forced assimilation and thus "achieve the mutual respect for all our traditions and backgrounds that is the deepest and ultimate goal of the American dream." Representing a unity-within-diversity position familiar to the revival, Studer emphasized that using the variants of folk culture to illustrate the diversity of American society would help children to "become the ideal citizens of a country whose official motto is *E Pluribus Unum.*"[18] Of the many revival programs, Folkways Records was perhaps the strongest proponent of using folk music to illustrate American cultural diversity, especially to schoolchildren.[19]

In 1960, Asch began releasing albums specifically tailored for junior high and high school history and social studies classes. Unlike his earlier educational series, which had focused on spoken word rather than music, these albums of American history alternated song tracks with narrated documents. The first album, *American History in Ballad and Song,* prepared by Albert Barouch and Theodore O. Cron, contains songs selected for their "maximum effective use" in seventh-, eighth-, and ninth-grade sections. Each song is followed by "thought questions," and every section concludes with homework assignments.

The albums celebrate civic ideals such as political democracy and emphasize the contributions that minority groups made to national development. For example, a homework question that follows the song "Shamrock," describing the plight of Irish immigrants, states, "What contributions have the different religious, ethnic, and national groups made to America? Can you list several specific examples?" The Development of Democracy section opens with "Free Elections," an eighteenth-century song on suffrage, which explains the importance of the vote. A homework question following this piece is even more relevant to both historical and contemporary problems: "Since the vote is so precious, some people would like to prevent fellow Americans from using it. Can you give examples of this?" If the message behind this question was too subtle, students were also instructed, "In a summary paragraph, explain why this is dangerous for everyone."[20] Subsequent sections include the Early Republic, Nineteenth-Century Immigration, the Civil War, Industrialization, and the American Farmer. The Industrialization section largely focuses on the poor working conditions early industrial workers suffered, as well as the unionization drives they embraced to uphold their rights. Songs such as "My Children Are Seven in Number" teach about the 1933 coal strikes in Davidson and Wilder, Tennessee, and the students are asked to list the miners' grievances, as well as the advantages that mine owners had—and "exploited over"—the workers. The section continues with songs from textile mill strikes, such as "Mill Mother's Lament" by Ella May Wiggins, a union organizer who was killed during a textile strike in Gastonia, North Carolina, in 1929, and "The Death of Harry Simms," about another union organizer who was killed by company guards during a coal strike in Harlan County, Kentucky, in 1932. Students are again asked to recognize the grievances that the workers had and to determine what the government could have done to help them. The "thought question" directs students to explain why workers would want to unionize, and one of the homework assignments asks students to imagine being a union organizer for mill workers and write a speech that would convince them to organize. After this, the American Farmer section begins with the nineteenth-century Populist Movement, then explores injustices of the sharecropping and tenant farming systems, and concludes with the Dust Bowl through the songs "Raggedy," "Seven Cent Cotton and Forty Cent Meat," and "Dust Storm Disaster." The collection ends with the section The World of Man, which features Japanese Buddhist, Hindu, Muslim, Polish, Hungarian, and South African songs. It also includes the song "It's the Same All Over," which summarizes the section's theme of "present[ing] the case that all men are basically alike in their hopes, fears, and dreams."[21]

The second volume of the *American History in Ballad and Song* series was geared for high school social studies classes—specifically, for students at the sophomore through senior levels. Taking a thematic rather than chronological approach, it explores variations of "democracy" with sections dedicated to cultural, political, economic, and international democracy. The first section, on cultural democracy, delves into investigating the components of American national identity. Again, attention is paid to the influence of immigrant cultures. Students are asked to examine what factors pulled different immigrants to the United States, where various groups settled, what hardships they faced, and how these hardships had been eased through legislation. The discussion of immigration soon turns into an investigation of American xenophobia through Woody Guthrie's "Two Good Men," about the trial of Nicola Sacco and Bartolomeo Vanzetti, and "Sherman Wu." Closing the section on cultural democracy is a popular contemporary Puerto Rican song and a documentary clip of Puerto Rican migrants arriving at Idlewild (Kennedy) Airport in New York. The entire emphasis in the section is on cultural diversity, and students are asked to examine how the United States has dealt with the plurality of ethnic cultures. Although the songs chosen for the section highlight the importance of cultural diversity, students are asked to ponder the costs and benefits of living in a heterogeneous society.

The economic democracy section continues to investigate American history from the people's perspective. Illustrating laissez-faire capitalism and the public-versus-private debate are songs such as Les Rice's "Banks of Marble": "Then we'd own those banks of marble. . . . And we'd share those vaults of silver / That we all have sweated for! (repeat)."[22] The theme of the downtrodden challenging conditions of inequality continues throughout the next section, political democracy. It opens by claiming that universal suffrage is essential for a democratic government but that throughout American history, several groups, such as women, have been excluded from voting. Students are asked to list other groups who did not have the right to vote and to identify any groups who were still denied this right; the third part of the section features a speech by Martin Luther King Jr. calling for the right to vote for African Americans in the South. The section continues with the hardships that migrant workers have endured and closes with the McCarthy committee's "abuse" of Americans' constitutional rights during the 1950s.[23]

These albums continued in the same vein as Asch's educational albums of the prior decade, articulating a version of U.S. history reminiscent of progressive history, which highlighted conflicts between social and economic groups and had fallen out of favor after the rise of consensus historians in the 1950s. By presenting an interpretation of the nation's past that championed the working class, internationalism, and civil rights, they also presented a left-wing view of American history and identity reminiscent of the Popular Front. Even though it was imparting historical interpretation that was academically and politically out of step with mainstream trends, Folkways Records received many letters commending it specifically for its educational endeavors. In 1960, George G. Dawson, an assistant professor in the Social Studies Department of New York University, wrote to Asch about an article that he wrote on the use of folk music as a teaching tool. In the letter he compliments Folkways for its albums and notes how successful they have been in his American history classes. Even students wrote to express their appreciation. In a letter to Marion Distler, a student named Dan Harris states, "I respect [Folkways] . . . as an instrument for the promotion of culture and education." Furthermore, he notes the political persuasion of Folkways—or, at least, of those who were fans of the company—by commenting that he was introduced to the company's records when his history teacher, "a bit of a leftist," played some albums of social protest music: "I was tremendously impressed (and one doesn't have to have any particular political leanings to love the records)."[24] Even the writers at the *Little Sandy Review,* a magazine that often lambasted the revivalists who used folk music for political purposes, commended Asch's educational efforts. Edmund Gilbertson praised the album *American History in Ballad and Song, Volume 1,* writing, "I absolutely turn green with envy of today's enlightened junior high social classes when I find that they can study the problems of the American farmer by listening to Woody Guthrie sing 'Dust Storm Disaster'; learn about colonial hardship with Peggy Seeger's 'When I Was Single'; study the causes of industrial fair play legislation by hearing Pete Seeger sing 'The Blind Fiddler'; and so on. Ah, progress!"[25] On these recordings Asch did sometimes fall into the trap of romanticizing the American folk as well as American history, but he did so to promote a more just, inclusive, and egalitarian national community. Asch's respect for

civil rights and his conception of American identity as rooted in cultural pluralism and social justice drove his recording ventures, especially in the realm of
education.

Despite Asch's efforts to release educational albums, the Newport Folk Festival's attempts to popularize traditional music, and *Sing Out!* magazine's critical examination of the various directions in which the revival was moving,
many feared that the message of the revival was becoming increasingly lost in
the commercial morass of the folk boom. Revivalists such as Seeger and Lomax
were most dismayed that commercial companies and agents who had no interest
in what folk music represented, or the context from which it came, had taken
the reins in bringing it to the masses. The "folk" music that the commercializers
pushed—rearranged and performed by white, middle-class singers—was a far
cry from the traditional music that the revivalists championed.

## "Neo-ethnics"

During the height of the commercial boom, a different group of musical enthusiasts emerged that defined folk music solely as traditional music. In response
to rampant popularization, these enthusiasts embraced a conservative view of
folk music that emphasized rural white and black traditions, largely to the exclusion of political or contemporary music. Figures such as Ralph Rinzler, a
member of the string band the Greenbrier Boys, believed that they, like Seeger,
served as a conduit channeling authentic folk music to the American public.
This cohort first emerged in the *Anthology of American Folk Music* generation
during the previous decade. In the liner notes that Rinzler wrote for the Greenbrier Boys' album, he insisted that if listeners liked their music, they should then
go back to the real thing (i.e., traditional musicians). Rinzler then took this
stance a step further and left the band to manage the traditional musicians Bill
Monroe and Tom (Clarence) Ashley, the latter of whom had appeared on *Anthology.* To help facilitate a wider appreciation of traditional singers, Rinzler,
Izzy Young, and John Cohen organized Friends of Old Time Music. The group
organized concerts of traditional performers who recorded albums sold under
the race and hillbilly categories of the 1920s and 1930s. By showcasing traditional music, these programs were reminiscent of the kind that Alan Lomax had
staged during the 1940s in New York City and that, more recently, Rinzler had
staged at the Newport Folk Festival.[26] Rinzler recognized that his turn to managing and promoting traditional performers stemmed from his anger at commercial culture for dismissing the musical traditions that he found both
aesthetically pleasing and culturally profound. As did Lomax, Rinzler lamented
the commercial music industry's refusal to record people who played the music
of their own communities, while people from outside the tradition achieved
fame and fortune for singing the very same songs.[27]

Rinzler was not alone in his effort to scrape away the commercialism of the
folk boom and stay on course by promoting traditional folk music and singers.

While he turned his attention to managing musicians, others such as the New Lost City Ramblers recorded albums of traditional—or, at least, antiquated—music. Focusing primarily on white rural music, and even old Tin Pan Alley songs, the Ramblers (Mike Seeger, John Cohen, and Tom Paley) were music collectors in the Harry Smith vein. They painstakingly studied commercial hillbilly recordings from the 1920s and 1930s and re-created that style as much as they could in their own performances in the effort to perfect what they viewed as an authentic sound unadulterated by musical interpreters.[28]

These musical purists even had a "fanzine" directed at their segment of the revival: the *Little Sandy Review*. Paul Nelson and Jon Pankake, the two University of Minnesota undergraduates who created the magazine, described themselves and their mission this way: "We are two people who love folk music very much and want to do all we can to help the good in it grow and the bad in it to perish. . . . [I]f you disagree, fine. More power to you." The rather cantankerous and humorous editors were unrelentingly critical of anything they saw as tainted by commercialism. For example, in response to a letter to the editor that asked whether it is wrong to rearrange a song to enhance its ability to communicate to a wider audience, the editors wrote, "The idea of 'arranging a song to communicate to most people' is a pretty nauseating one to us. This is what the Weavers and the Kingston Trio do. People must come to folk music themselves. You don't change or dilute the music and make it come to them. The real music is there, open to anyone who is willing to come take it in its purest form."[29] By accepting only traditional music as folk music, Pankake and Nelson represented a community of folk enthusiasts who rejected the work of even revival stalwarts such as Pete Seeger. Instead, they sought musical purity, believing that authentic folk music could be found among traditional performers reared in rural communities or in these artists' early recordings.

The number of purist sympathizers grew during the early 1960s, although not all of them agreed with Pankake and Nelson and their black-and-white definition of folk music. Largely situated on college campuses, these enthusiasts tended to form folk music clubs. At the University of Texas, Austin, Roger Abrahams organized "Thursday night folk sings," and at the University of Illinois, Archie Green helped form the Campus Folksong Club. In many ways, the college enthusiasts' interest in traditional folk music seems to be an example of the sociologist Anthony Giddens's argument that some communities rely on traditions in an effort to create or re-create a "personal and collective identity."[30] Many college-age folk fans dating back to the early 1950s used traditional folk music to establish their identities. The collective identity based on a shared interest in traditional music that came to define the traditionalist college "folkies" unified them as a cultural group. The networks that they developed with fellow folk devotees provided the students with a community, which was particularly valuable to those who constituted a small minority at their colleges, as was the case for the folkies at Austin.[31] In fact, they represented a form of counterculture protest, aligning themselves with an "imagined past with a rural or country tradition" that contrasted sharply with their urban or suburban upbringings.[32]

Initially, the students who became involved in these organizations were cultural outcasts, but soon their efforts to put the traditional back into folk music began to influence larger trends in the revival, and even the boom. In the winter of 1962, students at the University of Chicago hosted a folk festival that featured only traditional performers, a musical event that garnered much praise from older revivalists and young purists alike. Not only did the purists generate forums such as the *Little Sandy Review* to voice their opinions, but they also had record labels such as Folkways that catered to their tastes. By the mid-1960s, however, Folkways no longer dominated this field. Other record labels, including Vanguard, Prestige, and even Elektra, brought folk singers from the 1920s and 1930s—Mississippi John Hurt, Clarence Ashley, Furry Lewis, Son House, and others—back into the recording studio. Many purist revivalists also worked to bring these musicians on-stage and included them in popular music festivals such as the Newport Folk Festival, the Berkeley Folk Festival, and the NFF in addition to programs that had always included traditional musicians, such as the University of Chicago and Philadelphia festivals.

The purists responded to the commercialization of the folk boom by cultivating their own community of believers. As other revival programs attempted to broaden their horizons to adapt to the cultural changes of the era, the purists maintained conservative definitions of what qualified as authentic folk music—usually, rural music. Yet at the same time, they also broadened the politics of the movement. On the surface, many seemed to reject the overt political stances that had characterized the revival during the People's Songs era. However, as Van Ronk explained, just because musicians did not have a political repertoire, it did not mean that they were "apolitical." For instance, he refrained from performing topical songs because they did not suit his aesthetic style, but he often sang at rallies and other political events.[33] Other members of this cohort saw their actions as unambiguously political, although their views and actions differed from those of the first generation of revivalists. Like the earlier revivalists, they were strong proponents of cultural heterogeneity and wanted this diversity reflected musically. The folklorist Archie Green explained that he and others who shared his views wanted folk music to remain culturally distinctive and performed by people who came from these traditions rather than interpreted by groups such as the Kingston Trio, or even the Weavers, that made little to no effort to capture the songs' original styles. In fact, he considered Mike Seeger and other purists far more radical than other revivalists, including Pete Seeger, because the purists made painstaking efforts to emulate the style of traditional musicians, and thus preserve their techniques, during the middle of the folk boom, when most audiences were far more interested in the interpreters.[34] This radicalism may have been more cultural than political, in a strict sense, but cultural aspects were increasingly acquiring political dimensions as the era of identity politics grew on the margins of social activism.

## Neo-Almanacs?

Throughout much of the 1950s, the left wing of the revival struggled to weather the storm of anticommunism. Near the end of the decade, the political and social freeze that had seemed to envelope American politics and society started to thaw, and activism—or, at least, progressive social and political consciousness—began to reemerge. Of course, the Civil Rights Movement had been active in the South for much of the 1950s, but by the beginning of the following decade, a reform sentiment focusing on issues of economic as well as political inequality began to sweep across the national political landscape. One of the first signs of this shift in the political wind was a growing realization that many citizens' poverty, disfranchisement, and social and geographical isolation impeded their access to the American dream. Some social scientists began to study African American and Puerto Rican communities that were isolated in urban ghettoes. Others turned their attention to the rural poor, many of whom came from the regions where folklorists and enthusiasts had flocked to record music in previous decades. Michael Harrington's *The Other America* (1962) and Harry Caudill's *Night Comes to the Cumberlands* (1963), a study of poverty in the southern Appalachian Mountains, particularly ignited public interest in the plight of the "invisible poor" and influenced policies in the Kennedy and Johnson administrations.[35]

Despite the gross inequalities in American life, most Americans in the 1950s and early 1960s believed that the nation could be reformed through social and political change, which would bring previously marginalized groups into the national body politic. The Cold War may have prompted anxiety and fear, but it also simultaneously made Americans cling steadfastly to ideals such as democracy and civic participation.[36] The championing of civic ideals, combined with a realization that many Americans faced barriers to these ideals, helped the Civil Rights Movement to achieve its initial goals of federally mandated integration and voting rights through the U.S. Supreme Court's decision in *Brown v. Board of Education* (1954), the Civil Rights Act of 1964, and the Voting Rights Act of 1965. New reform energy also fed programs such as President John F. Kennedy's Peace Corps and President Lyndon B. Johnson's War on Poverty, which included the Economic Opportunity Act of 1964 and the Volunteers in Service to America (VISTA).

The revivalists were very much in tune to the possibilities of the new liberal era. In 1961, the folklorist Gene Bluestein linked the young fans of folk music to the era's Zeitgeist of hope: "This is still a young movement, composed of students who are filled with the stubborn idealism that permeates the songs of Negro slaves, miners, hoboes, and blues singers. If the Kennedy administration is serious in its proposal to recruit them into a corps which will work to push into new frontiers, they will respond en masse and bring their guitars with them."[37] Indeed, many revivalists did become active in programs for social and political change and often used their voices, guitars, and banjos to advance social causes. The folklorist Alan Jabbour described the revival in the early 1960s as a musical movement filled with idealistic fervor: "We in our revival sought out—and created—a music to express simultaneously our quest for cultural roots, our admiration of democratic ideals and values, [and] our solidarity with the culturally neglected."[38]

Even though the liberals who dominated the federal government gradually took notice of domestic problems and attempted to proffer solutions, young activists, much like their radical predecessors of the 1930s and 1940s, gravitated toward political alternatives. The baby boom generation of activists turned to the left largely because liberals only partially succeeded in helping the underclass; they made these struggles newsworthy but often failed to implement strong programs that would change the status quo. This half-success made people aware of the disjuncture between promises and reality: liberals promoted equality but did too little to make it a reality on the ground for people who needed it the most. While they called for political fairness, they steered clear of policies or programs that crossed the line from economic reform to economic restructuring. Eventually, the emerging activists would come to define their movement in opposition to liberalism. Liberalism, in their view, saw traditional politics and the electoral process as the key way to solve domestic problems, whereas the new activists sought to transform American society politically, to "redeem" the nation's "democratic values," through direct action. If change was to be had, liberals wanted it to be gradual so as not to cause any reaction against it; keeping things in order was key. This, to young activists, was too slow, at best, and something that stifled any meaningful reform, at worst. Therefore, they took it upon themselves to be the impetus for change.[39]

Thus, the "old" New Left, as the historian and former participant Todd Gitlin refers to the movement during its early years, "aspired to be the voice, the conscience, and goad of its generation," and it served as a catalyst for the rise of student activism in the late 1960s. Initially, however, the New Left was a fringe movement, and members proudly wore their badge of marginality, believing that their support for socially and economically disadvantaged citizens ran contrary to mainstream, middle-class America—a social, political, and economic stratum from which most of the members came.[40]

Many members of the New Left believed that the movement was sui generis, wholly unconnected to the leftist movements that had preceded it. This "self-flattering idea of a virgin birth" allowed the young activists not only to break out of definitional confines that bound members of the Old Left but also to separate themselves from the politics of anticommunism. However, they were connected, at least ideologically, to many progressive groups that predated the Cold War. For example, Students for a Democratic Society (SDS), an organization that became the locus of the New Left, formed as the student branch of the socialist League for Industrial Democracy, which began as a socialist organization in 1905.[41] The new members of SDS, however, began to reject the rhetoric of their parent organization. Michael Harrington, the young spokesman for the

Socialist Party, explained that at one point he tried to get Tom Hayden, a leading member of SDS, to join the Young People's Socialist League (YPSL). Hayden agreed on almost every reform issue that Harrington advocated: the importance of the Civil Rights Movement, social justice, and economic reform. He believed in everything but the word "socialism," because to him the term was too bound up in a European context and thus disconnected from the American public. Hayden deliberately "wanted to speak American."[42]

Al Haber, the president of SDS, shared Hayden's sentiment. In 1961, he wrote that SDS should become an intellectual source for activism, its purpose to provide student activists, many of whom were skittish about "ideologies," with a framework for action. However, even though they eschewed labels such as "socialist," many worked to achieve the same kind of political and economic equality as did their socialist—and communist—forebears. After all, Haber's ultimate hope for SDS was that it would generate the kind of reforms necessary to bring marginalized and disfranchised citizens into the political process.[43] Essentially, that meant that SDS members would fight to make American political and economic institutions more democratic, to *reform* the system rather than overthrow it. Their words may have marked a disjuncture from the ideological Old Left, but their desire to open the American political system to all citizens was reminiscent of the goals of activists who emerged during the Popular Front.

One clear connection between the two generations is that many early activists in the New Left were children of Old Leftists. These "red diaper babies" maintained what the sociologists Ron Eyerman and Andrew Jamison refer to as a "habitus of protest" that was embedded in their families and the communities in which they were raised.[44] These New Left activists were raised in families that valued political agitation, even during the era of the Red Scare when political protest was a risky endeavor. Abrahams explains that he, like many other activists, grew up in a "highly political" German Jewish family; as a teenager, he, unlike Hayden, did become a member of YPSL. During the early 1960s, Abrahams observed that the political activism of the era had seeped into the growing folk community, noting that the crowd that gathered to swap songs on Sunday afternoons in Washington Square Park in New York City was "highly politicized," meaning that it was highly leftist.[45]

Through this observation, Abrahams substantiates another aspect of the "habitus of protest" that Eyerman and Jamison attribute to the American left. As they explain, protest songs have been used in various movements that spanned generations and thereby "have been important in linking generations and in connecting movements."[46] Through folk music, the leftist revivalists of the 1930s and 1940s expressed political views via the same mode of cultural expression that many young activists adopted in the early 1960s. Gitlin also recognizes that the folk music that political revivalists popularized in the 1940s not only linked the Old Left activists to the New Left generation but also connected these young activists to other politically minded youth who were not raised within political families. Folk music "was the main bridge between red-diaper babydom as a whole and the rest of their generation," and Gitlin recounts that he first learned of political folk music through the father of his "red diaper" girlfriend.[47] Richard Flacks, another leading member of SDS, partly attributes his political awakening to folk music, and he credits folk music for influencing the political development of many in his cohort, declaring, perhaps jokingly, "To understand the *Port Huron Statement,* you have to understand Bob Dylan."[48]

The 1960s activists did not turn to an established political party to help push their goals; nor did they adopt a clear ideological position. Yet the New Left, much like the Old Left of the Popular Front generation, continued to believe in the promise of democratic Americanism and civic equality. Although heyday of the Popular Front had long since ended, Gitlin declares, "The idea of it could be sung. . . . [F]olk [music] was the living prayer of a defunct movement, the consolation and penumbra of its children, gingerly holding the place of a Left in American culture." If the spirit of the Popular Front was carried through to the 1960s via folk music, then the "idea" that the folk revival channeled into the new era of activism was the promise of American democracy—cultural and political. Many of the student activists in the Student Nonviolent Coordinating Committee (SNCC), and the Economic Research and Action Project (ERAP) tried to become "instruments of the voiceless voices" that would make the plight of the American poor visible on a national scale.[49] Furthermore, many former members of the Popular Front joined in the revival of overt activism, which served to provide physical as well as spiritual connections between the two eras of left-wing activity.

During the boom, folk music magazines, shows, and radio programs proliferated, yet the revival did not provide a literary outlet for its left-leaning members, young and old. With the increased competition, *Sing Out!*—the former political mouthpiece of the left side of the revival—had discontinued polemics and focused on the dynamics of the revival and the boom. During *Sing Out!* magazine's political and topical lull, a new periodical made its debut on the folk music scene and quickly became a key forum for young folk music fans who participated in, or sympathized with, New Left activism. Intended as a source for spreading topical songs, *Broadside* began in the apartment of former Almanac Singer Agnes "Sis" Cunningham and her husband, Gordon Friesen, both of whom were involved in People's Songs. *Broadside* was actually the brainchild of a few revivalists from the People's Songs era: the songwriter Malvina Reynolds, who initiated the idea, and Pete Seeger, who enthusiastically endorsed the plan. Cunningham and Friesen had suffered hard times during the blacklist of the previous decade, but they remained strong in their political beliefs and welcomed the opportunity to revive the mission of printing and distributing socially significant songs that began with the *People's Songs* bulletin. Cunningham and Friesen printed *Broadside* on a mimeograph machine, giving it a production quality that reflected their limited budget. Despite the magazine's modesty, many folk revivalists believed in its message, and major figures, including Pete and Toshi Seeger and Moses Asch, lent their financial support.

Friesen and Cunningham printed the first issue of *Broadside* in February 1962 and continued to issue the magazine every other month. The debut issue opened with an explanation of the magazine's purpose. Friesen reasoned that because so many songwriters were composing topical songs, "The only way to find out if a song is good is to give it wide circulation and let the singers and listeners decide for themselves." The opening editorial then continued to shield the magazine from the authenticity debates: "BROADSIDE may never publish a song that could be called a 'folk song,' but let us remember that many of our best folk songs were topical songs in their inception."[50] Following the opening editorial are songs by Malvina Reynolds and Agnes Cunningham; Bob Dylan also contributed his "Talking John Birch Blues" to the magazine's inaugural issue.

When Cunningham and Friesen began *Broadside,* they were riding a wave of interest in topical songs. They believed that the popularity of topical material stemmed from the rising dissatisfaction among American youth about how the nation was operating. The growing disillusionment over the failure of liberal promises prompted songwriters to generate music that directly addressed social, political, and economic problems. To the writers of these songs, the folk revival to which they belonged was not merely a musical fad. Rather, it was a large part of the movement culture of the 1960s. Moreover, as with People's Songs, the topical songwriters were still connected to the people. Many became active in movements that sought to correct injustices in American life. From walking picket lines to traveling south to participate in voting registration drives and singing during the Berkeley Free Speech Movement, Phil Ochs, Tom Paxton, Bob Dylan, Joan Baez, and singers like them appeared to practice what they preached. Cunningham and Friesen sought to spread the songs that helped sustain this activism among a wider audience, mainly to support the causes themselves. They had no illusions that the songs printed in *Broadside* would be commercially successful; they just hoped that the material would help boost the morale of those engaged in people's struggles. Friesen explained, "We began *Broadside* for the purpose of providing an outlet for song writers deeply motivated by local struggles rather than aiming at becoming 'stars.'"[51] Ultimately, Cunningham and Friesen hoped to preserve the new songs as documents of American grassroots activism.

One theme that was prevalent in the early issues of *Broadside* was nuclear war. The magazine featured numerous songs on the topic, including Dylan's "Let Me Die in My Footsteps," and several articles on the fears and health effects of nuclear testing. Friesen commented on this trend in an editorial in the fifth issue, in which he explained, "If our songwriters reflect the mood of the country, the number one concern of Americans today is the problem of peace and the deadly nuclear arms race. For the theme of peace—and related subjects such as renewed atomic bomb testing and fallout shelters—occurs in the largest percentage of songs being submitted."[52] In addition to antinuclear songs, the magazine printed songs that preached environmentalism, such as "The Indiana Dunes," which called for protection of the dunes around Lake Michigan that were in danger of being destroyed to make way for a new steel plant. Julius Lester contributed songs from the Civil Rights Movement in the South and black freedom songs from the North. After 1963, *Broadside* began featuring songs protesting the escalating military presence in Vietnam.

In addition to new songs, *Broadside* kept its reading audience apprised of protest activities. In 1964, Bob Cohen contributed "The Mississippi Caravan of Music," an article about a group of folk singers to which he belonged and that included Barbara Dane, Judy Collins, Peter La Farge, Phil Ochs, and Pete Seeger. The group had performed at more than thirty Mississippi Freedom Centers. The caravan, Cohen wrote, "demonstrated the important contribution of Negro music in every aspect of American musical and cultural history. For children who have been educated—or rather brainwashed—by the public school system to accept the myth of their own inferiority this was an exhilarating revelation."[53] Shortly before the rise of Black Nationalism, the political folk revivalists advocated racial pride along with political activism.

*Broadside* was the political antidote to the commercialism of the boom. Ochs, a singer, songwriter, and frequent *Broadside* contributor, noted the need for the type of music that the magazine published, writing in 1963 that before the era of mass media, folk singers acted as "a traveling newspaper spreading tales through music." Now, during an era of "forced conformity," the folk singer of the 1960s served this role again by breaking the silence of media censorship.[54] While the political revivalists, young and old, appreciated the mission that *Broadside* undertook, other revivalists did not. For example, *Broadside* became a perennial whipping boy in the *Little Sandy Review*. Nelson and Pankake regularly criticized *Broadside*'s political focus, which led the magazine to print musically weak songs as long as they contained a progressive message. The "protesteer" songwriters featured in *Broadside* composed heavily formulaic songs, according to Nelson and Pankake, to the extent that "in place of talent, we get a sort of reverse–Norman Rockwell Formula for Protest in which the key words are Negro, Bomb, Brotherhood, Shelter, Black and White Together, Capitalist, Politician, Win, Fight, Boss, Worker, Freedom, etc. (Try writing your own *Broadside* song by using this Formula; it shouldn't take you over five minutes.)"[55] While the editors of the *Little Sandy Review* excoriated the quality of the songs and songwriters in *Broadside,* many of those songs (and songwriters) soon found their way into another major revival outlet: *Sing Out!*

At the beginning of their thirteenth anniversary issue in 1964, the editors of *Sing Out!* reaffirmed their political commitment and began to include material by the topical songwriters from the *Broadside* group.[56] Although it may not have been as obvious as it was in the past, the editors wrote, "We have always been partial to songs of social protest and topical comment—and readers will continue to find this type of material in every issue of SING OUT!"[57] The editorial also calls for readers to submit folk songs that are both traditional and contemporary, addressing the social and political concerns of America of the 1960s. In 1965, Irwin Silber debuted his column "Fan the Flames," which became a regular feature during the rest of his tenure at the magazine. In the column, Silber strung together political musings, social commentaries, and general complaints about the contemporary state of affairs. Taking his title from the Industrial Workers of the World's *Little Red Songbook* slogan "Songs to Fan the Flames of Discontent," Silber wrote in the first column, "Sometimes it seems as though America's conscience, at best a lonesome waif in this 'affluent' society, has found a home in the folk song coffee houses."[58] In a column a few months later, Silber commented that a new group was taking up the torch that he and other revivalists had carried through People's Songs and People's Artists: "A new generation of young songwriters, talented and with social consciences honed to the cutting edge by the silent frustration of the 1950s, began to produce a dizzying crop of songs that did not fear to comment on the social realities of the times. This has been one of the healthiest developments in American cultural life of the past decade."[59]

Topical songwriters of the early 1960s were the heirs to the People's Songs tradition of composing songs to aid in the people's struggles; for this generation, those struggles included the Civil Rights Movement, free speech, and protesting the escalation of the war in Vietnam. Other commentators on the revival also noted this turn. Robert Shelton of the *New York Times* cited Ochs as exemplifying this new trend. A topical folk singer, Ochs, Shelton wrote, "has become a sort of musical editorial writer" of his generation. With songs like "Talking Cuban Crisis" and "The Ballad of Billie Sol," Ochs's "satire is trenchant and his opinions are controversial."[60] Indeed they were, and many young folk singers began to follow the path of politically relevant folk music. *Sing Out!* lauded these efforts and encouraged topical songwriters such as Peter La Farge, Tom Paxton, Mark Spolestra, Phil Ochs, and Bob Dylan, by printing their songs and explaining their meaning. In 1965, the magazine featured another symposium on "Topical Songs and Folksinging." Josh Dunson, also a writer for *Broadside,* explained the trend. "In these songs," he wrote, "there is anger and disgust with the values of the preceding generation: the political values that have dictated war, the cultural values that have supported segregation, and the social values that have ordered chastity until marriage."[61] Like the first generation of revivalists, the members of the new generation expressed their anger at the status quo through song.

Yet at the same time, the new topical songs differed from the topical songs of the People's Songs era in several respects. Many veered away from an agitprop approach and instead addressed broad themes or targeted specific issues through personal perspectives. Some older revivalists criticized this trend. Moses Asch wrote, "Most protest songs that have existed and are still meaningful in today's world use a militant action, a 'for-something' expression as opposed to the 'let's-weep, let's-look-into-our-souls, let's-reflect, let's-examine' attitude of the so-called school of contemporary 'poets' writing and singing songs of today."

Dunson noted the new approach that young topical songwriters were taking, as well. "You will never find the endorsement of a world system or even of an organization," he wrote. "These songs are written in the first person. Although there is compassion, there are no proposals. This is in contrast to the pretty clear goals of earlier social protest songwriters of the IWW through People's Songs."[62] Although Dunson's observation ignores the fact that many of these songwriters did support specific organizations, such as SDS, SNCC, and the Congress of Racial Equality (CORE), he correctly notes that the topical songwriters of the baby boom imbued their songs with individualism, a perspective that was largely lacking in topical songs from the People's Songs era. Michael Denning provides a good way to understand what created this generational disjuncture. He explains that while the Popular Front generation may have trained—or, at the very least, influenced—the activists of the New Left, the later activists responded to their own set of circumstances, to the unique conditions they faced as the postwar generation.[63] Therefore, even if they had the same concerns as the Popular Front generation, the means by which they sought to change the system differed. The area where this disjuncture was perhaps the most apparent, and where the New Left clearly charted its own path, was in civil rights activism.

Of all of the social and political causes, the Civil Rights Movement was the primary galvanizing force for political activism in the early 1960s. Many students in SDS participated in this struggle because they believed that achieving political rights was the first step toward securing economic and social justice. During the early 1960s, black and white students in civil rights organizations such as SNCC initiated voter registration drives for disfranchised African Americans in the South, particularly in Mississippi. Yet it was not simply a matter of getting southern blacks the right to vote, but the prospect of helping to bring them into a democratic political process, that inspired many of the activists to move from southern cities to rural towns and to travel from Michigan to Mississippi to assist in the voting rights efforts.

Collectively, these student activists believed in the promise of "participatory democracy." According to Tom Hayden, the phrase meant "action"; students were now rebelling against the previous decade of apathy and, as Hayden later explained, "What's the opposite of apathy? Active participation. Citizenship. Making history. Voting was not enough. Having a democracy in which you have an apathetic citizenship spoon-fed information by a monolithic media, periodically voting was very weak, a declining form of democracy." In a participatory democratic system, citizens become directly involved in the process of decision making regarding decisions that will affect their lives. Political decisions are made collectively rather than by representatives so that everyone can weigh in equally on local and national issues. Advocates of participatory democracy call for active citizenship wherein citizens become fully engaged in the decision-making process so that "participation" becomes one with "control."[64]

It is clear that these were guiding principles for SNCC and SDS programs that stressed community mobilization, such as the Mississippi field projects that educated sharecroppers, farmers, and domestic workers with little to no formal education and no experience in leadership positions—civic or religious—to become leaders in the freedom struggle. According to the Mississippi project head Robert Moses, "They were not credentialed people. . . . Yet, through the process, they became leaders." Collective decision making became the way to ensure that future black leaders remained "responsible to their constituents."[65] In voter registration drives and freedom schools that SNCC members organized throughout the Deep South, activists taught the people how to become active citizens, and this is what inspired their northern counterparts. Although the meaning of "participatory democracy" would change over the course of the decade, its emphasis on directing disfranchised people into the political system through grassroots action was, as the journalist James Miller argues, "what was *new* about this left."[66]

Amid this renewed activism, many folk revivalists—young and old—traveled to the South to join in the grassroots civil rights efforts. Pete Seeger and Theodore Bikel were the first to participate in southern marches, but others soon followed. Odetta, Joan Baez, Bob Dylan, and Peter, Paul, and Mary performed in Washington, D.C., on the morning of the March on Washington in 1963; the SNCC Freedom Singers, Seeger, Dylan, Marian Anderson, Mahalia Jackson, and Peter, Paul, and Mary performed at the evening concert. For three days in May 1964, Guy Carawan hosted a "Sing for Freedom" workshop at the Gammon Theological Seminary in Atlanta that brought the southern activists Fannie Lou Hamer, Bernice Johnson Reagon, and Andrew Young together with the northern topical folk singers Tom Paxton, Phil Ochs, and Len Chandler.[67]

Back in the North, Irwin Silber and Robert Shelton kept folk fans apprised of the freedom struggle in *Sing Out!* and the *New York Times,* respectively. Folkways also kept listeners informed about the civil rights efforts in the South by releasing albums of music from the movement that Guy Carawan compiled, such as *The Nashville Sit-In Story: Songs and Scenes of Nashville Lunch Counter Desegregation (by the Sit-In Participants)* (1960); *WNEW's Story of Selma* (1965), which featured songs that Pete Seeger and Len Chandler collected during the march; and *The Story of Greenwood, Mississippi* (1965), a documentary narrated by Robert Moses about the voter registration drives. Asch also released educational albums such as *Songs of the American Negro Slaves,* which included liner notes written by the historian John Hope Franklin, and two albums featuring W. E. B. Du Bois commenting on American racial conditions: *Socialism and the American Negro* (1960) and *W. E. B. Du Bois: A Recorded Autobiography, Interview with Moses Asch* (1961). Asch saw the Civil Rights Movement as history in the making and set out to document it, much as he sought to record other critical aspects of American (and global) life. In doing so, Asch sought to aid in what he believed to be a greater good, which he explained to Carawan in 1959 as giving "dignity and understanding to ALL peoples." This is what he hoped to do by recording the struggles of black Americans to secure their democratic rights.[68]

Many of the musicians who became directly involved in the Civil Rights Movement were connected to the Newport Folk Festival. These affiliations further politicized the festival and rendered it a staunch advocate in this struggle for political and social justice. The Newport program of 1963 reflected its intensifying politicization, first by including the Freedom Singers, a group formed of SNCC members that Bernice Johnson Reagon organized and Toshi Seeger managed. The politics of Newport became even more overt when SNCC leaders and Joan Baez led a group of more than six hundred movement supporters who had been in the audience of the Saturday night concert down the streets of Newport to Truro Park for a rally in support of the impending March on Washington.[69] Even those who did not participate in the impromptu march were provided with a history of the movement in Shelton's article "Battle Hymns of the Republic," which described the role of folk music in the Civil Rights Movement and emphasized the Freedom Singers' significance. The 1963 festival also provided the iconic picture of Pete Seeger, Bob Dylan, Joan Baez, and Peter, Paul, and Mary linking arms with Bernice Johnson Reagon and other Freedom Singers in a rendition of "We Shall Overcome" at the end of the first evening concert.

By 1964, musical activists were openly praised in the festival program. In his article "The Year of the Topical Song," Ochs complimented Carawan in particular for his work in disseminating protest music and gathering socially active musicians for the Freedom Movement. As Shelton remarked in the *New York Times* after the 1964 festival, "The festival closed in a symbolic finale merging music and social meaning. Odetta led other performers and an audience of 15,000 in two songs of the Negro integration movement. The social commitment of folk music blended with its aesthetic core in a triumphant conclusion. There was a democratizing spirit about this fusion of Negro and white musical forms and about the people who are the conveyor belts of these traditions that was little short of inspiring." Shelton also quoted a "recording official" commenting that the festival was "almost a utopian dream. All this love, brotherhood and good music seem unreal compared to what is happening in the country today."[70] With 47,000 admissions paid for the 1963 festival and 15,000 attendees at the first concert of the 1964 festival alone, the Newport Folk Festival was a prime vehicle for illustrating the importance of the Civil Rights Movement in the South to a predominantly white, northern public audience. Through these efforts, the organizers of Newport encouraged the new generation to ensure that the promise of civil rights applied to all Americans and to mobilize music in the effort to secure this promise.

At the beginning of 1966, *Sing Out!* printed a long article about a conference held at the Highlander Folk School that aimed "to encourage and promote grassroots southern Negro culture." When the conference was held, the Civil Rights Movement was undergoing sweeping changes. Many people had begun to question the compatibility of black identity and American identity. In this climate of mounting identity crisis, Carawan and other revivalists tried to initiate a last-ditch effort to bring the movement back to its cultural roots and to ensure that folk traditions played a role in the new black consciousness movement. The conference connected white topical singers from the North to black activists from the South. Together, they drafted the following statement:

> This is an effort to confront ourselves with the problem of our identity in American culture. Negroes have created world-wide musical language in ragtime, jazz, blues, gospel, rock 'n' roll, etc., but they are ashamed to accept the richer root music and folk tradition out of which all this emerged. It will be our attempt through community gatherings and other projects to counteract this feeling of shame and this mis-education and thereby to renew the interest of the Negro community in its own artistic output, to the end that much beautiful music be saved from oblivion, and that the habits which produce it to stay alive, so that more songs will grow in the future.

To accomplish these goals, the attendees—civil rights workers, folklorists, black academics, and field project workers—from across the South agreed to work to alter educational curricula to encourage cultural pride, conduct research on black musical forms, and develop community projects to encourage local people to become involved. The conference members drafted resolutions that combined cultural democracy with the ideas of cultural and racial pride that were burgeoning within the movement: "We intend to encourage the Negro Community to come alive in its own spirit and on its own terms: We stand firmly opposed to those who hold that because the Negroes are winning their Civil Rights that they must be assimilated into the sterile ways of Main Street America. Political and economic progress do not have to mean conformity. A rich and beautiful America should be as culturally varied as possible." Yet at the same time, there was a sense of togetherness, a unity within diversity that stood in marked contrast to the separatist position that later came to characterize racial nationalism. Through folk music, according to the attendees, blacks could develop a sense of pride both in their racial distinctiveness and as members of the national community: "In our folk music we will discover a bridge toward a prideful and democratic meeting ground with the white people of the South."[71] For the time being, racial pride still seemed compatible with a pluralist Americanism.

During the first half of the 1960s, the Civil Rights Movement brought political folk revivalists together, spanning the generations of revivalists from the People's Songs era to the baby boomers. By mid-decade, the escalation of the Vietnam War also prompted members of the New Left to mobilize. While the media tended to focus on the youth element of the antiwar protests, especially since many occurred on college campuses, the antiwar movement was not restricted to the young. As with civil rights, many older leftists were active in the movement, and many People's Songs members took up the banner against what they saw as a new phase of American imperialism.

After Lyndon Johnson sent ground troops into Vietnam in 1965, the American protest movement began to pick up steam. That same year, SDS organized a March on Washington to protest the escalation of the war. The march attracted fifteen thousand marchers, by one conservative estimate, five thousand more than SDS expected. As Ochs, Judy Collins, and the Freedom Singers sang about peace, the marchers walked in lines of eighty abreast.[72] Many folk revivalists threw themselves into the antiwar movement as the war progressed. Folkways Records captured the developing movement in *Berkeley Teach-In: Vietnam* (1965), in which students and professors gathered to discuss the war and its consequences. This was symbolic for many, not just because it denounced American actions, but also because it marked an end to the pervasive timidity over displaying left politics that had dominated the academy during the previous decade.

Also in 1965, Irwin Silber and Barbara Dane suggested turning a hootenanny that was planned for Carnegie Hall into a "sing-in for peace" to protest the war. They invited folk singers from around the country to come and sing one song each for the two-night event. More than sixty performers participated, and the first night sold out. Even though much of the audience remained apathetic to the war and attended the event primarily for entertainment, a large coterie of antiwar folk revivalists was present. After the second performance ended at almost 4:00 AM, many audience members marched three miles to the Village Gate music club to continue the music.[73] Individual revivalists also protested the war in their own ways. Joan Baez followed the historian Staughton Lynd's lead and refused to pay the percentage of her income tax that she calculated went to the war effort. Ochs and other songwriters wrote numerous antiwar songs, such as "I Ain't Marching Anymore" and "The War Is Over." The war also inspired Pete Seeger to compose "Waist Deep in the Big Muddy," which he sang on the *Smothers Brothers Comedy Hour* in 1968. CBS initially censored Seeger's performance because he openly criticized Johnson's handling of the war through lyrics such as, "We're waist deep in the Big Muddy / And the big fool says to push on." That year, Silber and Dane published *The Vietnam Songbook,* which contained topical songs by contemporary songwriters and traditional songs from Vietnam—north and south.

The combination of civil rights and antiwar protests indicates that the early activists of the New Left and the Old Leftists of the People's Songs generation united through a mutual faith that the nation could be reformed and that they could lead the way. They believed in the promise of constitutional ideals and that the American political system could work if it became inclusive of, and accessible to, all citizens. Tom Hayden went as far as to suggest in 1965 that SDS should organize a national convention to generate a Constitutional Congress "as a symbolic gesture that would dramatize the political philosophy of the New Left to the rest of the country" and bring underrepresented minorities together to challenge a system that excluded them.[74] Despite the radical—and unfeasible—nature of this proposal, it was grounded in American political thought.

During its early years, SDS and the New Left in general were motivated by domestic problems such as the suppression of civil liberties, of intellectual inquiry, and of any social activism during the anticommunist crusades, as well as the vast inequities in American society. Ultimately, the activists believed that "an American radical's first and overwhelming priority was radical change in America," according to Todd Gitlin.[75] This same belief had inspired political revivalists and other activists to join the Popular Front in the 1930s and sustain that effort into the postwar and Cold War years. Many of them continued to believe in the possibility of reforming America into the 1960s and joined forces with the young activists of the New Left. In 1968, Pete Seeger reiterated this message to an audience attending a forum at the Ford Hall in Boston. In a talk replayed over the radio, Seeger told listeners that "freedom and peace begin in your own home and your own community" and that they should continue to fight for social justice, even if the cause seemed hopeless. Rather than withdraw from society in disgust, they should "figure that the world's got at least a 50-50 chance, and maybe your little grain of sand as much as mine might help tip the scale and it might be the grain of sand which would mean the human race will keep going."[76] All the activists had to do was keep moving forward.

Together, the revivalists of the Old Left and the New Left promoted a culturally and politically democratic Americanism that had begun to take shape during the 1930s. Unlike liberals, Old Leftists were committed to direct action, particularly in the form of strikes and marches. The days of singing folk songs on picket lines alongside striking workers and at union rallies may have ended, but the age of civil rights marches in the South was in full swing, and the era of antiwar rallies in the North had just begun. Further connecting these two generations were the ideas of civic education. The educational initiatives that young civil rights activists and SDS members taught in the Freedom Schools in the rural South had many similarities to the older leftist revivalists' educational programs in centers such as the Highlander Folk School. In fact, Highlander served as one of the main conduits between the revivalists and activists of the Popular Front and the New Left. In 1932, Don West and Myles Horton established Highlander in Monteagle, Tennessee, as a labor college designed to both protect southern mountain culture and improve the lives of local residents through education. West and Horton strongly advocated civil rights for southern blacks, but Highlander initially focused on labor conditions that affected local residents—most of whom were white. By the early 1950s, however, the school had shifted directions and turned from labor organization to facilitating civil rights mobilization in the South.[77] Zilphia Horton, music director at Highlander, worked to bring folk music into the labor movement in the 1930s and 1940s and continued the effort in civil rights activism during the 1950s. Horton was responsible for teaching Pete Seeger the song "We Shall

Overcome," which she had learned in 1946 from striking members of the Food, Tobacco, Agricultural and Allied Workers of America. Seeger then published the song in the *People's Songs* bulletin, and eventually it filtered into the Civil Rights Movement.[78] Horton died in 1956, but her efforts to use Highlander as a way to bring folk music—particularly, traditional black folk songs—into civil rights activism was sustained by Carawan and his wife, Candie, throughout the 1960s.[79]

In addition to uniting activists of different generations, sites such as Highlander generated tools used to sustain social and political activism. As a white Californian, Carawan was an outsider to both the South and the black civil rights struggle. Yet he believed in the cause, and like the members of People's Songs before him, he believed that folk music could serve as a powerful tool in the fight for social and political justice. As early as 1959, Carawan wrote in a letter to Moses Asch, "There is such a great potential here [at Highlander] for developing a program around folk music and to make the integration movement in the south into a singing movement." The movement was already a "singing" movement, but Carawan wanted "to develop a musical program suiting today[']s needs," and he even used his own talent to support that effort, further noting, "A lot of the singing I'll be doing in the south I'll do for free because I believe in it." Activists from the Popular Front era, the Cold War era, and the New Left era also believed in it, but despite the commonality, generational differences did exist such that when the young activists began to increasingly respond to political circumstances in their own way, many older activists found it difficult to relate to the young members. While this created a divide between the Old Left and New Left activists, it also generated schisms within the New Left itself—schisms that widened as the decade wore on.

## Conclusion

During the early 1960s, folk music had become a cultural phenomenon that encompassed numerous groups. At the same time that teenage fans filled auditorium seats for episodes of *Hootenanny,* other young enthusiasts flatly rejected anything that seemed to lack authenticity—anything that was not traditional. These musical purists attempted to preserve and promote musical traditions that were in danger of being lost in American culture. For the more politically conscious purists, the politics of their programs were rooted in cultural preservation and cultural advocacy. Essentially, what had begun in the late 1950s as divergent segments of the revival had turned into independent trajectories by the middle of the 1960s.

Throughout the boom years, however, many core revivalists remained committed to promoting a democratic Americanism through folk music, aided by a new generation of movement members. Political revivalists of the People's Songs and baby boom generations once again brought folk music into democratic reform. Even revivalists who did not directly partake in the new wave of activism tried to teach children about social and cultural difference (and in-equality) via different types of folk music. The programs and rhetoric of the revival may have shifted over time, but the message of the movement remained the same. During the first few years of the 1960s, the revivalists, like many ac-tivists, still believed that the national cultural, political, and social systems *could* be reformed. Scraping the corrosion of commercialism from folk music, the revivalists tried to reclaim the music of their movement and use it again to publicize the democratic Americanism that had been at the core of the revival since the very beginning.

# 6

## A BUST AND A BEGINNING

The 1960s opened with a marked degree of optimism among those who sought social and political change. The decade closed with an equal amount of disillusionment and anger when those changes failed to become reality. By the end of the era, the political ideas that had united the early New Leftists dissolved; the folk revivalists experienced a similar fate as members, no longer interested in the message of the movement, increasingly went their separate ways. The fragmentation of both groups, the cultural and political anger that seethed across the country, and the political gains of the "Silent Majority" seemed to sound the final death knell for the politically progressive Americanism that was central to the revival. By the close of the decade, the revival as a movement had ended.

Of the many factors that precipitated the dissolution of the revival, the most obvious were the divisions between the revivalists. What had begun as divergent groups during the 1950s turned into factions by the middle of the 1960s, and more enthusiasts and revivalists began to openly reject what had been a primary objective of the revival: using folk music to generate a democratic, pluralist Americanism. In the midst of these internal shifts, the revivalists had to contend with the explosion of folk music in pop culture. Now, with a national spotlight fixed on folk music, what the revivalists did with the music—whether using it for political reform or merely expanding what could be classified under the rubric of folk music—became contestable on a much larger scale. The political revivalists of the New Left upheld the People's Songs mission of using songs for political and social activism. As these figures remained embedded in the revival, other folk music enthusiasts tried to sever the ties between folk music and social politics. The purists, for example, rejected the revival's connection between folk music and constructs of Americanism even before the folk boom. Furthermore, the rise of radical politics and cultural nationalism among young leftists in the later years of the 1960s caused many older, formerly centrist revivalists to turn to the center right. Clinging to a vision of American unity that was becoming increasingly irrelevant in national life, these revivalists tried to sever the connection between folk music and political radicalism or counter-culture movements. In the midst of this turmoil, still other revivalists tried to alter the movement to appease everyone—the traditionalists, the conservative revivalists, the leftists, and the popular enthusiasts. Yet it was a lost cause. By the second half of the decade, the differences in views and opinions over-whelmed the movement.

The revival's internecine fighting closely mirrored what was occurring else-where in America. Reactions against the freedom struggle after it moved into northern cities, coupled with the Civil Rights Movement's own failures, led some activists to reject integration in favor of cultural separatism, a turn that was further inspired by the rise of Black Nationalism. As the Civil Rights Move-ment splintered, the New Left divided along fault lines of its own. Many activ-ists who faced their own challenges within the movement left to support the rise of identity-specific movements, while others joined Jerry Rubin's and Abbie Hoffman's absurdist and theatrical Yippies. In general, efforts at reforming the *nation* became almost obsolete as young activists carved out their own identi-ties and eschewed any connection to a national body.

Amid this factionalism, and what appeared to be the end of progressive Americanism, multiculturalism, a movement based on updated concepts of cul-tural democracy emerged. Many of the new multiculturalists were educational theorists who advocated multiethnic education. Through curricular reform, these figures sought to generate a version of Americanism that bore remarkable similarities to the unity-in-diversity view of national identity that first emerged with cultural pluralism, cosmopolitanism, and regionalism. While not a direct continuation of early twentieth-century pluralism, this wing of multicultural-ists sought to ensure that the overarching national identity incorporated the cultures of historically marginalized communities. In the midst of this, many former revivalists became involved in organizing a festival that aimed to give a voice to the voiceless and to encourage ethnic and racial minorities to take pride in their cultural traditions. The Smithsonian Festival of American Folklife (FAF), in effect, provides an epilogue to the narrative of the folk music revival. Although the revival as a movement had ended, some of the ideas that moti-vated core revivalists continued to inform the design and the mission behind the Smithsonian festival.

## The Turn

The end of the revival did not come as a great surprise to many involved; the seeds of its destruction were noticeably present during the height of the folk boom. This was partly revealed through the changes that the Newport Folk Festival began to undergo after it resumed in 1963. Rural fiddlers, urban song-writers, blues musicians, and American Indian dancers all contributed to the revived festival's "calliope of folk artists."[1] The Newport programs featured tra-ditional artists during smaller daytime performances and workshops, but the organizers often excluded these performers from the large evening concerts. This had begun to change by the middle of the decade, and the festival of 1966 marked a significant turn toward traditional music. This shift, however, took a toll on ticket sales, and the press coverage was not the same as it had been. To maintain a steady revenue stream, Newport continued to feature big names of questionable folk pedigree to attract an audience, and this led to confusion over Newport's identity as a festival. Even Robert Shelton observed that the festival was pulling in too many directions. The Newport committee's desire to cater to various tastes rendered the programs "kaleidoscopic" to the degree that it was difficult to determine what the festival's focus was anymore.[2]

The rise of the political singer-songwriter of the 1960s was an important trigger of this fragmentation. Despite the commercial nature of performers such as the Kingston Trio and even the Weavers, there was little dispute that the songs they covered came from a traditional folk canon. The songs of topical revivalist singer-songwriters, however, were not so easy to classify. Shelton dis-missed the debate altogether when he wrote, "The quibbling over definition—whether these are 'topical songs' or 'contemporary folk songs'—seems a waste of energy. Topical song writers Tom Paxton and Bob Dylan . . . are writing of universals in a folk vein. Some of the topical songs may endure, may enter oral tradition, and are definitely written in the cadences and language of folk expres-sion, so we'll continue to use the two terms interchangeably."[3] Irwin Silber also supported a broad definition of folk music when he asserted, "As a working definition to discuss the phenomenon of this folksong revival, we have to ac-knowledge that it is what these young people are singing, and not what we think they should be singing, that constitutes folk music."[4] By writing topical songs—or music for the people—they were continuing down a path that the Almanac Singers had established in the pre–World War II era and that People's Songs continued through the postwar years.

During the mid-1960s, many of the political songwriters began to take an introspective turn that ushered in a new definition of folk music. As early as 1959, John Cohen observed that the new generation of folk singers no longer emphasized "social reform or world-wide reform. The effort is focused more on a search for real and human values. We are not looking for someone to lead us. We are looking within ourselves."[5] Cohen's early observation of young folk en-thusiasts' "looking within ourselves" would come to describe the direction that many folk musicians followed during the final years of the movement. The art-ists who turned inward began to write from a personal perspective about issues that they faced and their emotional reactions to them. Rather than write songs for anyone else, they increasingly composed music to express themselves.

Bob Dylan offered the most dramatic symbol of the shift from protest to the personal. Emerging on the folk scene in 1961, Dylan followed in Woody Guthrie's musical footsteps and soon became the songwriting darling of the topical singers. That changed, however, in the summer of 1965, when Dylan released the rock-and-roll single "Like a Rolling Stone" and showed up on the stage of Newport clad in leather pants, backed by members of the Paul Butterfield Blues Band. Revival stalwarts such as Pete Seeger and Irwin Silber were mostly dismayed at Dylan's sharp, and sudden, turn away from socially and politically topical music. Other folk enthusiasts, however, commended Dylan's new musical and lyrical styles. The debate over introspective folk music in general, and over Dylan in particular, raged in the pages of *Sing Out!* After Dylan's notorious performance at Newport, Jim Rooney observed that his shift marked a clear generational schism within the revival: "The highway he travels is now is unfamiliar to those who bummed around in the thirties during the Depression. He travels by plane.... The mountains and valleys he knows are those of the mind.... 'The people' so loved by Pete Seeger are 'the mob' so hated by Dylan. In the face of violence he has chosen to preserve himself alone. No one else. And he defies everyone else to have the courage to be as alone, as unconnected . . . as he."[6]

Many older revivalists were unable to understand Dylan's changing perspective. In the November 1964 issue of *Sing Out!*, before Dylan's Newport performance, Silber printed "Open Letter to Bob Dylan," in which he questioned Dylan's new approach, noting that his "new songs seem to be all inner-directed now, innerprobing, self-conscious" and that he no longer tried to communicate with the audience.[7] Paul Nelson, a prominent voice of the young revivalists since his days as co-founder and editor of the *Little Sandy Review*, responded by leveling vehement attacks against Silber in several issues of *Sing Out!* Echoing, Rooney's differentiation between the neo-revivalists such as Dylan and the old guard, Nelson responded to Silber's concerns about Dylan, and the young revivalists in general, by writing, "Time, if nothing else, will vindicate Bob Dylan's 'New Music' from the sad and even pathetic charges of Social Irresponsibility and Artistic Decadence leveled by the current representatives of the Thirties and Forties.... Dylan's unyielding and poetic point of view represents a total commitment to the subjective over the objective, the microcosm over the macrocosm, man rather than Man, problems not Problems . . . knowing full well that unless the personal is achieved, the universal cannot follow."[8] By this time, Nelson and many other revivalists had ceased to have any interest in the "universal." How could folk music be used as a tool to define the nation when the young revivalists were increasingly interested in using music as a way to find and define themselves?

By 1966, groups that maintained only a tenuous connection to traditional or political music, such as the Lovin' Spoonful, Simon and Garfunkel, and the Mamas and the Papas, had surpassed such revival mainstays as Peter, Paul, and Mary and the Kingston Trio in "folk" record sales.[9] Many new groups adapted the topical songwriters' new, introverted approach to form folk rock. As a hybrid of folk protest music and rock-and-roll, folk rock grew louder and more electric as the decade progressed. The growing popularity of the music caused even some traditional musicians to trade in their acoustic guitars for electric ones. Part of folk rock's popularity stemmed from the student movement, in which students began to see themselves as a distinct, and beleaguered, group. This self-actualization pushed "proletarian protest" to the side to make way for a "youth revolution."[10] No longer was the music of the revival primarily from or for the marginalized people of America. While some critics praised folk rock as a breath of fresh air, others viewed it as symbolic of the revival's end. Even Pete Seeger's optimism about the widespread political possibilities of folk music had waned because the youth of America were no longer "interested in organizing, but in freeing [themselves] from organizational restraints." Many formerly political folk singers became preoccupied with exploring the depths of their emotions, and the British Invasion had snatched up much of the youth market. By the late 1960s, rock music had become so theatrical that folk singers performing with acoustic guitars appeared hopelessly dated to a new generation of teenage listeners.[11]

Another trend that signified a decline in the revival and the hope to use folk music to generate a democratic Americanism was growing anger among social activists. During the mid-1960s, *Sing Out!* continued to provide coverage of social movements that used folk music as part of the effort to gain political rights, as in the case of the United Farm Workers' grape strike. In his article about the strike, Silber included the song "La Peregrinacion (The Pilgrimage)," which plainly states, "From Delano I go / To Sacramento / To fight for my rights."[12] In the same issue, the magazine noted shifts in the Civil Rights Movement after its northward turn in David Llorens's article "New Birth in the Ghetto," which described the new antipoverty struggles in northern cities, particularly highlighting the "End the Slums" campaign. The article focused on the songwriter and black activist Jimmy Collier and featured his song "Burn, Baby, Burn," in which he expresses his frustration through the lines, "I heard people talking about a dream, now, a dream I couldn't catch. . . . If I can't enjoy the American dream, won't be water but fire next time."[13] Collier's song spoke to the rise of anger over the failures of the Civil Rights Movement to engender permanent changes in many black Americans' daily lives.

"Burn, Baby, Burn" reflected young black activists' loss of faith in American political ideals. In the wake of the riots in Watts and other cities and countless beatings and arrests, civil rights volunteers began questioning the plausibility of the "American dream" for which they initially believed they were fighting. The civic ideals that the nation allegedly espoused, and to which the civil rights volunteers sought access, seemed empty in the face of the unrelenting violence they had suffered in the South and urban North. Dovetailing with this disillusionment was the growing doubt in the tactical viability of nonviolence. These two circumstances, combined with a growing interest in racial identity, caused many activists to turn to the theories of Black Nationalism embodied in black power. Combining the racial pride elements embedded in the Black Is Beautiful ethos with the separatism of Black Nationalism, black power marked a new form of radicalism that emerged from the ranks of young black activists.[14] The concept of black power had roots in Black Nationalist movements that began in the late nineteenth century and periodically reemerged in the twentieth century. Even though Black Nationalism took different forms over the years, all of the variations were predicated on the view that African Americans would never be fully included in the American national community on par with whites. Black power emerged from the belief that any cultural change would have to come entirely from within the black community. After years of being depicted in popular culture as comical minstrels, as sexless mammies and Uncle Toms, or as primitive savages, black activists began to write of their own culture and their own history and thus generated an identity that emerged entirely from within the black community—a task that activists such as Marcus Garvey, W. E. B. Du Bois, Carter G. Woodson, and Langston Hughes had encouraged since the early decades of the century. The calls for a new black identity that emerged from this process served as both the "adhesive" and the "guiding force" for the emergence of black power during the late 1960s.[15]

Both *Sing Out!* and *Broadside* closely monitored these changes in the Civil Rights Movement. Julius Lester's "The Angry Children of Malcolm X" encapsulated the anger that many young black activists felt. Opening his article with the blanket statement, "The world of the black American is different from that of the white American," Lester described how white America had consistently refused to allow black Americans to assimilate into the national mainstream. Initially, the Civil Rights Movement encouraged black Americans to fight to achieve assimilation, but gradually, by the mid-1960s, the movement had turned into a "War of Liberation," and Lester credited Malcolm X for inspiring the rise of black militancy. The black man of this era, according to Lester, "has stopped being a Negro and has become a black man in recognition of his real identity. 'Negro' is an American invention which [shut] him off from those of the same color in Africa. He recognizes now that part of himself is in Africa." Not only had this newfound racial awareness given black Americans a distinct identity, but it also allowed them to break free from the fight to become full members of the American national body. For many, the era of integration and nonviolence had ended. "Now it is over," Lester wrote. "The days of singing freedom songs and the days of combating billy clubs with Love. We Shall Overcome (and we have overcome our blindness) sounds old, out-dated and can enter the pantheon of the greats along with IWW songs and the union songs."[16] According to Lester's assessment, traditional folk songs had no place in the newfound social and cultural changes that were sweeping the nation.

In the late 1960s, the Black Nationalist style of social and cultural protest had moved beyond black communities and extended into groups of ethnically marginalized Americans, including Hispanics, American Indians, Asian Americans, and even white ethnics such as Jews, Italians, and Poles.[17] Radical groups such as the Chicano Brown Berets on the West Coast and the Puerto Rican Young Lords of the East Coast, the Chinese Red Guard, the American Indian Movement, the Asian American Political Alliance, and even an organization of white Appalachians calling themselves "the Patriots," adopted the rhetoric of black power to buttress their struggles for cultural and social equality. Many of these activists adopted the same demands, style of dress, community programs, and machismo of the quintessential black power organization, the Black Panthers. Perhaps the most significant aspect of the Panthers that these groups incorporated into their own movements was a deep sense of pride. Rather than seeing their ethnic and racial lineage as a source of weakness, these young activists generated movements of cultural nationalism in which they viewed ethnic traditions as sources of strength that contrasted with the cultural bankruptcy of white America.[18] Although the government never collapsed during the social and political crisis of the 1960s and 1970s, the rise of cultural nationalism severely damaged the belief in a unified American identity. Large swaths of the American youth population ceased to identify with the national body and national civic ideals.[19]

As identity politics critically wounded the revivalists' pluralist Americanism during the late 1960s, the movement against the Vietnam War hammered the final nail into its coffin. Viewing U.S. involvement in Vietnam as a violation of the ideals for which the country allegedly stood—for example, anticolonialism and self-government—many Americans had turned against the war by the close of the decade. Young, black civil rights activists believed it was just another instance of an imperialist white America trying to subjugate a colored race. Young, white activists also adopted this view and began to sympathize with the Vietcong and other revolutionaries from developing nations. This turn against a national war prompted many to question mainstream national values and augmented their identification with groups operating on the fringes of society.[20] To young activists on the left, the American image was tarnished and the nation corroded beyond the point of salvaging; they wanted nothing to do with the conservative patriots who cloaked themselves with the American mantle.[21] By leading many to question the sanctity of national civic ideals and their place in American society, the war helped open the floodgates of anger and resentment over the civic conformity of the Cold War era and the forced assimilation to an Anglo suburban lifestyle that many experienced during the post–World War II years.[22]

The revival was not immune to these changes in American society. Many revivalists attempted to accommodate the cultural and political shifts by broadening their musical and political approaches, whereas others steadfastly refused to alter their programs in any way. The Newport Folk Festival and the National Folk Festival (NFF), respectively, illustrate these two reactions. Throughout the 1960s, Newport diversified its representation of both folk music and political causes. In 1967, the festival began to feature Luis Valdez's El Teatro Campesino (Farm Workers' Theater), the cultural arm of the United Farm Workers that staged performances based on the Hispanic experience in America, particularly emphasizing migrant farmers' struggles. That same year, Bread and Puppet Theater, a politically progressive troupe that became famous for the giant puppets it used in antiwar demonstrations, made its debut. In 1968, the Newport Folk Festival Foundation organized musical events for the Poor People's March on Washington. The foundation members had designed these events in much the same way that they designed the more recent festivals: the people would present their own musical traditions. The folklorist Bruce Jackson explained that the organizers hoped to ensure that the music of the march came *from* the marchers, "rather than stars brought in from outside their world."[23] During the festival of that year, Joan Baez recounted on-stage her experiences being jailed for civil disobedience, Reverend Kirkpatrick sang songs about Resurrection City (the culmination of the Poor People's Campaign in Washington, D.C.), and Pete Seeger and the Pennywhistlers commented about the injustices of the war in Vietnam.

Newport's attempts to adapt to the political changes enabled it to remain politically relevant to a degree, particularly among the younger generation of leftist folk fans. The National Folk Festival, however, was situated at the opposite end of the spectrum. Sarah Gertrude Knott blatantly refused to reflect the new politics and incorporate new forms of folk music that emerged over the course of the 1960s, and the popularity of her festival foundered as a result. Although she appreciated the rising popularity of folk music during the boom years, Knott and others in the National Folk Festival Association (NFFA) were horrified that the media portrayed both folk performers and enthusiasts as members of the counterculture. In 1964, Melvin Hussey, the executive vice-president of the NFFA, wrote an irate letter to the editor of a newspaper in St. Petersburg, Florida (the location of the 1964 festival), complaining about a cartoon that personified the festival as a "bewhiskered, beslippered beatnik, with vacuous eyes, unshorn hair and eternal guitar, plainly a refugee from a hootenanny." The National Folk Festival, he explained, presented authentic American traditions "gaily but in dignity" by people who maintained this heritage in their everyday lives rather than putting "pseudo folk entertainers" such as Peter, Paul, and Mary and other popular groups on their stage.[24] The music featured on the NFF stages remained traditional both in style and presentation—the performers came from regional and ethnic communities, and the music and dance they presented was intended to illustrate a cultural heritage. The festival stayed true to Knott's historical understanding of folk music; new forms of music that emerged out of the boom, and popular boom musicians, were not welcome in the NFF. The National Folk Festival was unable to curry favor among many young folk enthusiasts of the 1960s precisely because the fans of the boom era tended to be more interested in the urban "pseudo folk" groups. In a move that perhaps further alienated young "folkniks," Knott dismissed the products of the urban folk boom. In the introduction of the festival's program for 1967, Knott wrote, "It is doubtful that the new city-born songs and dances, reflecting a new kind of civilization, will build the kind of foundation necessary to cast their influence on the future. Few have the enduring characteristics that have distinguished earlier folklore."[25]

The NFFA leaders also faced problems with their continued celebration of American nationalism and unity. At the beginning of the 1960s, Knott had argued that folk music appreciation could help in the fight against communism as much as it did in the struggle against fascism. She continued to believe that American citizens could be united through mutually shared civic ideals, asserting that the festival enabled Americans to "strengthen our belief in the ideals of our country through the unifying influence of a common culture and beloved by all our people."[26] While the festival illustrated American cultural heterogeneity, it adhered to a view of ideological homogeneity—meaning that the organizers believed that Americans continued to uphold the same civic ideals as they did during the World War II era. It was a vision of national unity based on shared ideals that became increasingly outdated as the 1960s wore on. In 1965, for example, Hussey asked President Lyndon Johnson to endorse the festival with the following words: "[The festival's] programs demonstrate the strength and beauty of a cultural pattern, woven of many threads, but distinctively American in the completed fabric. These programs eloquently refute the alien doctrines which would divide us, and the spirit of Americanism which they engender makes them worthy of our wholehearted support."[27] During a period marked by growing recognition of the failure of American democracy to include the poor and racial minorities, this kind of justification for the value of the NFF was grossly out of sync with the younger folk music enthusiasts of the 1960s.

As the decade progressed, the NFFA appeared to move even further to the right. Knott waded directly into the political maelstrom by writing in the 1968 program, "While protests and picket lines grab public attention and paint the United States as a cauldron of discontent, there are thousands who present a totally different picture of this country. They are the conservative, both rural and urban, people who are helping to hold the balance as they have done in older times and in other communities."[28] These were the kind of Americans, and this was the type of national identity, that Knott and the NFFA presented throughout the tumultuous decade. Despite all of the challenges to this view— or perhaps because of them—the NFFA persistently proclaimed that Americans appreciated the folk arts that it presented and that the nation needed the "assurance of national identity and tradition produced by such performance" during the social and cultural factionalism of the 1960s, although fewer and fewer people were listening.[29]

The political factionalism took its toll on the Newport Folk Festival, as well, despite the concessions and accommodations that the festival organizers had made. On the one hand, the inclusion of political protests illuminated the political differences between leftist revivalists and traditional musicians from rural, conservative communities. After the 1968 program, Buell Kazee, a Baptist minister and banjo player from rural Kentucky, summarized this political disjuncture, writing, "These people told me before I came here it wouldn't be like this. I don't want anything to do with tearing down America. I don't know why these folks don't do the honest thing and admit that this is ideology and not just music. If I'd known it was goin' to be like this I'd of stayed in Kentucky."[30] On the other hand, the festival was a place for like-minded people to gather in a community, people who largely rejected mass culture, supported civil rights, and were against the war.[31] Yet even the inclusion of leftist views did not appease the more politically radical folk music fans, for the kind of reform efforts that Newport continued to advocate were becoming increasingly irrelevant as both direct action techniques and violence escalated during the late 1960s. To many audience members, merely "singing about social and political problems was no longer adequate." These new activists found that the older organizers did not share their tactical views, and thus they no longer believed that Newport provided the kind of outlet that they needed.[32] The divisions and rancor within Newport all contributed to the festival's downward spiral. Riots during the Newport Jazz Festival of 1969 prompted the city authorities to place several restrictions on the folk festival days before it opened in 1969, creating an atmosphere that was rather repressive for an entertaining music festival. Financial problems forced the foundation to cancel the 1970 program. New uprisings at the jazz festival in 1971 prompted the town to revoke the folk festival's license. The Newport Folk Festival did not recover for well over a decade.

The trials and tribulations of the Newport festival also played out in the *Sing Out!* editorial room. In his remaining days as the editor of the magazine, Silber tried to push the magazine in an even more hard-line political direction, an effort that was reminiscent of the magazine's early days. This time, however, the idea of using the magazine as a political soapbox did not sit well with the rest of the board. By April 1968, Silber was fed up, and although he hoped to continue contributing articles, he tendered his resignation to *Sing Out!* Silber was not the only figure from the old guard who had become disillusioned with the magazine, and with the folk music revival as a whole, by the late 1960s. During an editorial meeting in 1967, Pete Seeger reminisced about old times, noting how he and Lee Hays had begun the magazine to challenge the forces of commercial music and protect traditional forms. Back then, they had clear enemies: Tin Pan Alley, Nashville, Hollywood, and other purveyors of mass culture, in addition to political and social reactionaries. Now that had changed. Folk music was big business, and those in the revival had turned on one another—the sectarianism among the revivalists was tearing *Sing Out!* and the rest of the movement apart.[33]

The problems at *Sing Out!* had plagued the magazine for years. Many of the disputes reflected the old factionalism within the revival: the debates over the rise of folk rock, the controversies over fusing politics with folk music, and questions over what the term "folk music" even meant. Ed Badeaux, one of the magazine's editors, drew the conclusion that this constant infighting was one of many indications that the revival had ended. In his article "'The Spectacle Moves On," Badeaux claimed that of all the things that the revivalists could disagree on, the one thing that they at *Sing Out!* knew for sure was that "folk music is very definitely not 'what's happening.' We may disagree almost to the point of violence as to what exactly has happened. But if we have eyes and ears, if we can interpret record sales charts, then we know this as fact." The youth of America had moved on to new types of music, especially the new type of rock-and-roll inspired by the British Invasion. Badeaux further described the state of the folk boom as "about as serious as the national craze for hula hoops. Period." Throughout the article, Badeaux echoed Seeger's disillusionment by describing the early revivalists as "dedicated idealists" who had believed that the revival would generate an "American awakening to true musical values" and who had become "victims of their own enthusiasms, blinding themselves to the truths of the American commercial music scene." Now folk music *was* commercial: "It is amplified. It is stoned. It is completely removed from life."[34] If anything signified the collapse of the revival, this judgment was it.

## *The End*

At approximately the same time that the revival began to implode, the old New Left started to disintegrate. Interestingly, James Miller illustrates the demise of the old New Left through Bob Dylan's stylistic change, a change that many historians point to when looking for the locus of the folk revival's decline. "Bob Dylan wasn't strumming an acoustic guitar and singing broadsides in the artless manner of Woody Guthrie any longer," Miller writes. "Now, he was shouting over a welter of amplified instruments, plunging headlong into dreamlike poems of betrayed love and apocalypse with the fevered, deranged conviction of a rock-and-roll Rimbaud." Similarly, the members of Students for a Democratic Society (SDS) and the rest of the New Left had turned away from promoting democracy through education and intellectual inquiry and toward something that "was impatient, raw, hard with anticipation."[35] Miller's comparison is significant not only because it reaffirms Dylan's connection to the generation that had turned SDS into a significant political force, but also because it illustrates the simultaneity of these two events: the end of the New Left and the end of the folk revival.

The rise of black power and racial nationalism among many black civil rights activists caused a contingent of civil rights activists to advocate cultural separation rather than political integration. Some antiwar protestors turned from peaceful demonstrations to fighting violence with violence. As the Black Panthers became the vanguard of militant black activism, the Weathermen, though never large in number, became the face of the new militant antiwar movement. Like the early New Leftists, they excoriated liberalism, romanticized revolutionaries from developing countries, and viewed Americans as numbed by affluence and comfort.

Despite the Weathermen's marginality, many activists believed that the group represented the vanguard of the antiwar movement. By 1969, SDS had collapsed under a leadership that rejected leaders, bureaucracies, and discipline. The New Left had splintered in many directions, and even those who remained within the main movement no longer sought to reform America because they no longer identified *with* America, to the extent that "contempt, even, for the conventions of the flag, home, religion, suburbs, shopping, plain homely Norman Rockwell order—had become a rock-bottom prerequisite for membership in the movement core," according to the activist Todd Gitlin.[36] The following year, the Weathermen wrote, "Tens of thousands have learned that protests and marches don't do it. Revolutionary violence is the only way."[37] Indeed, the radicalization of the left provided little room for the ideas of reform that had initially galvanized the movement.

The type of radicalism that the New Left adopted in the late 1960s severed any remaining threads that connected it to the Old Left of the Popular Front era. The initial members followed a political trajectory grounded in the ideals of inclusive democracy, political engagement, and social justice. By believing in the power of civic ideals, the early movement was predicated on making the principles found in the U.S. Constitution and the Declaration of Independence applicable to all citizens; thus, activists of both generations—the late 1930s–1940s and the early 1960s—had faith in American civic ideals.[38] They fought to achieve the realization of these ideas by promoting the labor, civil rights, and peace movements. This hope in the possibility of reform, however, fell by the wayside as activists increasingly adopted revolutionary rhetoric and tactics by the waning years of the decade. When reflecting on her political activism in 1977, Margaret Gelder Franz, an Old Left organizer, described her cohort as "revolutionaries." She further explained, "I am using the term loosely because looking back on the whole thing, none of us were ever revolutionaries—we were all left reformists, not revolutionaries. We thought we were; and everybody else thought we were, but we really weren't."[39] Indeed, that is a description that applies to the initial generation of the New Left. Before the social and political fracturing of the late 1960s, these activists believed that domestic problems could be solved through direct action and civic engagement. Yet by the end of the era, this dream had dissolved in the face of chaos and disillusionment.

Although the folk music revival had always been segmented, by the mid-1960s the differences had grown to such an extent that the revival "lost its semblance of a unified phenomenon."[40] Divergent definitions of folk music based on commercial products, political messages, and introspective songwriting had stretched the definitional boundaries of folk music to a breaking point. The more successful revivalists entered the pop or rock-and-roll musical mainstream, and others moved into the mini-revivals of Gaelic, Klezmer, and other ethnic music that became popular in the 1970s. While folk music continued to be popular among different political groups, and some revivalist singer-songwriters still used their music as a weapon for social justice, they largely operated as independent agents or as parts of other social movements.

Programs that were intrinsic to the revival had to either change with the times or face an end themselves. College music organizations such as the Illinois Campus Folksong Club, the Newport Folk Festival, and the careers of some singers ended with the movement. Others, such as *Sing Out!* and Folkways Records, revamped their programs to change with the political and social tide. In 1971 alone, Folkways produced such albums as *Angela Davis Speaks, From the Cold Jaws of Prison: By Inmates and Ex-Mates, Musicians and Poets from Attica, Rikers and the Tombs,* and *But the Women Rose, Volume 1: Voices of Women in American History.* The previous year, Irwin Silber and Barbara Dane had formed Parendon Records, an offshoot of Folkways, specifically to introduce people to the revolutionary movements that were occurring around the world and to the most "overtly political" music in the United States.[41] Many former revivalists took the academic route during the 1970s and enrolled in doctoral programs in folklore. Even Alan Lomax partially left the public realm to focus on honing his theory of cantometrics, a combination of ethnomusicology and anthropology that he started developing in the early 1960s to analyze indigenous music. Still others followed the path of institutional politics and joined with the folklorist Archie Green to push for a federal bill to protect folk culture. After undergoing several changes, the bill eventually passed in 1976 and established the American Folklife Center at the Library of Congress.[42]

The revival had experienced a thinning of its ranks before. Yet this time was different—first, because now even the stalwart members left the movement; and second, because the revivalists' vision of a pluralist democratic Americanism had largely lost its viability in American society. After the mid-1960s, the concept of a national "great community" based on common ideals began to dissolve. From the 1930s through the 1960s, progressive nationalists could feasibly promote national unity through a civic nationalism grounded in the "American Idea," in which culturally and ethnically disparate Americans came together as a national community that respected cultural difference. Yet this nationalism glossed over real divisions in American life such as socioeconomic disparity and racial marginalization, which tended to go hand in hand. The Civil Rights Movement and the sociological awareness of American poverty during the early 1960s made these inequalities impossible to ignore.

Programs such as the Poor People's Campaign and Resurrection City in 1968 revealed that liberals' attempts to address these matters through initiatives such as the Civil Rights Act and the War on Poverty had failed to solve the problems. Growing political frustration coupled with the social and cultural factionalism of the 1960s effectively closed the book on any hope for political, or even national, unity. Now cultural pluralists took an antinationalist stance, highlighting the "separateness" of ethnic groups, and, according to John Higham, "any affirmation of a unifying national culture, became *ipso facto* oppressive," even one based on shared civic ideals.[43] The era of democratic nationalism that characterized the revival had officially ended.[44] "Nationalism" and "patriotism" fell into the bailiwick of the growing right-wing movement, a movement that also employed populist rhetoric and iconography but used it to create a conservative national identity that sharply contrasted with the revivalists' progressive Americanism. Although the prospects for a progressive view of national identity were bleak by the end of the decade, all was not lost for those who tried to maintain their faith in democratic Americanism. A new movement, one that also elevated marginalized communities to insure their representation in the American national body, was growing on the horizon.

## The Beginning

In 1950, Alan Lomax gave a speech at the Midcentury International Folklore Conference in which he called for folklorists to act as advocates for marginalized peoples, many of whom came from the traditional "folk" communities that folklorists so treasured. By recording their music, folklorists had given minority peoples a voice. Lomax declared, "We have become in this way the champion of the ordinary people of the world, who aren't backed up by printing presses, radio chains, and B29s."[45] A decade later, Lomax reiterated this position in the *HiFi/Stereo Review*:

> The recording machine can be a voice to the voiceless, for the millions in the world who have no access to the main channels of communication, and whose cultures are being talked to death by all sorts of well-intentioned people—teachers, missionaries, etc.—and who are being shouted into silence by our commercially bought-and-paid-for loudspeakers. It took me a long time to realize that the main point of my activity was to redress the balance a bit, to put sound technology at the disposal of the folk, to bring the channels of communication to all sorts of artists and areas.[46]

This time, Lomax made these comments when social and political dissent was on the rise and when marginalized American citizens had increasingly begun to fight openly for their rights at home and around the world.

During the late 1960s through the early 1970s, progressive activists developed programs that aimed to do exactly what Lomax called for: to give a "voice" to the "voiceless." In the United States, these activists began a concerted effort to ensure that the American identity reflected the nation's culturally diverse population. Labeled "multiculturalism," this program was highly influenced by the Black Nationalist movement of the late 1960s, as well as by theories of cultural democracy. Rejecting forced assimilation to white, middle-class norms, multiculturalists returned to celebrating ethnic and racial diversity as the defining feature of American identity. Many early multiculturalists crafted a version of Americanism that emphasized the cultural distinctiveness of ethnic and racial minorities while simultaneously highlighting the contributions that these groups made to the development of local and national cultural identities.[47]

Many of these advocates specifically focused on educating children of these groups to appreciate their ethno-racial heritage. But rather than take the cultural gifts approach of forcing children to identify with a "homeland" that was not theirs, multiculturalists encouraged children to appreciate the cultures of their local communities, many of which were located in urban areas. They also redesigned curricula to make it more relevant to minority groups, as well as to incorporate themes of ethnic diversity into all subjects rather than isolate them into a separate unit. In her study *Educating for Diversity* (1965), the educational theorist Betty Atwell Wright explains that education had to shift to accommodate a post-segregation society, with the understanding that intraracial and interracial conflicts "can still defeat democracy." "Intergroup" education advocates therefore sought to end "*de facto* segregation in communities and schools" by valuing cultural diversity. This program had a strong socially progressive undercurrent, for intergroup educators ultimately aimed to contribute to "the development of cosmopolitan citizens who can function more effectively in culturally diverse communities, and who are free of racial, religious, regional, or social class provincialism." They also indicated their strong support for the Civil Rights Movement by working to secure a respect for equal rights and equal opportunity in public services, education, employment, and housing among schoolchildren.[48]

Intergroup advocates encouraged schools to use books, records, and filmstrips produced by antidiscrimination groups such as the Anti-Defamation League, the National Conference of Christians and Jews, and the Council on Human Relations. In a chapter in which she lists such resources for intergroup education, Atwell devotes a section to Folkways Records, mostly highlighting albums that pertained to African American history and the Civil Rights Movement. She also recommends songbooks such as Guy and Candie Carawan's *We Shall Overcome* (1963), Irwin Silber's *Soldier Songs and Home-Front Ballads of the Civil War* (1964), and Moses Asch and Alan Lomax's *The Leadbelly Songbook* (1962). Three years later, another intergroup education publication sponsored by the Anti-Defamation League again recommended Folkways Records, specifically citing *The Nashville Sit-In Story* and *The Negro Woman,* an album of selected writings from African American writers and activists.[49]

In the early 1970s, intergroup education morphed into "multiethnic education," which specifically encouraged ethnic pride and cross-cultural understanding. Multiethnic educators made up a segment of the emerging multicultural movement, which followed in the footsteps of intergroup education by designing school curricula to teach children about the importance of diversity.[50] According to these early multiculturalists, ethnic and racial identities were a fact of American life. However, the lines separating ethnic and racial groups were permeable, and citizens formed their own identities by adopting elements from a variety of social groups. Multiethnic programs therefore focused on the place of minority citizens within American society, and these advocates aimed to inculcate ethnic/racial pride among minority students, as well as to provide students with the requisite "skills, attitudes, and knowledge they need to function within their ethnic culture, the mainstream culture, and within and across other ethnic cultures."[51]

Multiculturalism is often viewed as a product of the identity politics of the late 1960s, most likely because the movement followed on the heels of the era of racial nationalism. However, focusing too much on the influence of cultural nationalism obscures several other movements and theories that contributed to the development of multiculturalism. In many respects, multiculturalists borrowed from the social theories of Randolph Bourne and Horace Kallen. By maintaining that ethnic diversity gave the United States its identity and encouraging the protection of the cultures of these groups, multicultural theorists incorporated aspects of Kallen's cultural pluralism into their programs. By focusing on individuals as well as groups, and by regarding identities as malleable, they also included elements of Bourne's cosmopolitanism. The Association for Supervision and Curriculum Development, which became an early advocate of multicultural education, articulated an approach akin to Kallen's cultural pluralism by emphasizing the importance of ethnic group identities: "Cultural heritage is the essence of relationship patterns, linguistic and expressive communication, and the fundamental values and attitudes through which each child grows. To ignore, or invalidate this living experience for any individual is, in effect, to distort and diminish the possibilities for developing that person's potential." At the same time, the organization's recognition that "no group lives in isolation, but that, instead, each group influences and is influenced by others" bears strong similarities to the social fluidity embodied in cosmopolitanism.[52] By adopting elements of cosmopolitanism, these early multiculturalists displayed qualities of "hybrid" multiculturalism, meaning that they believed that identities evolved as individuals expanded their cultural experiences and hence advocated cultural mixing rather than racial or ethnic purity.[53]

By combining elements of pluralism and cosmopolitanism in their programs, these early multiculturalists fell under the category of "soft" multiculturalism, meaning that while they advocated cultural diversity, they still believed that Americans belonged to a unified national body. They maintained that cultural differences were "compatible" with patriotism and that ethnic and racial diversity were actually sources of America's strength.[54] While multiculturalism emerged from a longer historical trajectory, the movement was not simply a wholesale revival of cultural pluralism and cosmopolitanism. As much as early multiculturalists borrowed from these earlier theories, they also incorporated concepts from contemporary social and cultural movements. Embedded in their recognition of the contributions that ethnic and racial groups made to national life was an understanding that racial *pride* stemmed from racial *power*. Since the late 1960s, black power advocates had demanded that schools acknowledge more than just the cultural contributions of racial and ethnic groups and recognize the power that came from racial or ethnic identities themselves.[55] This element of multiculturalism became known as the "new pluralism" and was based on a form of racial pride that stemmed from the Civil Rights Movement. The education theorist James Banks explains that the black struggle for civil rights "legitimized ethnicity"; soon members of other racial minorities began to seek out their own racial heritage, as well. As a result, many young activists began to direct their efforts to attaining representation in secondary and higher education curricula.[56]

From the heyday of pluralist populism during the New Deal era to the rise of cultural nationalism during the 1960s, folk revivalists had worked alongside other progressive reformers—and radicals—to include racial and ethnic minority groups in the national body on an equal footing with Anglo-Americans. Alan Lomax, for instance, had always emphasized the importance of racial minorities in shaping American culture. He ardently believed that collecting, preserving, and recording the music of socially ostracized, politically disfranchised, and economically marginalized peoples would aid them in their struggles for equality—political and cultural. In an unpublished letter to the *New York Times* from 1968, Lomax expressed a view akin to that of the early multiculturalists regarding the significance of racial pride; while he lauded the political successes of the Civil Rights Movement, he argued that the message of racial equality had to become a stronger feature of American culture. Children needed to be taught about the importance of black culture and history, and he called for the media to do more than "a few token specials and Sunday afternoon shows." In Lomax's view, schools, the media, politicians, and philanthropic organizations all had to work to generate the kind of "cultural equality" that the nation continued to lack.[57]

During the early 1970s, after the collapse of the movement, many former revivalists joined with public folklorists and multiculturalists to publicize the notion, in Archie Green's words, "that traditional artistry and folk wisdom were integral to the American experience."[58] Many of these figures also borrowed concepts that had become prevalent in the revival. Specifically, they adopted ideas of cultural preservation and the encouragement of ethnic and racial minority groups to take pride in their cultural practices, which they hoped would lead to stronger and more widespread preservation efforts. In advancing these ideas, the members of this cohort of folk music enthusiasts held many of the same aims as the emerging multiculturalists. The program that provided the nexus between multiculturalism and folk music during this decade was the Smithsonian Festival of American Folklife.

In 1966, S. Dillon Ripley, the secretary of the Smithsonian Institution, endorsed James Morris's plan for a folk festival to be held on the National Mall. The Smithsonian had recently attempted to soften its image and make the institution more accessible to the public. As head of the Division of Performing Arts, Morris believed that a folk festival would bring the institution closer to the public, and he soon tapped the folk performer, manager, and preservationist Ralph Rinzler to help organize it. Rinzler envisioned the festival as a "holistic" enterprise—one that included music, dance, food, and crafts—with the aim to celebrate and teach about folk culture. Therefore, the festival would be called a "Folklife" rather than simply a "Folk" festival, as all of the music-centric festivals were labeled. Through an educational folklife display, Rinzler sought to "establish the fact that folklife was not just fun and games, people dressing up and dancing around a maypole." Instead, he wanted the audience to learn that these traditions served important functions in community life and were not colorful replicas of a distant past or the strange practices of quaintly archaic people.[59]

One way to impart this message was through audience participation. Rinzler structured the festival as a series of simultaneous cultural demonstrations. Rather than placing the participants on a stage, he situated them on the same level as the audience and stipulated that the ropes separating the two groups would be lowered after the demonstration, thus allowing the audience to mingle with presenters. By collapsing the boundaries that divided presenters from the audience, the FAF organizers worked to enhance the experience that participants gained from watching folk traditions by making that experience interactive. Directly engaging with the tradition-bearers enabled audience members to continue learning about the significance of these traditions even after the performances ended.[60]

Rinzler's views on folk music profoundly shaped the development of the FAF.[61] Even before he began designing the festival, he sought to introduce Americans to folk traditions that had persisted in communities, despite the fact that they were commercially unpopular. Seeking to understand "music as behavior," Rinzler was fascinated by how certain musical forms—for example, hillbilly music from the 1920s—lasted for years after a decline in commercial popularity, and he wanted to know how this music and these musicians could survive well past their prime. He was amazed that traditional musicians such as Clarence Ashley and Doc Boggs were still playing regional music into the 1960s, long after the rise of commercial country and the Grand Ole Opry, and he "had an intense desire to make sure that it stayed around." This is one of the primary reasons he began managing these musicians during the years of the folk boom. Rinzler believed that he could function as a mediator between traditional folk music and a "world that was moving away from it" or that was trying to repackage it to fit commercial expectations of how the music should sound. This desire spoke to Rinzler's traditionalist sympathies, and it set him apart from many revivalists during the movement. He disdained the way some revivalists had treated the music, using it as a raw material to construct something new—for example, compositions and dramatic arrangements such as "Ballad for Americans" or other adaptations that musicians such as the Kingston Trio and Richard Dyer Bennett had generated. Instead, Rinzler sought to "scrape" away the adaptations and get to the heart of the music itself.[62]

This understanding placed Rinzler squarely in the company of folk music purists who began to form their own trajectory independent from the revival during the mid-1960s. Rinzler recognized that the notion of a folk*life* festival came from the "inside-outside" concept. Rinzler and other preservationists, such as Bernice Johnson Reagon, a prominent singer and activist from the Civil Rights Movement, believed that the people from *inside* a cultural tradition, not *outside* musical interpreters, should be the ones presenting the music. By adopting a strictly inside-outside position, the FAF was effectively giving voice to folk communities, many of which continued to be marginalized from mainstream culture and society. Having *only* these Americans teach the larger public about their communities was the festival's first foray into the cultural politics of the late 1960s.[63]

By creating a festival with the express intention of protecting traditional cultural practices and presenting them to a wide, public audience without the filter of interpreters, the FAF followed in the trajectory that purists initiated during the height of the folk boom. At the same time, it also sustained the revival's goal of altering how Americans related to their culture and understood their national identity. Through the festival, Rinzler promoted a clear vision of cultural democracy, a view that drew inspiration from Carl Sandburg's and Woody Guthrie's populism, Charles Seeger's leftist politics, and civil rights activism. Richard Kurin, a later director of the Smithsonian Center for Folklife and Cultural Heritage, argues that Rinzler combined these influences to generate a festival that let tradition-bearers present their own traditions. This stipulation that *only* tradition-bearers would be the performers revealed Rinzler's goal of democratizing American culture by introducing attendees to music, dance, foodways, and handicrafts that were ignored in commercially dominated pop culture. This larger, more overtly political goal came at a good time, because the idea of using the National Mall "as a pulpit" to challenge the status quo grew prominent in the aftermath of the March on Washington in 1963.[64] Cultural advocacy may have been the primary intention of the festival, but through its presentation of folk culture, the FAF also helped to generate a new understanding of Americanism during the social, cultural, and political fragmentation of the late 1960s and 1970s, one that both borrowed and differed from the democratic Americanism that folk revivalists had promoted.

In all, more than 431,000 people attended the first FAF, a turnout that encouraged the Smithsonian "to establish the Festival as an annual Independence Day tribute to our folk heritage." Over the course of four days, fifty-eight traditional craftspeople and thirty-two musical and dance groups participated in the program. The festival featured "Mountain banjo-pickers and ballad singers, Chinese lion fighters, Indian sand painters, basket and rug weavers, New Orleans jazz bands and a Bohemian hammer-dulcimer band from east Texas combined with a host of participants from many rural and urban areas of our country to weave the colorful fabric of American traditional culture."[65] The festival took on an explicitly preservationist, and romanticized, tone when the program book described several of the featured traditions as the survivals of a preindustrial age that managed to persist, even after "the advent of mass media and rapid transportation."[66] Initially, Rinzler and Morris also envisioned a large academic conference to be held in conjunction with the festival. They sought to bring folklore scholars, government officials, and foundation organizers together to discuss the importance of traditional crafts to the American economy and national heritage. Rinzler also wanted the conference participants to discuss how to publicize the important contributions that folk culture made to the nation's "total cultural heritage."[67]

In the festival of the following year, the FAF began to develop a stronger ideological vision, one that connected the festival both to the changing social climate of the late 1960s and to the rising trend of multiculturalism. Like other "soft" multiculturalists, the FAF organizers maintained a unity-within-diversity view that recognized the ways in which ethnic diversity formed the essence of the nation's identity. In his opening to the 1968 festival program, S. Dillon Ripley noted the importance of presenting a *public* display of folk culture in America. Situating the festival in the context of an increased awareness of cultural and ethnic difference, Ripley acknowledged that the program provided an opportunity to display "some aspects of the cultural roots of the people of the United States." This was because the festival was "a living exhibition of the creativity of the many ethnic groups that make up the culture of the country." Unfortunately, schools and other American institutions had done little to study and preserve the variants of folk culture in the United States, and this was precisely why the FAF was a necessary cultural endeavor, something that the organizers hoped would "serve to bring American people more fully in touch with their own creative roots, and that from this acquaintance the way [might] be pointed toward a richer life for some and a more meaningful understanding of the roots of our society."[68] Could an appreciation of ethnic traditions provide the much needed sense of identity—and thus, pride—that the multiculturalists argued ethnic and racial minorities needed to develop? Ripley is vague about the answer, but by recognizing the important cultural contributions that ethnic minorities made to American life, as well as recognizing their intrinsic cultural value, the FAF organizers used folklife to encourage Americans to appreciate the various cultural traditions of their own communities and the nation at large.

In another article, Samuel Stanley, the anthropology program coordinator for the Smithsonian Institution, articulated the festival's importance for understanding the pluralist nature of American identity. Although many of the ethnic traditions of naturalized Americans had merged into the dominant culture, there were "still numerous enclaves of viable culture groups who have remained on the banks of the river," such as the Japanese, Chinese, Russians, Norwegians, Poles, and Basques. Stanley argued, "Now is the time to seriously tackle the problem of identity of American culture. We must do it by understanding the culture of the ethnic groups which have successfully nourished and been nourished by the mainstream."[69] Here again he emphasized the importance of understanding cultural minorities as key components of the multifarious American identity. At the same time, he recognized that there had been a cultural exchange, that minority traditions had also been shaped by other cultural trends and had not remained static, isolated subcultures. By adopting a cosmopolitan view, Stanley challenged the rhetoric of racial nationalism of the late 1960s that emphasized the purity and sanctity of group identity.

The second festival, in 1968, sustained much of the same focus on traditional music as the debut program. That year also marked the beginning of the festival's emphasis on a particular state, with Texas as the inaugural feature. In 1969, the festival moved northward and highlighted Pennsylvanian traditions. Although annual programs emphasized different states, the organizers maintained their pluralist approach and continued to include various traditions found throughout the country. The program in 1969 added groups presenting Turkish, Afro-Cuban, and Greek traditions to the roster of festival performances. In his summary of the previous year's festival, Ripley explained, "While we as a people commonly share a national culture, each American also enjoys the distinctive ways of his family, ethnic groups, region and occupation which comprise his traditional or folk culture."[70] Through this statement, Ripley illustrated the cosmopolitan bent of the festival. By recognizing that each American participated in several cultural communities, he reflected the view of multiculturalists such as James Banks, who maintained that ethnic diversity "enriches a society by providing all citizens with more opportunities to experience other cultures and thus become more fulfilled as human beings" by having a more well-rounded "total human experience." Similar to the multiethnic educational programs that aimed to "provide students with cultural and ethnic alternatives," the FAF tried to teach Americans that there was a wide array of cultural traditions in the United States of which they could partake.[71]

While the FAF emphasized the centrality of the so-called insider in presenting traditional cultures, it also depended heavily on the work of outsiders. Several of the organizers were academics in the field of folklore, others were musicians themselves, and many participated in both groups. These figures ultimately decided what traditions and which performers would be presented to the public as authentic folk musicians and thus who would be "given voice." Even though the program was predicated on cultural inclusiveness, Rinzler observed that the organizers, as cultural brokers, had to weed out some traditions. Recognizing that not all folk culture was positive—some traditions preserved racial prejudices and other regressive practices—led Rinzler to conclude that "all that is folk cannot and should not be presented at festivals, though it may well be worth studying and understanding in the context of the culture that nourishes it." Despite the restrictions the organizers placed on the program, Rinzler reaffirmed the underlying message of the festival: to show that "American culture is varied. It's not a homogeneous or a melting-pot culture at all."[72]

Some critics observed that although the organizers structured the festival to showcase a variety of traditions, the early programs focused almost exclusively on the past. Green particularly criticized the initial festivals as reinforcing the notion that folk music was a preindustrial art form, which indicated that authentic folklore was "antiquated" and "backward-looking."[73] Prompted by his urging, the 1971 program included a section called "Working Americans," which Green coordinated. By 1973, the festival widened its representation even further by featuring new sections titled "Native American Program" and "Old Ways in the New World" (a segment entirely devoted to ethnic folklore). The following year, "African Diaspora," "Family Folklore," and "Children's" material were added to the program. In an effort to reach an even wider audience, Alan Lomax encouraged a nationwide broadcast of the festival on Public Broadcasting Service and National Public Radio such that people from across the country could experience the program, and people from the small towns that the program featured could witness the celebration of their cultures.[74]

Each year, the FAF expanded, including an ever more diverse array of traditions. The largest festival to date was the bicentennial celebration. The 1976 festival was a twelve-week phenomenon that included more than five thousand performers from across the United States and thirty-five other countries. The language of cultural democracy, advocacy, and preservation was at its strongest. Rinzler again used his position with the Smithsonian as an example of how cultural brokers could serve as cultural advocates: "The Smithsonian, as a national cultural institution, is an arbiter of taste and through the Festival acts as the cultural advocate of participants and cultures presented on the Mall. In our nation, where commercially dominated media determine the direction and accelerate the rate of cultural change, this cultural activist role of the national museum is decisive." By advocating cultural diversity through a festival of myriad folk traditions, Rinzler noted, the FAF helped Americans to "reaffirm our pluralism and cherish our differences while singing each other's songs" during a turbulent time when the future was filled with uncertainty.[75]

In the program book for the 1976 festival, Gary Everhardt, the director of the U.S. National Park Service, contributed an article in which he emphasized a unity-within-diversity view of American identity. "The Festival of American Folklife is an expression of these beliefs that we are different in many ways," he wrote, "but we are still one nation, one people whose individual differences have helped shape a great nation." He continued, "Everywhere you look there will be America—even in the performances of our friends from abroad, whose national traditions have contributed so much to the richness of our own culture." Alan Lomax pushed a particularly strong message of cosmopolitanism and unity in his own contribution. Calling for citizens to practice cultural equality by celebrating the variegated traditions of the American people, he declared, "By giving every culture its equal access to audiences, its equal time on the air, and its equal weight in education, we can come closer to the realization of the principles of Jefferson's declaration."[76] The idea that the music of the folk was intrinsic to the American identity permeated the festivals during the 1970s and continued to influence subsequent programs through the end of the century. In 1991, Richard Kurin remarked that the Smithsonian festival was still trying to uphold a mission that originated with the inaugural festival. "An unfinished agenda from 1967 still resonates today," he wrote. "Not all culture is or will be produced in Hollywood, Paris, Nashville, or on Madison Avenue. Local folks, people in families, communities, tribes, regions, and occupations continue to make culture."[77] These "local folks" were the groups that the Smithsonian credited with creating and sustaining an American heritage.

The Smithsonian festival illustrates how some former folk revivalists were able to adjust their understanding of Americanism, a vision of national identity that combined cultural pluralism, cosmopolitanism, and even cultural nationalism, to suit the changing cultural and political landscape. The FAF organizers reflected the identity politics of the late 1960s by encouraging racial and ethnic minorities to develop a sense of pride in their cultural traditions. By borrowing concepts of American heritage that came from the revival and combining them with early ideas of multiculturalism, members of the FAF were able to craft a version of American national identity that remained inclusive, democratic, and rooted in the diversity of the American people during an era of factionalism and disillusionment. This effort has lasted without interruption for more than forty years. Even in the twenty-first century, the festival's organizers continue to provide a voice for people in America, and the rest of the world.

## Conclusion

The revivalists were able to carry their movement through an economic depression, war, political repression, and even an invasion of commercial forces that threatened to commandeer American folk music. They were able constantly to move forward because, despite social and cultural tribulations, the revivalists believed in the movement's message. The folk revivalists sought to infuse folk music into mainstream culture with the intention of reforming the nation in the process. At the core of the revival was a goal to spread a version of Americanism that was inclusive of all citizens. If Americans understood that political democracy and cultural pluralism were the ideals that defined the nation, then they would be more likely to put those ideals into practice by bringing marginalized citizens into the political process—or so the revivalists believed. Even when the political climate did not particularly favor their version of Americanism, the revivalists continued to push forward, using folk music to challenge the status quo.

While they had withstood hardship and competing visions of Americanism before, the revivalists had not previously encountered anything like the turmoil of the late 1960s. At that time, ideas of a universal national identity—no matter how inclusive—became irrelevant in many leftist circles. Programs of reform equally fell by the wayside, as activists grew disillusioned with their failed efforts. Many remained politically active but now channeled their energy into specific programs rather than broad-based movements to change the nation as a whole. As leftists shed their affiliation with the nation, nationalism became the domain of their political counterparts. A climate such as this left little room for the Americanism of the revival. Although they remained committed to folk music, they no longer sustained the vision that had guided the movement.

Even before the dust settled from the turbulent end of the 1960s, a new generation of political activists combined ideas of American pluralism that originated in cultural pluralism and cosmopolitanism with aspects of the racial and ethnic nationalism that emerged during the decade. These figures belonged to the first generation of multiculturalists, with many channeling their efforts into educational reform via multiethnic initiatives. In so doing, they created a new space for the emergence of a democratic, pluralist Americanism similar to the kind that the revivalists had articulated. While this movement would change over the remaining decades of the century, during the 1970s a contingent of multiculturalists believed that cultural difference was the essence of American identity. Furthermore, they argued that racial and ethnic pride were not anathema to national unity and encouraged members of minority groups to be proud of their traditions and of their contributions to the country.

This was the same message that the former revivalists and cultural preservationists channeled into the Smithsonian Festival of American Folklife. The organizers of the program aimed to preserve folk traditions, not necessarily by going into folk communities armed with recording devices, but, rather, by getting the communities to protect their own traditions. They would do so, the organizers believed, if their members developed a sense of pride in their heritage. A public audience would also learn about the importance of these traditions both for their own sake and for their contribution to the cultural fabric of American life by learning them firsthand through the festival. In designing a festival with these intentions, the organizers did not seek to revive the revival. Rather, they sought to borrow aspects of the movement and channel them into a new program—and, perhaps, even a new movement.

# CONCLUSION

⌢

Every revival contains within itself the seed not only of its
own destruction . . . but also of new revivals.

—BENJAMIN A. BOTKIN,
"THE FOLK SONG REVIVAL: CULT OR CULTURE?"

The beginning of the folk music revival in the United States did not sig-
nify the beginning of popular interest in folk culture—music, lore,
crafts, and dance. Folk enthusiasts had sought to study and preserve folk
culture in America since the mid-nineteenth century. The revival, however, was
a distinct movement, predicated on preserving folk music and infusing it into
mainstream American culture. The revivalists believed that folk music, as
music of the people, reflected the nation's diverse cultural heritage. Furthermore, they argued that this music illustrated the cultural and political democracy that lay at the core of the nation's identity, for in their eyes, American folk
music included songs that came from and songs that were written for the people. This in turn led them to use folk music as a tool in securing social justice.
These principles lay at the heart of the folk revival, and they guided the movement from its beginning in the 1930s through its end in the late 1960s.

In popular culture, the revival is generally perceived as encompassing the
period of the folk boom of the 1950s and 1960s, when folk music became a pop
culture phenomenon. Many scholars take a more nuanced approach and date
the emergence of the revival to the 1940s, when urban listeners first began to
take interest in the genre. Yet even this interpretation uses popularity as the
litmus test for determining the chronological parameters of the movement. Defining the revival according to the criterion of popularity not only robs it of any
theoretical underpinnings but also does not provide a way of understanding the
revivalists' motivations. According to this assessment, there does not seem to be
a way to distinguish the revival from any other musical phenomenon.

The folk music revival, however, was far more than merely a musical fad.
Rather, the revivalists actively used music to promote a larger political agenda,

which entailed generating an Americanism rooted in political democracy and cultural pluralism. To ensure that their interpretation of American identity took root, the revivalists brought folk music into programs of activism that aimed to make the nation live up to its democratic ideals in practice as much as in rhetoric. The revivalists used folk music to secure Americans' commitment to democracy during World War II, to generate a singing labor movement during the 1940s, and to fight for civil rights and combat prejudice in American society from the 1930s through the 1960s. While many revivalists who adhered to this progressive interpretation of Americanism were inspired by Popular Front Americanism, this view was not restricted to members of the left. Even politically centrist revivalists, such as Sarah Gertrude Knott, believed that a pluralist version of democracy was the crux of Americanism.

What complicates the story of the revival is that it did not remain cohesive for long. Over time different subgroups developed within the movement that eventually would contribute to the revival's undoing. After the collapse of People's Songs, arguably at the forefront of the movement during the post–World War II era, the revivalists separated into diffuse programs. Despite the harsh political climate of 1950s America, most revivalists, ranging from those involved in People's Artists and *Sing Out!* to those involved in the National Folk Festival and Folkways Records, continued to promote democratic Americanism through folk music. In the midst of these groups, a new offshoot emerged: the cultural radicals of the *Anthology of American Folk Music* generation. These folk enthusiasts, however, used folk music to carve out an identity for themselves rather than to articulate an interpretation of national identity. During the 1950s, at least, these figures remained connected to the movement because they were inspired by older revivalists such as Pete Seeger and revival programs such as Folkways Records. Yet the advent of this group marked the beginning of a coterie of folk music enthusiasts that would eventually break away from the core of the revival in the following decade.

By the 1960s, many of the college enthusiasts of the previous decade—figures such as Ralph Rinzler, Roger Abrahams, Mike Seeger, John Cohen, and Izzy Young—joined with a new cohort of musical purists to form a cadre of cultural preservationists who actively sought to disentangle folk music from interpretations of Americanism, programs of political reform, and efforts at popularization. The last part of their mission was particularly relevant after the advent of the folk boom. Even though the enthusiasts of the popular boom were the cultural opposite of the purists, they, too, largely separated folk music from the articulations of Americanism that the core revivalists had worked to sustain. For many of them, folk music was just another part of the consumer culture of the early 1960s. In one sense, then, the revivalists had succeeded in their efforts to popularize folk music. However, the boom was actually one of the seeds of the revival's destruction. In the midst of these opposing trajectories— the folk music purists' cultural preservation efforts and the commercialization of the folk boom—the core revivalists tried to keep their message alive. Many became immersed in the democratic activism of the Civil Rights Movement and the New Left, bringing folk music to these new programs of democratic political reform.

The one quality that the boom, the left, and concepts of progressive Americanism shared in this era was instability. Like any fad, the boom lasted as long as the fickle fans of pop music remained interested, and by the end of the decade, rock-and-roll had captured the youth market once again. Many folk musicians of the boom turned to rock music, segued into the singer-songwriter movement of the late 1960s, or found a home in the new genre of adult contemporary music. The New Left and the Civil Rights Movement suffered from their own internal divisions that fractured both movements and instigated the advent of new, specialized forms of activism. Similarly, visions of a unified America had collapsed by the end of the decade. In the growing cacophony that resulted from an increasingly violent antiwar movement, cultural radicalism and separatism, and the not so Silent Majority, the pluralist version of democracy that the revivalists advocated was drowned out.

Even though this period marked the end of a sustained era of efforts to generate a democratic American identity, it was not the end of democratic Americanism altogether. Rather, the ideas that made up this nationalism—democracy, pluralism, cosmopolitanism—continued to inform a new concept of American identity embodied in multiculturalism. Multiculturalism combined ideas of cultural democracy with concepts of cultural pride that came out of the racial nationalism of the late 1960s. At the same time that multiculturalism emerged, a group of cultural preservationists became involved in the Smithsonian Festival of American Folklife (FAF), which was designed to bring traditional folk music back into the public sphere. Using rhetoric akin to that of the multiculturalists, the festival's organizers argued that folk music could help members of ethnic and racial minorities develop pride in their traditions and thus work to preserve their cultural practices. This had been one of the guiding principles of the folk revival, and the many people who participated in the FAF had been the folk music purists of the 1950s and 1960s. This cohort of preservationists had severed ties with the revival in the midst of the folk boom and charted their own path, which had perhaps enabled them to survive the end of the movement. Even though the FAF began during the waning years of the revival, organizers like Rinzler insisted that the festival was not a revival program. Despite their disengagement from the movement, these preservationists did borrow concepts that had first emerged in the revival. The FAF organizers argued that the program provided a way for ethnic, racial, and socioeconomic minorities to speak for themselves directly to a public audience. This idea was crucial to the revival, and even though the FAF was not *of* the movement, it carried many of the revivalists' core ideas into a new era.

By understanding what connected the revivalists and what motivated them throughout the movement, historians can gain a deeper understanding of both the revival itself and the role that it played in American cultural politics over the course of the mid-twentieth century. For forty years, the folk music revivalists worked to use folk music in efforts to bring all citizens into the national community in a figurative sense, by ensuring their representation in concepts of national identity, and in a literal sense, by securing their participation in the political, cultural, and economic systems. In their hands, folk songs became the music of the kind of America that they worked to achieve.

# APPENDIX:
# A NOTE ON RESOURCES FOR
# RECORDED MUSIC

There are several ways readers can access the music discussed in this book. Most of the mainstream artists' albums are available on compact disc, as are various "best of" and bootleg collections. Many of the obscure artists' songs and albums have been made available either in their original form or through box sets. For instance, all of the albums released on Folkways Records can be ordered through Smithsonian Folkways; the liner notes for the albums are available on the Smithsonian Folkways website at http://www.folkways.si.edu. In 1997, Smithsonian Folkways released Harry Smith's Anthology of American Folk Music on compact disc; the box set is still available with the original liner notes that Harry Smith wrote, along with new notes that provide a history of the collection and its cultural influence and a biography of Harry Smith. Smithsonian Records has also released several collections of folk music from the late 1950s and early 1960s—most notably, Friends of Old Time Music: The Folk Arrival, 1961–1965 (2006), an assortment of fifty-five live recordings from the New York City performances. The label issued a collection bringing together traditional artists and interpreters from the 1940s through the 1960s in Classic Folk Music from Smithsonian Folkways Recordings (2004).

For those interested in the political material, the definitive collection of left-wing folk songs from the late 1920s through the Almanacs era and into the early 1950s is *Songs for Political Action* (1996), a ten album set released on Bear Family Records. In addition to being the most thorough collection of this kind of music, the set comes with extensive liner notes that situate the recordings within their historical context. A strong collection of relatively obscure political songs from the later years of the revival is *The Best of Broadside: 1962–1988* (2000), released on Smithsonian Folkways Records. This set covers highlights from the political singer-songwriters of the *Broadside* community spanning the period covered in this book and beyond.

There are many albums of recordings from folk festivals. Newport alone has several that highlight the best performances of different genres during the early to mid-1960s. Examples include *Newport Folk Festival: The Best of Blues, 1959–1968* (Vanguard, 2000) and *Newport Folk Festival: The Best of Bluegrass, 1959–1966* (Vanguard, 2001). Vanguard has also released an album devoted to the concert highlights from 1963, *The Newport Folk Festival 1963: The Evening Concerts, Volume 1* (1996). For Bob Dylan fans, a collection of his Newport performances is available on the DVD *The Other Side of the Mirror: Live at Newport Folk Festival, 1963–1965* (Sony Music, 2007). The Smithsonian Center for Folklife and Cultural Heritage has established a radio station of performances from the Festival of American Folklife (currently called the Folklife Festival) dating back to the late 1960s; it is available at http://www.festival.si.edu.

The American Folklife Center (AFC) at the Library of Congress retains all of Alan Lomax's field recordings, as well as those of his father, in the Lomax Family Collections. Recently, the AFC released all of Alan Lomax's recordings—more than 17,400 digital audio files—through the Cultural Equity Project, available at http://research.cultural equity.org. A sampling of this collection is also available on the compact disc *The Alan Lomax Collection from the American Folklife Center* (Odyssey Productions, 2012). In addition, the AFC contains recordings of several of Alan Lomax's radio shows, which are available in the center's archives and through the Cultural Equity Project website.

# NOTES

<br>

## INTRODUCTION

1. Pete Seeger, "Why Folk Music?" in *The American Folk Scene: Dimensions of the Folksong Revival,* ed. David A. DeTurk and A. Poulin Jr. (New York: Dell, 1967), 46, 48.

2. Ron Eyerman and Andrew Jamison, *Music and Social Movements: Mobilizing Traditions in the Twentieth Century* (New York: Cambridge University Press, 1998), 6–11.

3. Rogers M. Smith, *Civic Ideals: Conflicting Visions of Citizenship in U.S. History* (New Haven, Conn.: Yale University Press, 1997), 477.

4. David A. Hollinger, *Postethnic America: Beyond Multiculturalism* (New York: Basic Books, 1995).

5. Richard Reuss and JoAnne C. Reuss, *American Folk Music and Left-Wing Politics, 1927–1957* (Lanham, Md.: Scarecrow Press, 2000).

6. Michael Denning, *The Cultural Front: The Laboring of American Culture in the Twentieth Century* (New York: Verso, 1996), 5.

7. While George Hertzog is often credited with coining this phrase in the *Encyclopedia of Folksong* (1949), it is a definition that has more or less applied to American folk music from the turn of the twentieth century.

8. Thomas Rochon, *Culture Moves: Ideas, Activism, and Changing Values* (Princeton, N.J.: Princeton University Press, 1998), 9, 16.

9. William G. Roy, *Reds, Whites, and Blues: Social Movements, Folk Music, and Race in the United States* (Princeton, N.J.: Princeton University Press, 2010), 5.

10. Benjamin Filene, *Romancing the Folk: Public Memory and American Roots Music* (Chapel Hill: University of North Carolina Press, 2000), 24–25; David Whisnant, *All That Is Native and Fine: The Politics of Culture in an American Region* (Chapel Hill: University of North Carolina Press, 1983), 105, 112, 119, 124; John Alexander Williams, *Appalachia: A History* (Chapel Hill: University of North Carolina Press, 2002), 211–212.

11. Simon J. Bronner, *Following Tradition: Folklore in the Discourse of American Culture* (Logan: Utah State University Press, 1998), 131–133; Rosemary Zumwalt, *American*

*Folklore Scholarship: A Dialogue of Dissent* (Bloomington: Indiana University Press, 1988), 5, 7.

12. Regina Bendix, *In Search of Authenticity: The Formation of Folklore Studies* (Madison: University of Wisconsin Press, 1997), 131.

13. John Lomax, *Adventures of a Ballad Hunter* (New York: Hafner, 1971 [1947]), viii, 1.

14. John Lomax, *Cowboy Songs and Other Frontier Ballads* (New York: Macmillan, 1922 [1911]).

15. Daniel J. Walkowitz, *City Folk: English Country Dance and the Politics of the Folk in Modern America* (New York: New York University Press, 2010), 3.

16. Nolan Porterfield, *Last Cavalier: The Life and Times of John A. Lomax, 1867–1948* (Urbana: University of Illinois Press, 1996), 168.

17. Lomax, *Adventures of a Ballad Hunter*, 121.

18. Ibid., 98.

19. Lynn Moss Sanders, *Howard W. Odum's Folklore Odyssey: Transformation to Tolerance through African American Folk Studies* (Athens: University of Georgia Press, 2003), 11–12, 14; D. K. Wilgus, *Anglo-American Folksong Scholarship since 1898* (New Brunswick, N.J.: Rutgers University Press, 1959), 152–153; Howard W. Odum, "Folk-Song and Folk-Poetry as Found in the Secular Songs of the Southern Negroes," *Journal of American Folklore* 24, no. 93 (July–September 1911): 255–294.

20. Sanders, *Howard W. Odum's Folklore Odyssey*, 18–19, 42.

21. Lomax, *Cowboys Songs and Other Frontier Ballads*, xxvi.

22. Phillips Barry, "The Collection of Folk-Song," *Journal of American Folklore* 27, no. 103 (March 1914): 77.

23. James Henry Powell, "The Concept of Cultural Pluralism in American Thought, 1915–1965" (Ph.D. diss., University of Notre Dame, Notre Dame, Ind.), 13; Everett Helmut Akam, *Transnational America: Cultural and Pluralist Thought in the Twentieth Century* (Lanham, Md.: Rowman and Littlefield, 2002), 3, 57; Rivka Shpak Lissak, *Pluralism and Progressives: Hull House and New Immigrants, 1890–1919* (Chicago: University of Chicago Press, 1989), 150–152, 155.

24. Lissak, *Pluralism and Progressives*, 40–42, 164–165.

25. Simon J. Bronner, *Folk Nation: Folklore in the Creation of American Tradition* (Wilmington, Del.: Scholarly Resources, 2002), 17.

26. Randolph Bourne, "Transnational America," in *History of a Literary Radical and Other Essays,* ed. Van Wyck Brooks, ed. (New York: B. W. Huebsch, 1920), 267, 295–297.

27. Robert Dorman, *Revolt of the Provinces: The Regionalist Movement in America, 1920–1945* (Chapel Hill: University of North Carolina Press, 1993), xi–xiii, 83; Benjamin Botkin, "Regionalism and Culture," in *The Writer in a Changing World,* 2d ed., ed. Henry Hart (New York: Equinox Cooperative Press, 1937), 140.

28. Dorman, *Revolt of the Provinces*, 9–10, 33, 66.

29. Benjamin Botkin, *Folk-Say: A Regional Miscellany* (Norman: University of Oklahoma Press, 1929–1932), 14.

30. "The Boom in Regionalism," editorial, *Saturday Review of Literature* 10, no. 38, April 7, 1934, 606, in Howard W. Odum and Harry Estill Moore, *American Regionalism: A Cultural-Historical Approach to National Integration* (New York: Henry Holt, 1938), 180.

31. Carl Sandburg, *The American Songbag* (New York: Harcourt Brace, 1927).

32. Karl Hagstrom Miller, *Segregating Sound: Inventing Folk and Pop Music in the Age of Jim Crow* (Durham, N.C.: Duke University Press, 2010), 244.

33. Sandburg, *The American Songbag*, viii.

34. Ibid., vii.

## CHAPTER 1

1. Michael Denning, *The Cultural Front: The Laboring of American Culture in the Twentieth Century* (New York: Verso, 1996), 129–131.

2. Gary Gerstle, "The Protean Character of American Liberalism," *American Historical Review* 99, no. 4 (October 1994): 1044–1045, 1068–1069.

3. Warren Susman, *Culture as History: The Transformation of American Society in the Twentieth Century* (New York: Pantheon, 1984), 157.

4. Terry Cooney, *Balancing Acts: American Thought and Culture in the 1930s* (New York: Twayne, 1995), 109; Gerstle, "The Protean Character of American Liberalism," 1068.

5. Michael C. Steiner, "Regionalism in the Great Depression," *Geographical Review* 73, no. 4 (October 1983): 432–433; Barbara Allen, "Regional Studies in American Folklore Scholarship," in *Sense of Place: American Regional Cultures*, ed. Barbara Allen and Thomas Schlereth (Lexington: University of Kentucky Press, 1990), 2–3, 6

6. Steiner, "Regionalism in the Great Depression," 430. In his assessment of the regionalist community, Steiner includes intellectuals associated with the Agrarian Fugitives at Vanderbilt University (the authors of *I'll Take My Stand*, a collection of essays bemoaning the loss of traditional southern culture in the face of industrialization and other effects of modernity) as the conservative wing of regionalism because they sought to use regionalist tactics to stem the tide of industrialism and regress to a more traditional, agrarian era. Several scholars include the Agrarians in the regionalist movement, but the Fugitives' understanding of the South and its place in America was antithetical to the premises of regionalism. The Fugitives were involved in a sectional campaign to identify a particularly southern way of life and to return the South to a romanticized past and re-entrench a racial hierarchy. Renowned southern regionalists such as Howard Odum, however, recoiled against this sectionalism because it focused on the South as an entity unto itself and did not seek to incorporate it into the national whole. As Odum argued, the goal of regionalism was to use a "cultural-historical approach to national unity and to translate the older historical sectionalism into a dynamic doctrine of national development": Howard W. Odum and Harry Estill Moore, *American Regionalism: A Cultural-Historical Approach to National Integration* (New York: Henry Holt, 1938), v. Botkin even attacked the Agrarian mission as incompatible with regionalism not only because it was "reactionary and regressive," but also because "regional writers do not make the mistake of identifying culture with a *way* of life; rather, they describe *ways* of living": Benjamin Botkin, "Regionalism and Culture," in *The Writer In a Changing World*, 2d ed., ed. Henry Hart (New York: Equinox Cooperative Press, 1937), 152, 155. The Fugitives, for their part, also had little to do with the southern regionalists like Odum, who were centered at the University of North Carolina.

7. Paul Sporn, *Against Itself: The Federal Theater and Writers' Projects in the Midwest* (Detroit: Wayne State University Press, 1995), 50–51.

8. Alan Lomax and Benjamin Botkin, "Folklore, American: Ten Eventful Years," in *Encyclopedia Britannica* (Chicago: University of Chicago Press, 1947), 359.

9. Diana Selig, *Americans All: The Cultural Gifts Movement* (Cambridge, Mass.: Harvard University Press, 2008), 15.

10. Ronald D. Cohen, *A History of Folk Music Festivals in the United States: Feasts of Musical Celebration* (Lanham, Md.: Scarecrow Press, 2008), 2.

11. John M. Hurley, "Hartford's Racial Cultural Program," *Recreation Magazine* 28 (January 1936): 501–507, 522.

12. Annabel Morris Buchanan, "The Function of a Folk Festival," *Southern Folklore Quarterly* 1, no. 1 (March 1937): 32, 34.

13. Michael Ann Williams, *Staging Tradition: John Lair and Sarah Gertrude Knott* (Urbana: University of Illinois Press, 2006), 16–18.

14. Ibid., 13–14; David Glassberg, *American Historical Pageantry: The Uses of Tradition in the Early Twentieth Century* (Chapel Hill: University of North Carolina Press, 1990), 243–247, 251.

15. Williams, *Staging Tradition*, 13.

16. Zoe Burkholder, *Color in the Classroom: How American Schools Taught Race, 1900–1954* (Oxford: Oxford University Press, 2011), 21; Selig, *Americans All*, 2, 4.

17. Burkholder, *Color in the Classroom*, 27.

18. Sarah Gertrude Knott, "The National Folk Festival USA: A Flashback to 1934," undated ms., drawer 1, folder 30, Sarah Gertrude Knott Collection, Folklife Archives, Kentucky Library and Museum, Western Kentucky University, Bowling Green (hereafter, FA).

19. Allen, "Regional Studies in American Folklore Scholarship," 2–3, 6.

20. Williams, *Staging Tradition*, 25; 1934 National Folk Festival Program book, n.p.; Sarah Gertrude Knott, "The First National Folk Festival—St. Louis, MO, 1934," drawer 1, folder 58, Sarah Gertrude Knott Collection, FA.

21. Selig, *Americans All*, 6, 13.

22. Second festival program, 1935, Chattanooga, drawer 1, folder 59, Sarah Gertrude Knott Collection, FA.

23. Williams, *Staging Tradition*, 29, 32–35.

24. Sarah Gertrude Knott, "Texas Celebrates its Hundredth Birthday," *Recreation* 30 (October 1936): 374.

25. Sarah Gertrude Knott, "General Plan" of the National Folk Festival Association (1939), drawer 1, folder 28, Sarah Gertrude Knott Collection, FA.

26. Williams, *Staging Tradition*, 38; Daniel J. Walkowitz, *City Folk: English Country Dance and the Politics of the Folk in Modern America* (New York: New York University Press, 2010), 170.

27. Radio broadcast on WCFL, Chicago, April 3, 1937, 3, 5, drawer 1, folder 61, Sarah Gertrude Knott Collection, FA.

28. Archie Green, "The National Folk Festival Association: Commercial Music Graphics #32," *John Edwards Memorial Foundation Quarterly* 11, no. 37 (Spring 1975): 24.

29. Burkholder, *Color in the Classroom*, 21; Selig, *Americans All*, 275.

30. Benjamin Botkin, "WPA and Folklore Research: 'Bread and Song,'" *Southern Folklore Quarterly* 3, no. 1 (March 1939): 10–11.

31. Jerrold Hirsch, "Folklore in the Making: B.A. Botkin," *Journal of American Folklore* 100, no. 395 (January–March 1987): 3–4.

32. Botkin, "WPA and Folklore Research," 10, 13, 14.

33. Benjamin Filene, *Romancing the Folk: Public Memory and American Roots Music*. Chapel Hill: University of North Carolina Press, 2000, 137–138; Simon J. Bronner, *Following Tradition: Folklore in the Discourse of American Culture* (Logan: Utah State University Press, 1998), 151.

34. From the Library of Congress's "Report of the Librarian of Congress for the Fiscal Year Ending June 30, 1928," 143–144, and from the Library of Congress's "Report of the Librarian of Congress for the Fiscal Year Ending June 30, 1929," 193, in box 5, Thesis Folklore and the New Deal, 1928–1985, folder, Richard A. Reuss Papers, Indiana University Archives, Indiana University, Bloomington (hereafter, IUA).

35. Filene, *Romancing the Folk*, 56.

36. Alan Lomax to Archive of American Folk Song, letter, September 18, 1941, in Ronald D. Cohen, ed., *Alan Lomax, Assistant in Charge: The Library of Congress Letters, 1935–1942* (Jackson: University of Mississippi Press, 2011), 242.

37. Alan Lomax to Harold Spivack, letter, June 8, 1938, in ibid., 79.

38. Lomax and Botkin, "Folklore, American," 359.

39. Cohen, *A History of Folk Music Festivals in the United States,* 22.

40. Alan Lomax to Olin Downes, letter, June 18, 1938, in Cohen, *Alan Lomax, Assistant in Charge,* 72.

41. Ibid. Despite his noble attempts and detailed plans, the festival as Lomax envisioned it never took place at the fair.

42. John Szwed, *Alan Lomax: The Man Who Recorded the World* (New York: Viking, 2010), 131.

43. Jeffrey E. Mirel, *Patriotic Pluralism: Americanization Education and European Immigrants* (Cambridge, Mass.: Harvard University Press, 2010), 159–164.

44. Ibid., 175; Burkholder, *Color in the Classroom,* 60–61.

45. Alfred Haworth Jones, "The Search for a Usable American Past in the New Deal Era," *Journal of American History* 23, no. 5 (1971): 718.

46. John Lomax, *Adventures of a Ballad Hunter* (New York: Hafner, 1971 [1947]), 117–118.

47. Gene Bluestein, "The Lomaxes' New Canon of American Folksong," *Texas Quarterly* 5, no. 1 (Spring 1962): 55, 58.

48. Alan Lomax, "America Sings the Saga of America," *New York Times Magazine,* January 26, 1947, 41.

49. Charles Seeger, *Music Manual for the Special Services Division of the Resettlement Administration, 1937,* box 8, Charles Seeger—Music Manual for the Resettlement Administration, 1937–1939, folder, Richard A. Reuss Papers, IUA.

50. Interview with Charles Seeger, tape 1, February 15, 1975 (Kate and Ralph), FP 2006-CT-00067, Ralph Rinzler Papers, Center for Folklife and Cultural Heritage, Smithsonian Institution, Washington, D.C. (hereafter, CFCH).

51. Nolan Porterfield, *Last Cavalier: The Life and Times of John A. Lomax, 1867–1948* (Urbana: University of Illinois Press, 1996), 390–391.

52. Charles Seeger to Nikolai Sokoloff, "Details for the Programming of Folk Music Units," memorandum, November 18, 1938, box 8, Charles Seeger—WPA Music Project, 1938–1939, folder, Richard A. Reuss Papers, IUA.

53. John Diggins, *The Rise and Fall of the American Left* (New York: W. W. Norton, 1992), 148–149.

54. Malcolm Cowley, *The Dream of the Golden Mountains: Remembering the Thirties* (New York: Viking, 1980), 22, 33–34, 43; Richard Pells, *Radical Visions and American Dreams: Culture and Social Thought in the Depression Years* (New York: Harper and Row, 1973), 159.

55. Interview with Harriet and A. B. Magil, April 3, 1976, 20–21, in David K. Dunaway Collection, American Folklife Center, Archive of Folk Culture, Library of Congress, Washington, D.C. (hereafter, AFC).

56. Harvey Klehr, *The Heyday of American Communism: The Depression Decade* (New York: Basic Books, 1984), 104.

57. Interview with Bess Lomax Hawes, May 6, 1977, 6, in David K. Dunaway Collection, AFC.

58. Klehr, *The Heyday of American Communism,* 217. While communists tried to

bury the hatchet with socialists, many did not respond in kind. After years of antipathy, many socialists refused to work with communists during the 1930s.

59. Denning, *The Cultural Front,* 4, 9.

60. Maurice Isserman, *Which Side Were You On? The American Communist Party during the Second World War* (Middletown, Conn.: Wesleyan University Press, 1982), 120; Klehr, *The Heyday of American Communism,* 207.

61. Denning, *The Cultural Front,* 133.

62. Interview with Norman Cazden, June 17, 1976, 16–17, David K. Dunaway Collection, AFC.

63. Richard Reuss and JoAnne C. Reuss, *American Folk Music and Left-Wing Politics, 1927–1957* (Lanham, Md.: Scarecrow Press, 2000), 59–61.

64. Michael Gold, "Change the World," *Daily Worker,* April 21, 1934, 7, box 5, Anthology—Worker's Chorus Movement ca. 1934–1940 folder, Richard A. Reuss Papers, IUA.

65. Interview with Charles Seeger, June 6, 1976, 25, in David K. Dunaway Collection, AFC.

66. Reuss and Reuss, *American Folk Music and Left-Wing Politics,* 46.

67. Gold, "Change the World."

68. Seeger interview, June 6, 1976, 32.

69. Julia L. Mickenberg, *Learning from the Left: Children's Literature, the Cold War, and Radical Politics in the United States* (New York: Oxford University Press, 2006), 76; Mark Naison, *Communists in Harlem during the Depression* (Urbana: University of Illinois Press, 1983), 11–19; Klehr, *The Heyday of American Communism,* 327–328, 333–340, 342; Isserman, *Which Side Were You On?* 21.

70. Steven Garabedian, "Reds, Whites, and the Blues: Lawrence Gellert, 'Negro Songs of Protest,' and the Left-Wing Folk-Song Revival of the 1930s and 1940s," *American Quarterly* 57, no. 1 (March 2005): 182, 192, 196–198. Gellert began collecting black music in Tryon, North Carolina, to advance the black freedom struggle. He claimed that because he worked for civil rights through the CPUSA, many blacks felt more comfortable around him and were more willing to reveal their protest songs to him—a situation that did not exist for either Lomax or Odum.

71. Reuss and Reuss, *American Folk Music and Left-Wing Politics,* xii, 21, 40, 57.

72. William H. Cobb, *Radical Education in the Rural South: Commonwealth College, 1922–1940* (Detroit: Wayne State University Press, 2000), 15–16, 133–134, 145.

73. Ibid., 214.

74. Robert S. Koppelman, ed., *"Sing Out, Warning! Sing Out, Love!": The Writings of Lee Hays* (Amherst: University of Massachusetts Press, 2003), 56.

75. Ibid., 5, 12, 14–15, 18.

76. Agnes "Sis" Cunningham and Gordon Friesen, *Red Dust and Broadside: A Joint Autobiography,* ed. Ronald D. Cohen (Amherst: University of Massachusetts Press, 1999), 182–194.

77. Denning, *The Cultural Front,* 72.

78. Richard Reuss, "Woody Guthrie and His Folk Tradition," *Journal of American Folklore* 83, no. 329 (July–September 1970): 281.

79. Woody Guthrie to Moses Asch, letter, January 2, 1946, 1, box 3 GS-505, Asch Project—Woody Guthrie: Letters from Woody to Moe folder, Peter Goldsmith Collection, CFCH.

80. Liner notes to Woody Guthrie, *Struggle: Documentary #1,* record album, 1976, 2, FA 2485, Folkways Records and Service Corporation, folder 40025, CFCH. Asch issued six of the songs in 1946, but he did not release the album in its entirety until 1976.

81. Guthrie to Asch, 3.

82. Denning, *The Cultural Front,* 13.

83. Reuss and Reuss, *American Folk Music and Left-Wing Politics,* 104, 116, 122, 128.

84. Earl Robinson and John Latouche, *Ballad for Americans,* record album, Vanguard VRS-9193, New York, 1976 [1940].

85. Denning, *The Cultural Front,* 125.

86. Earl Robinson, and Millard Lampell, *The Lonesome Train,* record album, Decca DL 9065, New York, 1945; Robert Cantwell, *When We Were Good: The Folk Revival* (Cambridge, Mass.: Harvard University Press, 1996), 105–106, 109.


## CHAPTER 2

1. Barbara Savage, *Broadcasting Freedom: Radio, War, and the Politics of Race, 1938–1948* (Chapel Hill: University of North Carolina Press, 1999), 15.

2. John Dewey, *Freedom and Culture* (New York: Putnam, 1939), 9–10.

3. Benjamin Filene, *Romancing the Folk: Public Memory and American Roots Music* (Chapel Hill: University of North Carolina Press, 2000), 133.

4. Zoe Burkholder, *Color in the Classroom: How American Schools Taught Race, 1900–1954* (Oxford: Oxford University Press, 2011), 101–102.

5. Philip Gleason, "WWII and the Development of American Studies," *American Quarterly* 36, no. 3 (1984): 344, 352–353.

6. Wendy Wall, *Inventing the "American Way": The Politics of Consensus from the New Deal to the Civil Rights Movement* (Oxford: Oxford University Press, 2008), 7, 68; Jeffrey E. Mirel, *Patriotic Pluralism: Americanization Education and European Immigrants* (Cambridge, Mass.: Harvard University Press, 2010), 177.

7. Howard W. Odum and Harry Estill Moore, *American Regionalism: A Cultural-Historical Approach to National Integration* (New York: Henry Holt, 1938), 3.

8. Cohen, *Alan Lomax, Assistant in Charge,* 338.

9. Ibid., 368.

10. Ibid., 318.

11. Ibid., 177.

12. Burkholder, *Color in the Classroom,* 68–69, 71.

13. James T. Sparrow, *Warfare State: World War II Americans and the Age of Big Government* (Oxford: Oxford University Press, 2011), 37.

14. Alan Lomax and John Lomax, *Our Singing Country: A Second Volume of American Ballads and Folk Songs* (New York: Macmillan, 1941), xiii.

15. John Szwed, *Alan Lomax: The Man Who Recorded the World* (New York: Viking, 2010), 211.

16. Alan Lomax BBC radio show script, n.d., 14, 17, in Alan Lomax Collection, Various Radio Scripts folder, box 4.01.15, American Folklife Center, Archive of Folk Culture, Library of Congress, Washington, D.C. (hereafter, AFC). Before writing the script Lomax devoted three days to investigating the neighborhood, recording as much of daily life as he could. As a result, even though the show was scripted, much of it was based on his own detailed observations: Szwed, *Alan Lomax,* 202.

17. Michele Hilmes and Jason Loviglio, eds., *Radio Reader: Essays in the Cultural History of Radio* (New York: Routledge, 2002), xi; Michele Hilmes, *Radio Voices: American Broadcasting, 1922–1952* (Minneapolis: University of Minnesota Press, 1997), 11; Lizabeth Cohen, *Making a New Deal: Industrial Workers in Chicago, 1919–1939* (Cambridge: Cambridge University Press, 1990), 327–331.

18. David Sarnoff, *Radio and Education: An Address at the 75th Convocation of the University of the State of New York,* October 31, 1939, 8, 19, box 45, folder 3116, Library of American Broadcasting, University of Maryland, College Park (hereafter, LAB).

19. Savage, *Broadcasting Freedom,* 14.

20. Alan Gevinson, "'What Neighbors Say': The Radio Research Project of the Library of Congress," *Performing Arts Broadcasting,* Winter 2002, 95.

21. Joseph Liss, "Regional Series," in *Report of the Radio Research Project, Library of Congress,* January 1941–February 1942, n.p., AFC.

22. Joseph Liss, "General Statement of Plan to Script Writers Working on Regional Documentary Programs," 2, Radio Research Project Manuscript Collection (hereafter, RRP Manuscript Collection), box 1941/005, untitled folder, AFC; Gevinson, "What Neighbors Say," 95–96.

23. Alan Lomax, "Documentary Activities," in *Report of the Radio Research Project, Library of Congress,* January 1941–February 1942, n.p., AFC.

24. "Okie Festival" transcript, box 1941/005, "Okie" folder, RRP Manuscript Collection, AFC.

25. "Outline of Proposed Defense Activities for the Radio Research Project," 1, "Hidden History" and "Americans Talk Back" box, RRP Manuscript Collection, AFC.

26. Letter from Alan Lomax, December 8, 1941, in RRP Manuscript Collection, box 1941/005, "Declaration of War" and "Declaration of War 2" folder, AFC.

27. Sparrow, *Warfare State,* 63.

28. Sarah Gertrude Knott to Teófilo Borunga, letter, March 14, 1940, drawer 1, folder 64, Sarah Gertrude Knott Collection, Folklife Archives, Kentucky Library and Museum, Western Kentucky University, Bowling Green (hereafter, FA).

29. Sarah Gertrude Knott to A. J. Campbell, Bureau of Information and Publicity, Halifax, Nova Scotia, letter, March 23, 1940, drawer 1, folder 64, Sarah Gertrude Knott Collection, FA.

30. Sarah Gertrude Knott to Mrs. Albert Miller, letter, January 30, 1941, drawer 1, folder 68, Sarah Gertrude Knott Collection, FA.

31. Sarah Gertrude Knott, "Cultures of Many Lands to Be Represented at the National Folk Festival," March 2, 1942, drawer 1, folder 69, Sarah Gertrude Knott Collection, FA.

32. Michael Ann Williams, *Staging Tradition: John Lair and Sarah Gertrude Knott* (Urbana: University of Illinois Press, 2006), 69.

33. "Notes on the Recognition of Change," Eleventh National Folk Festival in Philadelphia (1944), 1, drawer 1, folder 71, FA.

34. "A Glimpse of Folk Festivals in Others Lands through the Eleventh National Folk Festival," draft 2, 3, 5, drawer 1, folder 71, Sarah Gertrude Knott Collection, FA.

35. Burkholder, *Color in the Classroom,* 34–35.

36. "Friends through Recreation, Parts I and II," *Recreation* 39 (January 1946): 525, 526–527, 581. When citing the immigrants who should be credited for fighting for the United States, the author specifically mentions those from Europe, Asia, and Africa.

37. Burkholder, *Color in the Classroom,* 88–89.

38. Sarah Gertrude Knott, "Folk Lore in Our Day," *Recreation* 36 (April 1942): 24.

39. Sarah Gertrude Knott, "Demonstrations of Democracy—World War II Years," 1944, drawer 1, folder 71, Sarah Gertrude Knott Collection, FA.

40. W. P., "Leaders of Parent-Teachers Cites Value of Folk Music," April 4, 1941, drawer 1, folder 66, Sarah Gertrude Knott Collection, FA.

41. Henry Cowell, "Folk Music in a Democracy," in *Studies in Musical Education, History, and Aesthetics* (Pittsburgh: Music Teachers National Association, 1944), 172, 174.

42. James A. Banks, *Multiethnic Education: Theory and Practice*, 2nd ed. (Boston: Allyn and Bacon, 1988), 8.

43. William Vickery and Stewart G. Cole, *Intercultural Education in American Schools* (New York: Harper and Brothers, 1943); James Henry Powell, "The Concept of Cultural Pluralism in American Thought, 1915–1965," Ph.D. diss., University of Notre Dame, South Bend, Ind., 159–161, 163, 178.

44. From 1938 to 1939, CBS had aired a music program as part of the ASA called *Music of America*, but the show featured popular as well as folk music.

45. Sterling Fisher, dir., *Columbia's American School of the Air Teacher's Manual and Classroom Guide*, Department of Education, CBS, October 10, 1939, 16–17, box 45, folder 3156, LAB.

46. For the sake of consistency as well as brevity, the show hereafter will be referred to simply as *Folk Music of America*.

47. Script, *Folk Music of America*, February 20, 1940, 22, box 04.01.01, ASA Scripts 1939–1940 folder 2, AFC.

48. Script, *Wellsprings of Music*, March 1, 1941, 1, box 04.01, ASA scripts 1940–1941 folder 1, AFC.

49. Woody Guthrie, "Do Re Mi," Woody Guthrie Publications and TRO-Ludlow Music (BMI), 1961.

50. Script, *Folk Music of America*, April 9, 1940, 1, box 04.01.01, ASA Scripts 1939–1940 folder 2, AFC.

51. Cohen, *Alan Lomax: Assistant in Charge*, 232.

52. Script, *Wellsprings of Music*, April 14, 1941, 2, box 04.01, ASA Scripts 1940–1941 folder 1, AFC.

53. "The Composer Looks Abroad," *Folk Music of America Teacher's Manual*, 36, box 45, ASA 1940–1942 folder 3157, LAB.

54. Script, *Wellsprings of Music*, January 1, 1942, 1, box 04.01, ASA Scripts 1940–1941 folder 1, AFC.

55. Philip Gleason, "Americans All: World War II and the Shaping of American Identity," *Review of Politics* 43, no. 4 (October 1981): 500–503.

56. Fisher, *Columbia's American School of the Air Teacher's Manual and Classroom Guide*, 16.

57. Ibid.

58. Script, *Folk Music of America*, March 19, 1940, 1, box 04.01.01, ASA Scripts 1939–1940 folder 2, AFC.

59. Michael Denning, *The Cultural Front: The Laboring of American Culture in the Twentieth Century* (New York: Verso, 1996), xvii.

60. Savage, *Broadcasting Freedom*, 76.

61. Script, *Folk Music of America*, April 14, 1940, 2, box 04.01.01, ASA Scripts 1939–1940 folder 2, AFC.

62. Judith Smith, "Radio's 'Cultural Front,' 1938–1948," in *Radio Reader: Essays in the Cultural History of Radio*, ed. Michele Hilmes and Jason Loviglio (New York: Routledge, 2002), 217.

63. Fisher, *Columbia's American School of the Air Teacher's Manual and Classroom Guide*, 25.

64. Burkholder, *Color in the Classroom*, 99.

65. Script, *Wellsprings of Music*, April 1, 1941, 4, 8, box 04.01, ASA Scripts 1940–41 folder 1, AFC.

66. Correspondence Committee, Damascus High School, Damascus, Md., to Alan

Lomax, letter, February 26, 1940, 2, Alan Lomax CBS Radio Series Collection, box 139/002, folder 4, AFC.

67. Mrs. E. C. Ottoson to Alan Lomax, letter, February 5, 1940, and Cranford Public Schools, Cranford, N.J., to Alan Lomax, letter, November 15, 1939, both in Alan Lomax CBS Radio Series Collection, box 139/002, folder 4, AFC.

68. Alan Lomax to Mrs. David L. Wing, letter, October 14, 1940, Alan Lomax CBS Radio Series Collection, box 139/002, folder 1, AFC.

69. Peyton F. Anderson, M.D., to Alan Lomax, letter, February 25, 1940, Alan Lomax CBS Radio Series Collection, box 139/002, ASA Fan Mail folder, AFC.

70. Gary Gerstle, "The Protean Character of American Liberalism," *American Historical Review* 99, no. 4 (October 1994): 1070.


CHAPTER 3

1. Michael Denning, *The Cultural Front: The Laboring of American Culture in the Twentieth Century* (New York: Verso, 1996), 24–25.

2. Richard Reuss and JoAnne C. Reuss, *American Folk Music and Left-Wing Politics, 1927–1957* (Lanham, Md.: Scarecrow Press, 2000), 6.

3. Denning, *The Cultural Front,* 131.

4. During the 1940s, folk music also became popular among apolitical music enthusiasts in cities, particularly in the Northeast. Historians of the revival characterize this era as the beginning of the "urban" phase of the revival, a qualifier that would continue to describe the folk revival for the duration of the movement.

5. Robert S. Koppelman, ed., *"Sing Out, Warning! Sing Out, Love!": The Writings of Lee Hays* (Amherst: University of Massachusetts Press, 2003), 67.

6. Discussion between Pete Seeger and Ralph and Kate Rinzler, December 8, 1991, FP 2006-CT-00038, tape 2, Ralph Rinzler Papers, Center for Folklife and Cultural Heritage, Smithsonian Institution, Washington, D.C. (hereafter, CFCH).

7. "Interview with Millard Lampell," March 30, 1967, Ronald D. Cohen Papers, box 1.2, folder 110, Southern Folklife Collection, University of North Carolina, Chapel Hill (hereafter, SFC).

8. "Notes on a Conversation with Arthur Stern, Gordon Friesen, and Sis Cunningham," December 28, 1965, Ronald Cohen Papers, box 1.2, folder 105, SFC.

9. Denning, *The Cultural Front,* xvii.

10. Interview with Millard Lampell, October 29, 1979, 5, David K. Dunaway Collection, American Folklife Center, Archive of Folk Culture, Library of Congress, Washington, D.C. (hereafter, AFC).

11. Koppelman, *"Sing Out, Warning! Sing Out, Love!"* 84.

12. Interview with Bess Lomax Hawes, May 6, 1977, 30–31, David K. Dunaway Collection, AFC.

13. Ronald D. Cohen, *Rainbow Quest: The Folk Music Revival and American Society, 1940–1970* (Amherst: University of Massachusetts Press, 2002), 35.

14. Interview with Bess Lomax Hawes, May 6, 1977, 66, David K. Dunaway Collection, AFC.

15. Koppelman, *"Sing Out, Warning! Sing Out, Love!"* 69.

16. Interview with A. B. and Harriet Magil, April 3, 1976, 18, David K. Dunaway Collection, AFC.

17. Alan Lomax, quoted in Cohen, *Rainbow Quest,* 25.

18. Episode scripts, *Back Where I Come From,* October 21, 1940, 2, November 10, 1940, 8, February 10, 1941, box 4.01, folder 2, Alan Lomax Collection, AFC.

19. Cohen, *Rainbow Quest,* 28–35.

20. Reuss and Reuss, *American Folk Music and Left-Wing Politics,* 184; Robbie Lieberman, *My Song Is My Weapon: People's Songs, American Communism, and the Politics of Culture, 1930–1950* (Urbana: University of Illinois Press, 1989), 60–61.

21. Lieberman, *My Song Is My Weapon,* 5

22. Cohen, *Rainbow Quest,* 43–44. Political groups like Folksay did not corner the market on folk music activities in New York City and other urban areas. During the same time that they operated, Margaret Mayo organized another, apolitical square dance group that also became popular among folk music enthusiasts.

23. Cohen, *Rainbow Quest,* 35.

24. Maurice Isserman, *Which Side Were You On? The American Communist Party during the Second World War* (Middletown, Conn.: Wesleyan University Press, 1982), 1–2; Cohen, *Rainbow Quest,* 41.

25. Cohen. *Rainbow Quest,* 42–43; Lieberman, *My Song Is My Weapon,* xvi.

26. Interview with Mario Cassetta, September 26, 1976, 16, David K. Dunaway Collection, AFC.

27. Mike Gold, quoted in Cohen, *Rainbow Quest,* 42.

28. Aldon Morris, *The Origins of the Civil Rights Movement: Black Communities Organizing for Change* (New York: Free Press, 1984), 139–140.

29. Thomas Rochon, *Culture Moves: Ideas, Activism, and Changing Values* (Princeton, N.J.: Princeton University Press, 1998), 23, 31.

30. Denning, *The Cultural Front,* 131.

31. *People's Songs* 1, no. 1 (February 1946): 1.

32. Lieberman, *My Song Is My Weapon,* 71.

33. *People's Songs* 1, no. 1 (February 1946): 1.

34. "People's Songs: Songs of Labor and the American People," *People's Songs* 1, no. 12 (January 1947): 3.

35. Benjamin Botkin to Alan Lomax, memo, n.d., 4, Benjamin Botkin box, Richard A. Reuss Papers, Indiana University Archives, Indiana University, Bloomington.

36. "What Is People's Songs?" People's Songs folder, AFC.

37. *People's Songs* 1, no. 9 (October 1946): 3.

38. Lewis Allen, "The House I Live In," *People's Songs* 1, no. 11 (December 1946): 4.

39. Wendy Wall, *Inventing the "American Way": The Politics of Consensus from the New Deal to the Civil Rights Movement* (Oxford: Oxford University Press, 2008), 157.

40. *A People's Songs Workbook* (People's Songs, 1947), 1, 5–6, AFC.

41. Interview with Irwin Silber and Barbara Dane, May 26, 1977, 17–18, David K. Dunaway Collection, AFC.

42. "To the Readers," *People's Songs* 1, no. 2 (March 1946): 1–2.

43. "Song 27: Union Square Dance," *People's Songs* 1, no. 3 (April 1946): 7.

44. Interview with Irwin Silber and Barbara Dane.

45. Woody Guthrie to Moses Asch, letter, August 15, 1946, box 3, Asch Project—Woody Guthrie folder, Peter Goldsmith Collection, CFCH. Despite Guthrie's efforts, this album was never released.

46. Benjamin Botkin, "The Folk-Say of Freedom Songs," *Freedom Train,* October 21, 1947, 14, 16, in "Ben Botkin Correspondence," series 1, box 1, Archie Green Papers, SFC.

47. John Greenway, *American Folk Songs of Protest* (New York: Octagon, 1971), 12, 115.

48. Lord Invader (Rupert Grant), "God Made Us All," *People's Songs* 1, no. 6 (July 1946): 7.

49. Norma and Paul Preston, "Mister KKK," and "Hallelujah, I'm A-Travelin'," *People's Songs* 1, no. 8 (September 1946): 5, 8.

50. Bob and Adrienne Claiborne, "Listen, Mr. Bilbo," *People's Songs* 1, no. 2 (March 1946): 4.

51. Harold Preece and Celia Kraft, "Columbia Town," *People's Songs* 1, no. 5 (June 1946): 7.

52. "Singing Uncommercials," *People's Songs* 2, no. 5 (June 1947): 6; "Brown Skinned Cow," *People's Songs* 2, no. 11 (December 1947): 3.

53. "Housing Action Songbook: On to Sacramento," People's Songs of California, 1947, 5, AFC.

54. "Organize a People's Songs Branch," 1, AFC.

55. Marianne "Jolly" Robinson, *Out of the Frying Pan, Into the Fire: The Restless Journey of Marianne "Jolly" Robinson* (Berkeley, Calif.: Regent Press, 2010), 38–39.

56. Interview with Irwin Silber and Barbara Dane, 45–46.

57. Cohen, *Rainbow Quest*, 46–47, 55–56.

58. Interview with Irwin Silber, December 21, 1977, 2, David K. Dunaway Collection, AFC.

59. Reuss and Reuss, *American Folk Music and Left-Wing Politics*, 271.

60. Richard Weissman, *Which Side Were You On? An Inside History of the Folk Music Revival in America* (New York: Continuum International, 2005), 60.

61. Interview with Roger Abrahams, February 5 1986, SI-FP-1989-0032, tape 2, Robert Cantwell Collection, CFCH.

62. Interview with Pete Seeger, transcript, March 6, 1977, box 2000/019, folder 9, David K. Dunaway Collection, AFC.

63. From the liner notes to *Songs with Guy Carawan*, Folkways Records and Service Corporation, 1958, FG 3544, 3, Guy Carawan folder, CFCH.

## CHAPTER 4

1. For a detailed exploration of the emerging popularity of folk music during the 1950s, see Ronald Cohen and Rachel Donaldson, *Roots of the Revival: Folk Music in the United States and Great Britain in the 1950s* (Urbana: University of Illinois Press, 2014).

2. Although it is clear that she was not a communist sympathizer, Knott included left-wing performers in the NFF. In the 1950s, she included Pete Seeger, despite his political investigation, and in the early 1960s, she invited Jenny Vincent, another performer who was investigated by HUAC, to the NFF stage.

3. Quoted in Ronald D. Cohen, *A History of Folk Music Festivals in the United States: Feasts of Musical Celebration* (Lanham, Md.: Scarecrow Press, 2008), 32.

4. Sarah Gertrude Knott, "We Hold a Golden Key," 1955 Festival Program, 1, drawer 1, folder 82, Sarah Gertrude Knott Collection, Folklife Archives, Kentucky Library and Museum, Western Kentucky University, Bowling Green.

5. Stuart Foster, *Red Alert: Educators Confront the Red Scare in Public Schools, 1947–1954* (New York: Peter Lang, 2000), 85, 95; Andrew Hartman, *Education and the Cold War: The Battle for the American School* (New York: Palgrave Macmillan, 2008), 104–106.

6. Cohen, *A History of Folk Music Festivals in the United States*, 34.

7. Robert Baron, "Postwar Public Folklore and the Professionalization of Folklore

Studies," in *Public Folklore,* ed. Robert Baron and Nicholas Spitzer (Washington, D.C.: Smithsonian Institution Press, 1992), 310.

8. Ronald D. Cohen, *Rainbow Quest: The Folk Music Revival and American Society, 1940–1970* (Amherst: University of Massachusetts Press, 2002), 70.

9. Ibid., 70; Robbie Lieberman, *My Song Is My Weapon: People's Songs, American Communism, and the Politics of Culture, 1930–1950* (Urbana: University of Illinois Press, 1989), 86.

10. Interview with Pete Seeger, March 6, 1977, 70, 73, Box 1, Series 1, AFC 2000/019, folder 9, David K. Dunaway Collection, American Folklife Center, Archive of Folk Culture, Library of Congress, Washington, D.C. (hereafter, AFC).

11. Cohen and Donaldson, *Roots of the Revival,* 82.

12. Interview with Myles Horton, May 2, 1980, David K. Dunaway Collection, AFC.

13. *Red Channels* included Josh White and Burl Ives, who did testify, along with several other members of the folk music community, including Oscar Brand, Richard Dyer-Bennet, Tom Glazer, Millard Lampell, and Alan Lomax.

14. "Investigation of Communism in the Metropolitan Music School, Inc., and Related Fields—Part 2—'Testimony of Earl Robinson,'" in U.S. Congress, *Hearings of the House Un-American Activities Committee* (Washington, D.C.: U.S. Government Printing Office, 1957), 776–793.

15. John Greenway, *American Folksongs of Protest,* repr. ed. (New York: Octagon, 1971), 8.

16. Ibid., 9–10.

17. Interview with Irwin Silber, December 21, 1977, 2, David K. Dunaway Collection, AFC; Lieberman, *My Song Is My Weapon,* 140–144.

18. Irwin Silber, lecture presented at the Center for Folklife and Cultural Heritage, February 1, 1999, CDR no. 478, Center for Folklife and Cultural Heritage, Smithsonian Institution, Washington, D.C. (hereafter, CFCH).

19. Maurice Isserman, *If I Had a Hammer: The Death of the Old Left and the Birth of the New Left* (New York: Basic Books, 1987), 127–128, 147–148. Although Isserman does point out that communists had been against nuclear armaments since 1945, he goes to great lengths to disconnect the pacifists of the 1950s from the remnants of the Old Left. Isserman stipulates that the pacifists reacted against the health hazards of nuclear *testing* to avoid connection to the communist position of being against nuclear weapons, which would leave them open to attack by the anticommunist crusaders. This position, however, appears to have been a tactical rather than a strictly ideological difference between the pacifists and the leftists in respect to ending nuclear development.

20. Leo Cooper, "Alvin the Adamant Atom," *Sing Out!* 3, no. 7 (March 1953): 6–7.

21. "The Unity Chorus—Democracy at Work," *Sing Out!* 2, no. 6 (December 1951): 4.

22. "Lesson from Canada," *Sing Out!* 4, no. 4 (March 1954): 2.

23. "Heritage—U.S.A.," *Sing Out!* 2, no. 3 (August 1951): 2.

24. Ibid., *Sing Out!* 2, no. 9 (March 1952): 8; ibid., *Sing Out!* 3, no. 7 (March 1953): 9.

25. "Songs of Protest, Struggle in the Library of People's Music," *Sing Out!* 2, no. 9 (March 1952): 10.

26. "Heritage—U.S.A.," *Sing Out!* 2, no. 7 (January 1952): 8.

27. Irwin Silber, "'Male Supremacy' and Folk Song," *Sing Out!* 3, no. 7 (March 1953): 4–5, 10. Silber also cautions against taking this too far, noting that singers should not exclude all songs pertaining to love and marriage and peace songs that refer to "mankind" and universal "brotherhood."

28. *Sing Out!* 3, no. 6 (February 1953): 8.

29. "Saint Louis Builds an Inter-Racial Chorus," *Sing Out!* 2, no. 7 (January 1952): 6–7.

30. "Get Ballots with Ballads," *Sing Out!* 3, no. 1 (September 1952): 5.

31. Irwin Silber, "Racism, Chauvinism, Keynote U.S. Music," *Sing Out!* 2, no. 5 (November 1951): 6–7; ibid., *Sing Out!* 2, no. 6 (December 1951): 6.

32. "Heritage—U.S.A.," *Sing Out!* 3, no. 1 (September 1952): 8; *Sing Out!* 3, no. 9 (May 1953): 8.

33. Irwin Silber, "They're Still Writing Folksongs, Says *Sing Out!*'s Editor," *Sing Out!* 7, no. 2 (Summer 1957): 30.

34. "The Witch-Hunt Comes Closer," *Sing Out!* 2, no. 6 (December 1951): 2.

35. "The Un-American Subpoenas," *Sing Out!* 2, no. 9 (March 1952): 2.

36. "The Time of the Lists," *Sing Out!* 4, no. 2 (January 1954): 2.

37. Editorial, *Sing Out!* 6, no. 1 (Winter 1956): 2.

38. Irwin Silber, "Dear Reader," *Sing Out!* 4, no. 7 (Fall 1954): 2. See also Cohen and Donaldson, *Roots of the Revival.*

39. Verta Taylor, "Social Movement Continuity: The Women's Movement in Abeyance," *American Sociological Review* 54, no. 4 (October 1989): 761–762.

40. In the summer of 1949, People's Artists organized the infamous outdoor concert featuring Paul Robeson in Peekskill, New York. Threats of violence prevented the concert from taking place, but People's Artists regrouped and planned a second concert on September 4. This time, protestors followed through on their threats. After the concert, local police directed the exiting audience members down a narrow lane lined with local anti-communists shouting epithets and hurling rocks. Several concert attendees were injured in the melee.

41. Interview with Roger Abrahams, February 4, 1986, SI-FP-1989-CT-0031, tape 1, Robert Cantwell Collection, CFCH.

42. Interview with Irwin Silber, May 26, 1977, 2–3, David K. Dunaway Collection, AFC.

43. Lieberman, *My Song Is My Weapon,* 18; Cohen, *Rainbow Quest,* 42.

44. Interview with Peter Seeger, April 25, 1976, 19, box 1, series I, AFC 2000/019, folder 5, David K. Dunaway Collection, AFC.

45. Cohen, *Rainbow Quest,* 104.

46. Donaldson and Cohen, *Roots of the Revival.*

47. Morris Dickstein, "On and Off the Road: The Outsider as a Young Rebel," in *Beat Culture: The 1950s and Beyond,* ed. Cornelius A. Van Minnen, Jaap Van Der Bent, and Mel Van Elteren (Amsterdam: VU University Press, 1999), 34.

48. Ronald D. Cohen, "Singing Subversion: Folk Music and the Counterculture," in Van Minnen et al., *Beat Culture,* 124–125.

49. Benjamin Filene, *Romancing the Folk: Public Memory and American Roots Music* (Chapel Hill: University of North Carolina Press, 2000), 113, 115; Cohen, "Singing Subversion," 119.

50. Interview with Roger Abrahams.

51. John Cohen, "A Rare Interview with Harry Smith," *Sing Out!* 19, no. 1 (December 1968): 2, 4.

52. Jon Pankake, "The Brotherhood of the Anthology," in *A Booklet of Essays, Appreciations, and Annotations Pertaining to the Anthology of American Folk Music* (Washington, D.C.: Smithsonian Recordings, 1997), 26.

53. Interview with Peter Goldsmith, June 13, 1991, PG 043, Peter Goldsmith Collection, and interview with Ralph Rinzler, May 2, 1989, FP 2006-CT-00032, Ralph Rinzler Papers, CFCH.

54. Stephen Lee Taller to Moses Asch, letter, February 18, 1954, Moses and Francis Asch Collection, folder 45020, CFCH.

55. Lawrence Block, "Foreword," in Dave Van Ronk with Elijah Wald, *The Mayor of MacDougal Street: A Memoir* (Cambridge, Mass.: Da Capo Press, 2005), xii.

56. Van Ronk with Wald, *The Mayor of MacDougal Street,* 46.

57. Cohen, *Rainbow Quest,* 64.

58. Gene Bluestein, "Profiles: Moses Asch," draft of an article for *American Music,* Fall 1987, California State University, Fresno, 9, and interview with Moses Asch, PG044, both in Peter Goldsmith Collection, CFCH.

59. Cohen, *Rainbow Quest,* 40. Though Asch ran the company, Distler was officially named the president to avoid legal complications from Asch's financial disaster.

60. Interview with Moe Asch by Tony Schwartz, n.d., part 2 CDR-518-1, transcript, 1, CFCH; interview with Moses Asch, May 8, 1977, 2, David K. Dunaway Collection, AFC.

61. Michael Asch, "Folkways Records and the Ethics of Collecting: Some Personal Reflections," keynote address presented at the 51st Annual Meeting of the Canadian Society for Traditional Music, University of Alberta, Edmonton, November 2–4, 2007, 5, 9, 11, 15.

62. Peter D. Goldsmith, *Making People's Music: Moe Asch and Folkways Records* (Washington, D.C.: Smithsonian Institution Press, 1998), 98–99, 101–102.

63. David Bonner, *Revolutionizing Children's Records: The Young People's Records and Children's Record Guild Series, 1946–1977* (Lanham, Md.: Scarecrow Press, 2008), 36–38.

64. Beatrice Landeck, liner notes for *Who Built America: American History through Its Folksongs,* Folkways Records and Service Corporation (hereafter, FRSC), 1949, 1, Center for Folklife and Cultural Heritage, Smithsonian Institution, Washington, D.C. (hereafter, CFCH).

65. Liner notes for *Frontier Ballads,* FP5003 (FP 48-5, FP 48-6), FRSC, 1954, 2, CFCH.

66. Lary May, ed., *Recasting America: Culture and Politics in the Age of Cold War* (Chicago: University of Chicago Press, 1989), 5; Jackson Lears, "A Matter of Taste: Corporate Cultural Hegemony in a Mass-Consumption Society," in *Recasting America: Culture and Politics in the Age of Cold War,* ed. Lary May (Chicago: University of Chicago Press, 1989), 42.

67. Stephen J. Whitfield, *The Culture of the Cold War* (Baltimore: Johns Hopkins University Press, 1991), 57.

68. Charles Edward Smith, notes for *The Patriot Plan,* prod. Moses Asch, FRSC, 1958, 1, folder 5710, CFCH.

69. Ibid., 2–3, 5, 12.

70. Charles Edward Smith, text for *The Coming Age of Freedom,* FH 5006 FH 2191, FRSC, 1959, 10, CFCH. This is the "Documents and Speeches" album of the Heritage U.S.A. series.

71. Julia L. Mickenberg, *Learning from the Left: Children's Literature, the Cold War, and Radical Politics in the United States* (New York: Oxford University Press, 2006), 234.

72. Zoe Burkholder, *Color in the Classroom: How American Schools Taught Race, 1900–1954* (Oxford: Oxford University Press, 2011), 151.

73. Esther L. Berg and Florence B. Freedman, eds., *The Recording as a Teaching Tool: A Bulletin for Parents and Teachers,* FRSC, 1955, CFCH; Richard E. Du Wors and William B. Weist, "Records in Sociology," 5; Marguerite Cartwright, "The Use of Records in Intercultural Education," 5; Angelica W. Cass "Using Records of Folk Music in Adult Education," 5; Esther Brown, "Ethnic Dance in the Integrated Curriculum: Integration," 10, all in box 3, Folkways Catalogues folder, Peter Goldsmith Collection, CFCH.

74. Tony Schwartz, liner notes to *Nueva York: A Tape Documentary of Puerto Rican New Yorkers,* FD 5559, FRSC, 1959, CFCH; Robert Shelton, "New York on Tape," *New York Times,* April 12, 1959, 48, 50.

75. Charles Edward Smith, *The Coming Age of Freedom,* FH 5006, FRSC, 1959, 1, CFCH.

76. Bonner, *Revolutionizing Children's Music,* 74–75, 100–103.

77. Asch, "Folkways Records and the Ethics of Collecting," 18.

78. Mickenberg, *Learning from the Left,* 4–5, 15–16, 142.

79. NY 105-14276, box 3 GS-505, Asch Project—FBI Files folder, Peter Goldsmith Collection, CFCH.

80. *Gazette,* vol. 1, FN 2501, FRSC, 1958, 1, folder 2501, CFCH.

81. Andrew J. Dunbar, *America in the Fifties* (Syracuse, N.Y.: Syracuse University Press, 2006), 115.

82. Unprocessed material, folder of conference invitations, CFCH.

83. Mario J. Piriano to Moses Asch, letter, 1960, 1, in ibid.

84. Cohen, *Rainbow Quest,* 130–131.

85. Pete Seeger, "Johnny Appleseed, Jr.," *Sing Out!* 5, no. 4 (Fall 1955}: 44; ibid., *Sing Out!* 6, no. 1 (Winter 1956): 32; ibid., *Sing Out!* 4, no. 7 (Fall 1954): 30.

86. For example, Seeger had learned the song "Michael Row Your Boat Ashore," a black spiritual that white collectors collected in 1867, from Tony Saletan, another musical revivalist. He then taught it to the rest of the Weavers, who introduced it to the larger public by recording the song. The popularity of their recording landed the song in school books and summer camp programs, a process that rendered it "a pale wishy-washy piece of music compared to what it once was": interview with Pete Seeger, August 8, 1978, box 1, series 1, AFC 2000/019, David K. Dunaway Collection, AFC.

87. *Sing Out!* 6, no. 2 (Spring 1956): 2.

88. Letter from Jack Holtzman re[garding] Moses Asch, September 30, 1991, PG070, Peter Goldsmith Collection, CFCH.

89. Alan Lomax, "The 'Folkniks'—and the Songs They Sing," *Sing Out!* 9, no. 1 (Summer 1959): 30, reprinted in Alan Lomax, *Alan Lomax: Selected Writings, 1934–1997,* ed. Ronald D. Cohen. New York: Routledge, 2003.

90. Michael Denning, *The Cultural Front: The Laboring of American Culture in the Twentieth Century* (New York: Verso, 1996), 464.

## CHAPTER 5

1. Ron Eyerman and Scott Barretta, "From the 30s to the 60s: The Folk Music Revival in the United States," *Theory and Society* 25, no. 4 (August 1996): 522; Dave Van Ronk with Elijah Wald, *The Mayor of MacDougal Street: A Memoir* (Cambridge, Mass.: Da Capo Press, 2005), 167.

2. Robert Shelton, "Fad to Staple: Disks Reflect 'Arrival' of Folk Music as Part of Country's Popular Arts," *New York Times,* April 28, 1963, 144.

3. Tamara E. Livingston, "Music Revivals: Towards a General Theory," *Ethnomusicology* 43, no. 1 (Winter 1999): 79.

4. Izzy Young, "Frets and Frails," *Sing Out!* 11, no. 2 (April–May 1961): 49.

5. Irwin Silber, editorial, and Bob West, letter to the editor, *Sing Out!* 13, no. 4 (October–November 1963): 3, 5.

6. Benjamin Botkin, "The Folk Song Revival: Cult or Culture?" *Sing Out!* 15, no. 1 (March 1965): 32.

7. "Folk Songs and the Top 40," *Sing Out!* 16, no. 1 (February–March 1966): 12–14.

8. Ronald D. Cohen, *Rainbow Quest: The Folk Music Revival and American Society, 1940–1970* (Amherst: University of Massachusetts Press, 2002), 158, 160, 177, 193, 198, 200.

9. Ibid., 196–198, 200, 212.

10. Ronald D. Cohen, *A History of Folk Music Festivals in the United States: Feasts of Musical Celebration* (Lanham, Md.: Scarecrow Press, 2008), 46–47.

11. Newport Folk Festival program, 1959, 2, Ralph Rinzler Papers, Center for Folklife and Cultural Heritage, Smithsonian Institution, Washington, D.C. (hereafter, CFCH).

12. "Rinzler Interviews—Audio Tapes," FP 2006-CT-0003, tape 19, October 24–25, 1989, November 1, 1989, Ralph Rinzler Papers, CFCH.

13. Newport Folk Festival Program, 1959, 3.

14. Pete Seeger, "The American Folk Song Revival," in Newport Folk Festival program, 1960, n.p., Ralph Rinzler Papers, CFCH.

15. Cohen, *A History of Folk Music Festivals in the United States*, 75–76.

16. "Discussion between Pete Seeger, Ralph Rinzler, and Kate Rinzler," tape 2, December 8, 1991, FP 2006-CT-00039, Ralph Rinzler Papers, CFCH; Cohen, *A History of Folk Music Festivals in the United States*, 84.

17. John Anthony Scott, "Folklore and Folksong in Education," *New York Folklore Quarterly* 17, no. 4 (Winter 1962): 294–295.

18. Norman Studer, "The Place of Folklore in Education," *New York Folklore Quarterly* 18, no. 1 (Winter 1962): 3–5, 8–11.

19. Robert Shelton, "Folkways in Sound . . . or the Remarkable Enterprises of Mr. Moe Asch," *High Fidelity Magazine*, June 1960, 4.

20. *American History in Ballad and Song, Volume 1: Junior High Social Studies*, prepared by Albert Barouch and Theodore O. Cron, 1960, 1, 3, 8, Folkways Records, folder 5801, CFCH.

21. *American History in Ballad and Song, Volume 2: Senior High School Social Studies*, prepared by Albert Barouch and Theodore O. Cron, 1962, 9, 14–15, 16–17, 21, Folkways Records, folder 5802, CFCH.

22. *American History in Ballad and Song*, 2:8–10.

23. Ibid., 2:13–17.

24. George G. Dawson to Folkways Records, letter, March 29, 1960; Dan Harris to Marion Distler, letter, August 27, 1960, unprocessed material, CFCH.

25. Edmund Gilbertson, review of *American History in Ballad and Song, Volume 1*, *Little Sandy Review*, no. 9, 20.

26. John Szwed, *Alan Lomax: The Man Who Recorded the World* (New York: Viking, 2010), 337.

27. Interview with Ralph Rinzler, FP 2006-CT-0005, January 28, 1992, and interview with Ralph Rinzler, January 20, 1984, SI-FP-1989-CT-0039, Ralph Rinzler Papers, CFCH.

28. The Ramblers tried to re-create a 1930s aura in their look and sound. They adopted the blue eagle, the symbol of the New Deal's National Recovery Administration, as their logo and declared on one album, "I am lost—take me back to 1935": Van Ronk with Wald, *The Mayor of MacDougal Street*, 73.

29. Paul Nelson and Jon Pankake, "Introduction," *Little Sandy Review* 1, no. 1, 1; letter to the editor, *Little Sandy Review* 1, no. 4, 25.

30. Anthony Giddens, quoted in Ron Eyerman and Andrew Jamison, *Music and Social Movements: Mobilizing Traditions in the Twentieth Century* (New York: Cambridge University Press, 1998), 32.

31. Cohen, *Rainbow Quest,* 162–172.

32. Daniel J. Walkowitz, *City Folk: English Country Dance and the Politics of the Folk in Modern America* (New York: New York University Press, 2010), 166.

33. Van Ronk with Wald, *The Mayor of MacDougal Street,* 37.

34. Sean Burns, *Archie Green: The Making of a Working-Class Hero* (Urbana: University of Illinois Press, 2011), 97. It is important to note that the revival contained all of the factionalism that had plagued the American left. For instance, Archie Green was a staunch anticommunist, but he was a leftist in the IWW's anarcho-syndicalist tradition. Similarly, Dave Van Ronk was a libertarian who, along with others, started a Carlo Tresca club in which members had to reject Stalinism and capitalism and believe (and partake) in direct action as the means for achieving social change: Van Ronk with Wald, *The Mayor of Mac-Dougal Street,* 93.

35. Michael Harrington, *The Other America: Poverty in the United States,* repr. ed. (New York: Simon and Schuster, 1997 [1962]); Harry Caudill, *Night Comes to the Cumberlands: A Biography of a Depressed Area* (Ashland, Ken.: Jesse Stuart Foundation, 2001 [1963])

36. Gary Gerstle, *American Crucible: Race and Nation in the Twentieth Century* (Princeton, N.J.: Princeton University Press, 2001), 277.

37. Gene Bluestein, "Songs of the Silent Generation," *New Republic* 144, March 13, 1961, 22.

38. Alan Jabbour, "Foreword," in *Transforming Tradition: Folk Music Revivals Examined: Folk Music Revivals Examined,* ed. Neil V. Rosenberg (Urbana: University of Illinois Press, 1993), xiii.

39. Todd Gitlin, *The Sixties: Years of Hope, Days of Rage* (New York: Bantam, 1987), 59–60, 133; Allen J. Matusow, *The Unraveling of America: A History of Liberalism in the 1960s* (New York: Harper and Row, 1985), 310.

40. Gitlin, *The Sixties,* 26–27.

41. Ibid., 110.

42. James Miller, *Democracy Is in the Streets: From Port Huron to the Siege of Chicago* (New York: Simon and Schuster. 1987), 54.

43. Ibid., 54, 69.

44. Eyerman and Jamison borrow from Pierre Bourdieu's concept of the "habitus," which holds that an individual's identity is formed through personal preferences and learned practices, "patterns or frameworks," that one acquires through childhood socialization. The "habitus" is therefore a combination of personal taste and community values so that an individual's identity is based on their own choices as well as the traditions in which they were raised: Eyerman and Jamison, *Music and Social Movements,* 28.

45. Interview with Roger Abrahams, tape 1, April 2, 1986), SI-FP-1989-CT-0031, Robert Cantwell Collection, CFCH.

46. Eyerman and Jamison, *Music and Social Movements,* 28.

47. Gitlin, *The Sixties,* 75.

48. Interview with Happy Trau, July 14, 1984, 2, David K. Dunaway Collection, American Folklife Center, Archive of Folk Culture, Library of Congress, Washington, D.C. (hereafter, AFC); Richard Flacks, quoted in Miller, *Democracy Is in the Streets,* 161.

49. Gitlin, *The Sixties,* 166. ERAP was an SDS project that formed in 1963. The group focused on techniques of direct action by working within urban communities to teach economically marginalized people how to fight for their own rights. Beginning in 1964, SDS members of the group moved into slums in nine cities and attempted to organize local residents and pressure leaders to respond to the needs of the urban poor.

50. Gordon Friesen, editorial, *Broadside* 1, no. 1 (February 1962): n.p.

51. Agnes "Sis" Cunningham and Gordon Friesen, *Red Dust and Broadsides: A Joint Autobiography,* ed. Ronald D. Cohen (Amherst: University of Massachusetts Press, 1999), 285, 287, 289, 291–292.

52. Gordon Friesen, editorial, *Broadside* 1, no. 5 (May 1962): 2.

53. Bob Cohen, "Mississippi Caravan of Music," *Broadside,* no. 51 (October 1964): n.p.

54. Phil Ochs, "The Need for Topical Music," *Broadside,* no. 22 (March 1963): n.p.

55. John Pankake and Paul Nelson, "P-for-Protest," in *The American Folk Scene: Dimensions of a Folksong Revival,* ed. David A. DeTurk and A. Poulin Jr. (New York: Dell, 1967), 146.

56. The members of this group were musicians whose songs frequently appeared in *Broadside,* including Bob Dylan (during his musically formative years), Len Chandler, Phil Ochs, Mark Spolestra, Pete La Farge, Tom Paxton, Malvina Reynolds, and Janis Ian.

57. "We're Thirteen Years Old and Now Six Times a Year," *Sing Out!* 14, no. 1 (February–March 1964): 3.

58. Irwin Silber, "Fan the Flames," *Sing Out!* 15, no. 1 (March 1965): 47.

59. Ibid., *Sing Out!* 15, no. 3 (July 1965): 69.

60. Robert Shelton, "New Folk Singers in 'Village' Demonstrate a Pair of Trends," *New York Times,* June 11, 1963, 28.

61. Josh Dunson, "Topical Songs and Folksinging, 1965," *Sing Out!* 15, no. 4 (September 1965): 17.

62. Moses Asch and Josh Dunson, "Symposium: Topical Songs and Folksinging, 1965," *Sing Out!* 15, no. 4 (September 1965): 16–17.

63. Michael Denning, *The Cultural Front: The Laboring of American Culture in the Twentieth Century* (New York: Verso, 1996), 26.

64. Miller, *Democracy Is in the Streets,* 144; Dimitrios Roussopoulos and C. George Benello, *Participatory Democracy: Prospects for Democratizing Democracy* (Montreal: Black Rose Books, 2005), 6; Carol Pateman, *Participation and Democratic Theory* (Cambridge: Cambridge University Press, 1970), 42.

65. Quoted in Francesca Poletta, "Strategy and Democracy in the New Left," in *The New Left Revisited,* ed. John McMillian and Paul Buhle (Philadelphia: Temple University Press, 2003), 160–161.

66. Miller, *Democracy Is in the Streets,* 152–153.

67. Cohen, *Rainbow Quest,* 183–187, 204–208.

68. Marion Distler to Guy Carawan, letter, July 11, 1959, Guy Carawan folder 2, CFCH.

69. Cheryl Anne Brauner, "A Study of the Newport Folk Festival and the Newport Foundation," master's thesis, Department of Folklore, Memorial University of Newfoundland, Saint John's, 1983, 91–92.

70. Robert Shelton, "Symbolic Finale," *New York Times,* August 2, 1964, 89.

71. "Watering the Roots," *Sing Out!* 15, no. 6 (January 1966): 61, 63.

72. Miller, *Democracy Is in the Streets,* 231.

73. Irwin Silber lecture, February 1, 1999, CDR no. 478, CFCH; Cohen, *Rainbow Quest,* 245.

74. Miller, *Democracy Is in the Streets,* 234.

75. Gitlin, *The Sixties,* 121, 123.

76. "Pete Seeger Sings and Answers Questions at the Ford Hall Forum, Boston, Mass.," transcript. FH 5702 (BR 502), Folkways Record, 1968, 6, folder 5702, CFCH.

77. John Edgerton, *Speak Now against the Day: The Generation before the Civil Rights Movement in the South* (Chapel Hill: University of North Carolina Press, 1994), 158–160; Cohen, *Rainbow Quest,* 184.

78. Richard Reuss and JoAnne C. Reuss, *American Folk Music and Left-Wing Politics, 1927–1957* (Lanham, Md.: Scarecrow Press, 2000), 99. Originally, the lyrics were "We *will* overcome," but someone along the way, most likely Pete Seeger, changed it to the better-sounding "We *shall* overcome."

79. Guy Carawan to Moses Asch, letter, June 28, 1959, and Guy Carawan, undated memorandum, 1, Guy Carawan folder 2, CFCH.


CHAPTER 6

1. George Wein, quoted in Ronald D. Cohen, *A History of Folk Music Festivals in the United States: Feasts of Musical Celebration* (Lanham, Md.: Scarecrow Press, 2008), 84.

2. Robert Shelton, "A Fare-Thee-Well for Newport Sing," *New York Times,* July 25, 1965, 23.

3. Robert Shelton, "Guthrie's Heirs," *New York Times,* June 14, 1964, X13.

4. Irwin Silber's comments in "The Folksong Revival: A Symposium," *New York State Folklore Quarterly* 19, no. 2 (June 1963): 111.

5. John Cohen, "In Defense of Folk Singers," *Sing Out!* 9, no. 1 (Summer 1959): 33.

6. Jim Rooney, "Newport," *Sing Out!* 15, no. 5 (November 1965): 7.

7. Irwin Silber, "An Open Letter to Bob Dylan," *Sing Out!* 13, no. 5 (November 1964): 22–23.

8. Paul Nelson, "Bob Dylan: Another View," *Sing Out!* 16, no. 1 (February–March 1966): 69.

9. Robert Shelton, "Who's Leading the Folk Pack Now?" *New York Times,* November 20, 1966, D30.

10. Jerome Rodnitzky, *Minstrels of the Dawn: The Folk-Protest Singer as a Cultural Hero* (Chicago: Nelson-Hall, 1975), 21, 23, 146.

11. Ibid., 11, 139.

12. "La Peregracion," *Sing Out!* 16, no. 5 (November 1966): 5.

13. Jimmy Collier, "Burn, Baby, Burn," *Sing Out!* 16, no. 3 (July 1966): 8.

14. Peniel E. Joseph, ed., *The Black Power Movement: Rethinking the Civil Rights–Black Power Era* (New York: Routledge, 2006), 3.

15. William Van Deburg, *New Day in Babylon: The Black Power Movement and American Culture, 1965–1975* (Chicago: University of Chicago Press, 1992), 27.

16. Julius Lester, "The Angry Children of Malcolm X," *Sing Out!* 16, no. 5 (November 1966): 21–25.

17. Gary Gerstle, *American Crucible: Race and Nation in the Twentieth Century* (Princeton, N.J.: Princeton University Press, 2001), 329.

18. See Jeffrey O. G. Ogbar, "Rainbow Radicalism: The Rise of the Radical Ethnic Nationalism," in Joseph, *The Black Power Movement,* 193–228.

19. Gerstle, *American Crucible,* 345.

20. Ibid., 312–317.

21. David A. Hollinger, *Postethnic America: Beyond Multiculturalism* (New York: Basic Books, 1995), 99; David A. Hollinger "Ethnic Diversity, Cosmopolitanism and the Emergence of the American Liberal Intelligentsia," *American Quarterly* 27, no. 2 (May 1975): 149.

22. Gerstle, *American Crucible,* 329.

23. Bruce Jackson, quoted in Cheryl Anne Brauner, "A Study of the Newport Folk Festival and the Newport Foundation," master's thesis, Department of Folklore, Memorial University of Newfoundland, St. John's, 1983, 199.

24. Melvin Hussey, letter, November 5, 1964, and Melvin Hussey to Jim Gray, St. Petersburg Tourist Convention Bureau, letter, November 9, 1964, drawer 1, folder 90, Sarah Gertrude Knott Collection, Folklife Archives, Kentucky Library and Museum, Western Kentucky University, Bowling Green (hereafter, FA).

25. Sarah Gertrude Knott, introduction to the National Folk Festival program, 1967, 1, drawer 1, folder 96, Sarah Gertrude Knott Collection, FA.

26. Sarah Gertrude Knott, "Folksongs and Dances, U.S.A. The Changing Scene," *Southern Folklore Quarterly* 25, no. 3 (September 1961): 191.

27. Melvin Hussey to the White House, letter, February 21, 1965, drawer 1, folder 92, Sarah Gertrude Knott Collection, FA.

28. Sarah Gertrude Knott, "The Past Is Prologue," in National Folk Festival program, 1968, 1, drawer 1, folder 98, Sarah Gertrude Knott Collection, FA.

29. William High Jansen, NFFA, to Roger Stevens, Chairman, Arts Foundation, letter, 1969, drawer 1, folder 99, Sarah Gertrude Knott Collection, FA.

30. Anthony R. Dolan, "Heroes in the Seaweed: Letter from Newport," *National Review,* October 8, 1968, 1011.

31. Brauner, "A Study of the Newport Folk Festival and the Newport Foundation," 84, 93.

32. Bruce Jackson, "The Folksong Revival," in *Transforming Tradition: Folk Music Revivals Examined,* ed. Neil V. Rosenberg (Urbana: University of Illinois Press, 1993), 78.

33. Ibid., 265.

34. Ed Badeaux, "The Spectacle Moves On," *Sing Out!* 17, no. 4 (August–September 1967): 10–13.

35. James Miller, *Democracy Is in the Streets: From Port Huron to the Siege of Chicago* (New York: Simon and Schuster, 1987), 254.

36. Todd Gitlin, *The Sixties: Years of Hope, Days of Rage* (New York: Bantam, 1987), 184–185, 271, 353, 382, 396–397; Miller, *Democracy Is in the Streets,* 265, 311; Rodnitzky, *Minstrels of the Dawn,* 145.

37. "The Weather Underground Communique #1," in Timothy Patrick McCarthy and John McMillan, eds., *The Radical Reader: A Documentary History of the American Radical Tradition* (New York: New Press, 2003), 512.

38. Miller, *Democracy Is in the Streets,* 16, 254.

39. Interview with Margaret Gelder Franz, April 28, 1977, 9, David K. Dunaway Collection, American Folklife Center, Archive of Folk Culture, Library of Congress, Washington, D.C.

40. Gillian Mitchell, *The North American Folk Music Revival: Nation and Identity in the United States and Canada, 1945–1980* (Burlington, Vt.: Ashgate, 2007), 136.

41. Irwin Silber lecture, February 1, 1999, CDR no. 478, Center for Folklife and Cultural Heritage, Smithsonian Institution, Washington, D.C. (hereafter, CFCH).

42. Archie Green, *Torching the Fink Books on Vernacular Culture* (Chapel Hill: University of North Carolina Press, 2001), 141.

43. John Higham, "Multiculturalism and Universalism: A History and a Critique," *American Quarterly* 45, no. 2 (June 1993): 205–206.

44. Gerstle, *American Crucible,* 345.

45. Alan Lomax, quoted in Robert Baron, "Postwar Public Folklore and the Professionalization of Folklore Studies," in *Public Folklore*, ed. Robert Baron and Nicholas Spitzer (Washington, D.C.: Smithsonian Institution Press, 1992), 313.

46. Alan Lomax, "Saga of a Folksong Hunter: A Twenty-Year Odyssey with Cylinder Disc, and Tape," *HiFi/Stereo Review* 4, no. 5 (May 1960): 38.

47. Nathan Glazer, *We Are All Multiculturalists Now* (Cambridge, Mass.: Harvard University Press, 1997), 10–11.

48. Betty Atwell Wright, *Educating for Diversity* (New York: John Day, 1965), 16, 83, 106.

49. Jean Dresden Grambs, *Intergroup Education: Methods and Materials* (Englewood Cliffs, N.J.: Prentice-Hall, 1968).

50. Higham, "Multiculturalism and Universalism," 201.

51. James A. Banks, *Multiethnic Education: Practices and Promises* (Bloomington, Ind.: Phi Delta Kappa Educational Foundation, 1977), 8.

52. Carl A. Grant, ed., *Multicultural Education: Commitments, Issues, and Applications* (Washington, D.C.: Association for Supervision and Curriculum Development, 1977), 2–3.

53. Ibid. For example, the educational theorist H. Prentice Baptist Jr. took a cosmopolitan approach when he called for multiculturalists to recognize the various group cultures that contributed to urban teenagers' individual identities. He therefore strongly encouraged multiculturalists in cities to examine "the culture of poverty," "the youth culture," and "the urban culture" in addition to the cultures of ethnic and racial groups: H. Prentice Baptiste Jr., *Multicultural Education: A Synopsis* (Washington, D.C.: University Press of America, 1979), 10–11.

54. Gerstle, *American Crucible*, 348–349.

55. Higham, "Multiculturalism and Universalism," 205.

56. Banks, *Multiethnic Education*, 13. Black studies directly emerged out of the demand for courses on black history and culture in the late 1960s; courses in Chicano, Asian, and women's studies soon followed suit. As with early pluralists, multiculturalists tried to instill a sense of pride among children of ethnic and racial minorities in their cultural traditions. However, their messages were imbued with a rhetoric emphasizing that racial cultural traditions provided a source of strength for the people of these groups, a rhetoric that did not, and most likely could not, exist in the mainstream before the surge of racial and ethnic nationalism.

57. Alan Lomax, quoted in John Szwed, *Alan Lomax: The Man Who Recorded the World* (New York: Viking, 2010), 49, 361, 364.

58. Green, *Torching the Fink Books and Other Essays on Vernacular Culture*, 145.

59. Marc Pachter, "Oral History Interview with Ralph Rinzler," transcript, 1993, RU-009569, folder 9569, Ralph Rinzler Papers, CFCH.

60. Robert Cantwell, "Feasts of Unnaming: Folk Festivals and the Representation of Folklife," in *Public Folklore*, ed. Robert Baron and Nicholas R. Spitzer (Washington, D.C.: Smithsonian Institution Press, 1992), 273; interviews with Roger Abrahams, with Kate and Ralph Rinzler, June 28, 1993, FP 2006-CT-00039, Ralph Rinzler Papers, CFCH.

61. The organizers of the Smithsonian Festival of American Folklife eventually changed its name to the Smithsonian Folklife Festival, but, because I am concerned with the festival during its early years, I refer to it by its original name.

62. Interview with Ralph Rinzler, January 28, 1992, FP-2006-CT-0005, Ralph Rinzler Papers, CFCH.

63. Roger Abrahams, "Interview with Ralph Rinzler on His Life, Part 1," January 24, 1991, FP-2006-CT-00070, Ralph Rinzler Papers, CFCH.

64. Richard Kurin, "Pursuing Cultural Democracy," *Thirty-Fourth Festival Program Book, 2000,* 4, Ralph Rinzler Papers, CFCH; Richard Kurin, quoted in Cohen, *A History of Folk Music Festivals in the United States,* 116.

65. *Festival Program Book, 1967,* from a bound copy of the Smithsonian Festival of American Folklife, 1967–1973, 1, Ralph Rinzler Papers, CFCH.

66. Ibid., 1

67. Ralph Rinzler, quoted in Cohen, *A History of Folk Music Festival in the United States,* 116–117.

68. S. Dillon Ripley, "The Folk Festival Program," *Festival Program Book, 1968,* 3, Ralph Rinzler Papers, CFCH.

69. Samuel Stanley, "Why American Folklife Studies," *Festival Program Book, 1968,* 12, Ralph Rinzler Papers, CFCH.

70. S. Dillon Ripley, "Introduction," *Festival Program Book, 1968,* 5, Ralph Rinzler Papers, CFCH.

71. Banks, *Multiethnic Education,* 7–8.

72. Ralph Rinzler, "Introduction," *Festival Program Book, 1971,* n.p., Ralph Rinzler Papers, CFCH.

73. Sean Burns, *Archie Green: The Making of a Working-Class Hero* (Urbana: University of Illinois Press, 2011), 103.

74. Szwed, *Alan Lomax,* 369.

75. Ralph Rinzler, "A Festival to Cherish Our Differences," *The Smithsonian Festival of American Folklife, 1974–1976* (1976 program), 7, Ralph Rinzler Papers, CFCH.

76. Gary Everhardt, "Of Our National Heritage," 3; Alan Lomax, "Of People and Their Culture . . . and the Pursuit of Happiness," 4–5, both in *The Smithsonian Festival of American Folklife, 1974–1976* (1976 program), 7, Ralph Rinzler Papers, CFCH.

77. Richard Kurin, "The Festival of American Folklife: Building on Tradition," *Festival Program Book, 1991,* bound copy of program books, 1989–1991, Ralph Rinzler Papers, CFCH.

# BIBLIOGRAPHY

MANUSCRIPT COLLECTIONS

**American Folklife Center, Archive of Folk Culture, Library of Congress, Washington, D.C.**
Alan Lomax CBS Radio Series Collection
Alan Lomax Collection
David K. Dunaway Collection
Radio Research Project Manuscript Collection

**Center for Folklife and Cultural Heritage, Smithsonian Institution, Washington, D.C.**
Folkways Records and Service Corporation
Moses and Francis Asch Collection
Peter Goldsmith Collection
Ralph Rinzler Papers
Robert Cantwell Collection

**Folklife Archives, Kentucky Library and Museum, Western Kentucky University, Bowling Green**
Sarah Gertrude Knott Collection

**Indiana University Archives, Indiana University, Bloomington**
Richard A. Reuss Papers

**Library of American Broadcasting, University of Maryland, College Park**

**Southern Folklife Collection, University of North Carolina, Chapel Hill**
Archie Green Papers, 1944–2009
Ronald D. Cohen Papers, 1914–2005

## BOOKS, JOURNAL ARTICLES, RECORD ALBUMS, AND THESES

Akam, Everett Helmut. *Transnational America: Cultural and Pluralist Thought in the Twentieth Century.* Lanham, Md.: Rowman and Littlefield, 2002.

Allen, Barbara. "Regional Studies in American Folklore Scholarship." In *Sense of Place: American Regional Cultures,* ed. Barbara Allen and Thomas Schlereth. Lexington: University of Kentucky Press, 1990.

Banks, James A. *Multiethnic Education: Practices and Promises.* Bloomington, Ind.: Phi Delta Kappa Educational Foundation, 1977.

———. *Multiethnic Education: Theory and Practice,* 2d ed. Boston: Allyn and Bacon, 1988.

Baptiste, H. Prentice, Jr. *Multicultural Education: A Synopsis.* Washington, D.C.: University Press of America, 1979.

Baron, Robert. "Postwar Public Folklore and the Professionalization of Folklore Studies." In *Public Folklore,* ed. Robert Baron and Nicholas Spitzer, 307–338. Washington, D.C.: Smithsonian Institution Press, 1992.

Barry, Phillips. "The Collection of Folk-Song." *Journal of American Folklore* 27, no. 103 (March 1914): 77–78.

Bendix, Regina. *In Search of Authenticity: The Formation of Folklore Studies.* Madison: University of Wisconsin Press, 1997.

Bluestein, Gene. "The Lomaxes' New Canon of American Folksong." *Texas Quarterly* 5, no. 1 (Spring 1962): 49–59.

———. *The Voice of the Folk.* Amherst: University of Massachusetts Press, 1972.

Bonner, David. *Revolutionizing Children's Records: The Young People's Records and Children's Record Guild Series, 1946–1977.* Lanham, Md.: Scarecrow Press, 2008.

Botkin, Benjamin. *Folk-Say: A Regional Miscellany.* Norman: University of Oklahoma Press, 1929–1932.

———. "The Folk Song Revival: Cult or Culture?" *Journal of American Folklore* 84, no. 334 (October–December 1971): 399.

———. "Regionalism and Culture." In *The Writer in a Changing World,* 2d ed., ed. Henry Hart, 140–157. New York: Equinox Cooperative Press, 1937.

———. "WPA and Folklore Research: 'Bread and Song.'" *Southern Folklore Quarterly* 3, no. 1 (March 1939): 10–14.

Bourne, Randolph. "Transnational America." In *War and the Intellectuals: Essays by Randolph S. Bourne, 1915–1919,* ed. Carl Resek, 107–123. New York: Harper and Row, 1964.

Brauner, Cheryl Anne. "A Study of the Newport Folk Festival and the Newport Foundation." Master's thesis, Department of Folklore, Memorial University of Newfoundland, St. John's, 1983.

Bronner, Simon J. *Folk Nation: Folklore in the Creation of American Tradition.* Wilmington, Del.: Scholarly Resources, 2002.

———. *Following Tradition: Folklore in the Discourse of American Culture.* Logan: Utah State University Press, 1998.

Buchanan, Annabel Morris. "The Function of a Folk Festival." *Southern Folklore Quarterly* 1, no. 1 (March 1937): 32–34.

Burkholder, Zoe. *Color in the Classroom: How American Schools Taught Race, 1900–1954.* Oxford: Oxford University Press, 2011.

Burns, Sean. *Archie Green: The Making of a Working-Class Hero.* Urbana: University of Illinois Press, 2011.

Cantwell, Robert. "Feasts of Unnaming: Folk Festivals and the Representation of Folklife." In *Public Folklore,* ed. Robert Baron and Nicholas R. Spitzer, 263–305. Washington, D.C.: Smithsonian Institution Press, 1992.

———. *When We Were Good: The Folk Revival.* Cambridge, Mass.: Harvard University Press, 1996.

Caudill, Harry. *Night Comes to the Cumberlands: A Biography of a Depressed Area,* repr. ed. Ashland, Ken.: Jesse Stuart Foundation, 2001 [1963].

Cobb, William H. *Radical Education in the Rural South: Commonwealth College, 1922–1940.* Detroit: Wayne State University Press, 2000.

Cohen, Lizabeth. *Making a New Deal: Industrial Workers in Chicago, 1919–1939.* Cambridge: Cambridge University Press, 1990.

Cohen, Ronald D., ed. *Alan Lomax, Assistant in Charge: The Library of Congress Letters, 1935–1942.* Jackson: University of Mississippi Press, 2011.

———. *A History of Folk Music Festivals in the United States: Feasts of Musical Celebration.* Lanham, Md.: Scarecrow Press, 2008.

———. *Rainbow Quest: The Folk Music Revival and American Society, 1940–1970.* Amherst: University of Massachusetts Press, 2002.

———. "Singing Subversion: Folk Music and the Counterculture." In *Beat Culture: The 1950s and Beyond,* ed. Cornelius A. Van Minnen, 117–127. Amsterdam: VU University Press.

———. ed. *"Wasn't That a Time!": Firsthand Accounts of the Folk Music Revival.* Metuchen, N.J.: Scarecrow Press, 1995.

Cohen, Ronald D., and Rachel Clare Donaldson. *Roots of the Revival: Folk Music in the United States and Great Britain in the 1950s.* Urbana: University of Illinois Press, 2014.

Cooney, Terry. *Balancing Acts: American Thought and Culture in the 1930s.* New York: Twayne, 1995.

Cowell, Henry. "Folk Music in a Democracy." In *Studies in Musical Education, History, and Aesthetics,* 172–174. Pittsburgh: Music Teachers National Association, 1944.

Cowley, Malcolm. *The Dream of the Golden Mountains: Remembering the Thirties.* New York: Viking, 1980.

Cunningham, Agnes "Sis," and Gordon Friesen. *Red Dust and Broadsides: A Joint Autobiography,* ed. Ronald D. Cohen. Amherst: University of Massachusetts Press, 1999.

Denning, Michael. *The Cultural Front: The Laboring of American Culture in the Twentieth Century.* New York: Verso, 1996.

DeTurk, David, and A. Poulin Jr., eds. *The American Folk Scene: Dimensions of the Folksong Revival.* New York: Dell, 1967.

Dewey, John. *Freedom and Culture.* New York: Putnam, 1939.

Dickstein, Morris. "On and Off the Road: The Outsider as a Young Rebel." In *Beat Culture: The 1950s and Beyond,* ed. Cornelius A. Van Minnen, 31–47. Amsterdam: VU University Press, 1999.

Diggins, John. *The Rise and Fall of the American Left.* New York: W. W. Norton, 1992.

Dorman, Robert. *Revolt of the Provinces: The Regionalist Movement in America, 1920–1945.* Chapel Hill: University of North Carolina Press, 1993.

Dunaway, David King. *How Can I Keep from Singing: Pete Seeger.* New York: McGraw-Hill, 1981.

Dunbar, Andrew J. *America in the Fifties.* Syracuse, N.Y.: Syracuse University Press, 2006.

Edgerton, John. *Speak Now against the Day: The Generation before the Civil Rights Movement in the South.* Chapel Hill: University of North Carolina Press, 1994.

Eyerman, Ron, and Scott Barretta. "From the 30s to the 60s: The Folk Music Revival in the United States." *Theory and Society* 25, no. 4 (August 1996): 501–543.

Eyerman, Ron, and Andrew Jamison. *Music and Social Movements: Mobilizing Traditions in the Twentieth Century*. New York: Cambridge University Press, 1998.

Filene, Benjamin. *Romancing the Folk: Public Memory and American Roots Music*. Chapel Hill: University of North Carolina Press, 2000.

Foster, Stuart. *Red Alert: Educators Confront the Red Scare in Public Schools, 1947–1954*. New York: Peter Lang, 2000.

"Friends through Recreation, Parts I and II." *Recreation* 39 (January 1946): 525–530, 554.

Garabedian, Steven. "Reds, Whites, and the Blues: Lawrence Gellert, 'Negro Songs of Protest,' and the Left-Wing Folk-Song Revival of the 1930s and 1940s." *American Quarterly* 57, no. 1 (March 2005): 179–207.

Gerstle, Gary. *American Crucible: Race and Nation in the Twentieth Century*. Princeton, N.J.: Princeton University Press, 2001.

———. "The Protean Character of American Liberalism." *American Historical Review* 99, no. 4 (October 1994): 1043–1073.

Gevinson, Alan. "'What the Neighbors Say': The Radio Research Project of the Library of Congress." *Performing Arts Broadcasting*, Winter 2002, 94–121.

Gitlin, Todd. *The Sixties: Years of Hope, Days of Rage*. New York: Bantam, 1987.

Glassberg, David. *American Historical Pageantry: The Uses of Tradition in the Early Twentieth Century*. Chapel Hill: University of North Carolina Press, 1990.

Glazer, Nathan. *We Are All Multiculturalists Now*. Cambridge, Mass.: Harvard University Press, 1997.

Gleason, Philip. "Americans All: World War II and the Shaping of American Identity." *Review of Politics* 43, no. 4 (October 1981): 483–518.

———. "WWII and the Development of American Studies." *American Quarterly* 36, no. 3 (1984): 343–358.

Goldsmith, Peter D. *Making People's Music: Moe Asch and Folkways Records*. Washington, D.C.: Smithsonian Institution Press, 1998.

Grambs, Jean Dresden. *Intergroup Education: Methods and Materials*. Englewood Cliffs, N.J.: Prentice-Hall, 1968.

Grant, Carl A., ed. *Multicultural Education: Commitments, Issues, and Applications*. Washington, D.C.: Association for Supervision and Curriculum Development, 1977.

Green, Archie. "The National Folk Festival Association: Commercial Music Graphics #32." *John Edwards Memorial Foundation Quarterly* 11, no. 37 (Spring 1975): 23–32.

———. *Torching the Fink Books and Other Essays on Vernacular Culture*. Chapel Hill: University of North Carolina Press, 2001.

Greenway, John. *American Folk Songs of Protest*. New York: Octagon, 1971.

Hamilton, Marybeth. "Sexuality, Authenticity and the Making of the Blues Tradition." *Past and Present*, no. 169 (November 2000): 132–160.

Harrington, Michael. *The Other America: Poverty in the United States*, repr. ed. New York: Simon and Schuster, 1997 [1962].

Hart, Henry, ed. *The Writer in a Changing World*, 2d ed. New York: Equinox Cooperative Press, 1937.

Hartman, Andrew. *Education and the Cold War: The Battle for the American School*. New York: Palgrave Macmillan, 2008.

Highham, John. "Multiculturalism and Universalism: A History and a Critique." *American Quarterly* 45, no. 2 (June 1993): 195–219.

Hilmes, Michele. *Radio Voices: American Broadcasting, 1922–1952*. Minneapolis: University of Minnesota Press, 1997.

Hilmes, Michele, and Jason Loviglio, eds. *Radio Reader: Essays in the Cultural History of Radio*. New York: Routledge, 2002.

Hirsch, Jerrold. "Folklore in the Making: B. A. Botkin." *Journal of American Folklore* 100, no. 395 (January–March 1987): 3–38.

Hollinger, David A. "Ethnic Diversity, Cosmopolitanism and the Emergence of the American Liberal Intelligentsia." *American Quarterly* 27, no. 2 (May 1975): 133–151.

———. *Postethnic America: Beyond Multiculturalism*. New York: Basic Books, 1995.

Hurley, John M. "Hartford's Racial Cultural Program." *Recreation* 28 (January 1936): 501–507, 522.

Isserman, Maurice. *If I Had a Hammer—: The Death of the Old Left and the Birth of the New Left*. New York: Basic Books, 1987.

———. *Which Side Were You On? The American Communist Party during the Second World War*. Middletown, Conn.: Wesleyan University Press, 1982.

Jackson, Bruce. "The Folksong Revival." In *Transforming Tradition: Folk Music Revivals Examined*, ed. Neil V. Rosenberg, 73–83. Urbana: University of Illinois Press, 1993.

Jones, Alfred Haworth. "The Search for a Usable American Past in the New Deal Era." *Journal of American History* 23, no. 5 (1971): 710–724.

Joseph, Peniel E., ed. The *Black Power Movement: Rethinking the Civil Rights–Black Power Era*. New York: Routledge, 2006.

Klehr, Harvey. *The Heyday of American Communism: The Depression Decade*. New York: Basic Books, 1984.

Knott, Sarah Gertrude. "Folk Lore in Our Day." *Recreation* 36 (April 1942): 23–26.

———. "Folksongs and Dances, U.S.A.: The Changing Scene." *Southern Folklore Quarterly* 25, no. 3 (September 1961): 184–191.

———. "Texas Celebrates Its Hundredth Birthday." *Recreation* 30 (October 1936): 351–353, 374.

Koppelman, Robert S., ed. *"Sing Out, Warning! Sing Out, Love!": The Writings of Lee Hays*. Amherst: University of Massachusetts Press, 2003.

Lears, Jackson. "A Matter of Taste: Corporate Cultural Hegemony in a Mass-Consumption Society." In *Recasting America: Culture and Politics in the Age of Cold War*, ed. Lary May, 38–60. Chicago: University of Chicago Press, 1989.

Lieberman, Robbie. *My Song Is My Weapon: People's Songs, American Communism, and the Politics of Culture, 1930–1950*. Urbana: University of Illinois Press, 1989.

Lissak, Rivka Shpak. *Pluralism and Progressives: Hull House and New Immigrants, 1890–1919*. Chicago: University of Chicago Press, 1989.

Livingston, Tamara E. "Music Revivals: Towards a General Theory." *Ethnomusicology* 43, no. 1 (Winter 1999): 66–85.

Lomax, Alan. *Alan Lomax: Selected Writings, 1934–1997*, ed. Ronald D. Cohen. New York: Routledge, 2003.

———. "America Sings the Saga of America." *New York Times Magazine*, January 26, 1947, 16, 41.

Lomax, Alan, and John Lomax, eds. *Our Singing Country: A Second Volume of American Ballads and Folk Songs*. New York: Macmillan, 1941.

Lomax, John. *Adventures of a Ballad Hunter*. New York: Hafner, 1971 [1947].

———. *Cowboy Songs and Other Frontier Ballads*. New York: Macmillan, 1922.

Matusow, Allen J. *The Unraveling of America: A History of Liberalism in the 1960s*. New York: Harper and Row, 1985.

May, Lary, ed. *Recasting America: Culture and Politics in the Age of Cold War.* Chicago: University of Chicago Press, 1989.

McCarthy, Timothy Patrick, and John McMillan, eds. *The Radical Reader: A Documentary History of the American Radical Tradition.* New York: New Press, 2003.

McMillan, John, and Paul Buhle, eds. *The New Left Revisited.* Philadelphia: Temple University Press, 2003.

Mickenberg, Julia L. *Learning from the Left: Children's Literature, the Cold War, and Radical Politics in the United States.* New York: Oxford University Press, 2006.

Miller, James. *Democracy Is in the Streets: From Port Huron to the Siege of Chicago.* New York: Simon and Schuster, 1987.

Miller, Karl Hagstrom. *Segregating Sound: Inventing Folk and Pop Music in the Age of Jim Crow.* Durham, N.C.: Duke University Press, 2010.

Mirel, Jeffrey E. *Patriotic Pluralism: Americanization Education and European Immigrants.* Cambridge, Mass.: Harvard University Press, 2010.

Mitchell, Gillian. *The North American Folk Music Revival: Nation and Identity in the United States and Canada, 1945–1980.* Burlington, Vt.: Ashgate, 2007.

Morris, Aldon. *The Origins of the Civil Rights Movement: Black Communities Organizing for Change.* New York: Free Press, 1984.

Naison, Mark. *Communists in Harlem during the Depression.* Urbana: University of Illinois Press, 1983.

Odum, Howard W. *Folk, Region, and Society: Selected Papers of Howard W. Odum,* ed. Katherine Jocher. Chapel Hill: University of North Carolina Press, 1964.

Odum, Howard W., and Harry Estill Moore. *American Regionalism: A Cultural-Historical Approach to National Integration.* New York: Henry Holt, 1938.

Ogbar, Jeffrey O. G. "Rainbow Radicalism: The Rise of the Radical Ethnic Nationalism." In *The Black Power Movement: Rethinking the Civil Rights–Black Power Era,* ed. Peniel E. Joseph, 193–228. New York: Routledge, 2006.

Pankake, John, and Paul Nelson. "P-for-Protest." In *The American Folk Scene: Dimensions of a Folksong Revival,* ed. David A. DeTurk and A. Poulin Jr., 140–149. New York: Dell, 1967.

Pateman, Carol. *Participation and Democratic Theory.* Cambridge: Cambridge University Press, 1970.

Pells, Richard *Radical Visions and American Dreams: Culture and Social Thought in the Depression Years.* New York: Harper and Row, 1973.

Poletta, Francesca. "Strategy and Democracy in the New Left." In *The New Left Revisited,* ed. John McMillian and Paul Buhle, 156–177. Philadelphia: Temple University Press, 2003.

Porterfield, Nolan. *Last Cavalier: The Life and Times of John A. Lomax, 1867–1948.* Urbana: University of Illinois Press, 1996.

Powell, James Henry. "The Concept of Cultural Pluralism in American Thought, 1915–1965." Ph.D. diss., University of Notre Dame, Notre Dame, Ind., 1971.

Reuss, Richard. "Woody Guthrie and His Folk Tradition." *Journal of American Folklore* 83, no. 329 (July–September 1970): 273–304.

Reuss, Richard, and JoAnne C. Reuss. *American Folk Music and Left-Wing Politics, 1927–1957.* Lanham, Md.: Scarecrow Press, 2000.

Robinson, Marianne "Jolly." *Out of the Frying Pan, Into the Fire: The Restless Journey of Marianne "Jolly" Robinson.* Berkeley, Calif.: Regent Press, 2010.

Rochon, Thomas. *Culture Moves: Ideas, Activism, and Changing Values.* Princeton, N.J.: Princeton University Press, 1998.

Rodnitzky, Jerome. *Minstrels of the Dawn: The Folk-Protest Singer as a Cultural Hero.* Chicago: Nelson-Hall, 1975.

Rosenberg, Neil V., ed. *Transforming Tradition: Folk Music Revivals Examined.* Urbana: University of Illinois Press, 1993.

Roussopoulos, Dimitrios, and C. George Benello, eds. *Participatory Democracy: Prospects for Democratizing Democracy.* Montreal: Black Rose Books, 2005.

Roy, William G. *Reds, Whites, and Blues: Social Movements, Folk Music, and Race in the United States.* Princeton, N.J.: Princeton University Press, 2010.

Sandburg, Carl. *The American Songbag.* New York: Harcourt Brace, 1927.

Sanders, Lynn Moss. *Howard W. Odum's Folklore Odyssey: Transformation to Tolerance through African American Folk Studies.* Athens: University of Georgia Press, 2003.

Savage, Barbara. *Broadcasting Freedom: Radio, War, and the Politics of Race, 1938–1948.* Chapel Hill: University of North Carolina Press, 1999.

Scott, John Anthony. "Folklore and Folksong in Education." *New York Folklore Quarterly* 17, no. 4 (Winter 1962): 294–295.

Seeger, Pete. "Why Folk Music?" In *The American Folk Scene: Dimensions of the Folksong Revival,* ed. David A. DeTurk and A. Poulin Jr., 44–48. New York: Dell, 1967.

Selig, Diana. *Americans All: The Cultural Gifts Movement.* Cambridge, Mass.: Harvard University Press, 2008.

Smith, Judith. "Radio's 'Cultural Front,' 1938–1948." In *Radio Reader: Essays in the Cultural History of Radio,* ed. Michele Hilmes and Jason Loviglio, 209–230. New York: Routledge, 2002.

Smith, Rogers M. *Civic Ideals: Conflicting Visions of Citizenship in U.S. History.* New Haven, Conn.: Yale University Press, 1997.

Sparrow, James T. *Warfare State: World War II Americans and the Age of Big Government.* Oxford: Oxford University Press, 2011.

Sporn, Paul. *Against Itself: The Federal Theater and Writers' Projects in the Midwest.* Detroit: Wayne State University Press, 1995.

Steiner, Michael C. "Regionalism in the Great Depression." *Geographical Review* 73, no. 4 (October 1983): 430–446.

Studer, Norman. "The Place of Folklore in Education." *New York Folklore Quarterly* 18, no. 1 (Winter 1962): 3–11.

Susman, Warren. *Culture as History: The Transformation of American Society in the Twentieth Century.* New York: Pantheon, 1984.

Szwed, John. *Alan Lomax: The Man Who Recorded the World.* New York: Viking, 2010.

Taylor, Verta. "Social Movement Continuity: The Women's Movement in Abeyance." *American Sociological Review* 54, no. 4 (October 1989): 761–775.

Van Deburg, William. *New Day in Babylon: The Black Power Movement and American Culture, 1965–1975.* Chicago: University of Chicago Press, 1992.

Van Minnen, Cornelis A., Jaap Van Der Bent, and Mel Van Elteren, eds. *Beat Culture: The 1950s and Beyond.* Amsterdam: VU University Press, 1999.

Van Ronk, Dave, with Elijah Wald. *The Mayor of MacDougal Street: A Memoir.* Cambridge, Mass.: Da Capo Press, 2005.

Walkowitz, Daniel J. *City Folk: English Country Dance and the Politics of the Folk in Modern America.* New York: New York University Press, 2010.

Wall, Wendy. *Inventing the "American Way": The Politics of Consensus from the New Deal to the Civil Rights Movement.* Oxford: Oxford University Press, 2008.

Weissman, Richard. *Which Side Were You On? An Inside History of the Folk Music Revival in America.* New York: Continuum International, 2005.

Whisnant, David. *All That Is Native and Fine: The Politics of Culture in an American Region*. Chapel Hill: University of North Carolina Press, 1983.

Whitfield, Stephen J. *The Culture of the Cold War*. Baltimore: Johns Hopkins University Press, 1991.

Wilgus, D. K. *Anglo-American Folksong Scholarship since 1898*. New Brunswick, N.J.: Rutgers University Press, 1959.

Williams, John Alexander. *Appalachia: A History*. Chapel Hill: University of North Carolina Press, 2002.

Williams, Michael Ann. *Staging Tradition: John Lair and Sarah Gertrude Knott*. Urbana: University of Illinois Press, 2006.

Wright, Betty Atwell. *Educating for Diversity*. New York: John Day, 1965.

Zumwalt, Rosemary. *American Folklore Scholarship: A Dialogue of Dissent*. Bloomington: Indiana University Press, 1988.

# INDEX

**Rachel Clare Donaldson** is an independent scholar and the co-author (with Ronald D. Cohen) of *Roots of the Revival: Folk Music in the United States and Great Britain in the 1950s.*